BERLIOZ, ROMANTIC AND CLASSIC

WRITINGS BY ERNEST NEWMAN

Ernest Newman *circa* 1904

BERLIOZ,
ROMANTIC AND CLASSIC

Writings by Ernest Newman

Selected and edited by

PETER HEYWORTH

LONDON
VICTOR GOLLANCZ LTD
1972

The essay, "Berlioz, Romantic and Classic" first appeared
in *Musical Studies* by Ernest Newman, published by Bodley
Head in 1905.

Printed in Great Britain by
The Camelot Press Ltd, London and Southampton

Contents

Introduction

Introduction

Introduction

FOURTEEN WEEKS BEFORE Berlioz died in Paris on 8 March, 1869, Harriet Roberts, wife of a Welsh master-tailor living in Lancaster, gave birth to a son who subsequently assumed the *nom de plume* of Ernest Newman. Newman lived to witness (though not with much approval) the first professional stage performance of *Les Troyens* at Covent Garden in June 1957, and through much of his immensely long life he was a virtually single-handed champion of Berlioz. A generation before Harty and Beecham started to perform the less well-known works and advocates such as Turner and Wotton arrived on the scene, Newman had already put his formidable pen at the service of a composer whom he considered neglected and misunderstood.

He did in fact intend to write a full-length study of Berlioz's music. That even in the last years of his life he had not abandoned this project is clear from the fact that he allowed no articles on Berlioz to be included in the two anthologies of his writings in the *Sunday Times*, which appeared near the end of his life (*From the World of Music* and *More Essays from the World of Music*, edited by Felix Aprahamian, Calder, London 1957 and 1958). But by the time he had completed his studies on Wagner he was 82, and a large volume entitled *More Opera Nights* (a far less superficial book than its title might suggest) appeared in 1954, when he was 86. By then even Newman's prodigious intellectual energy had begun to flag and, to his dismay, his eyes started to fail him. As a result his book on Berlioz's music was never written.

That is the excuse for this small collection of selected writings. Over a period of almost sixty years (the earliest item I have been able to trace dates from 1899, the most recent from 1958), Newman wrote extensively on Berlioz, and in 1905 in his *Musical Studies* he published a lengthy essay, "Berlioz, Romantic and Classic", which Jacques Barzun has rightly described as "a pioneering study" and which stands at the head of this volume.

Many of the judgements expressed in it do not hold water today. Indeed, Newman himself, never a man who was afraid to change his mind, was to revise some of them drastically. In particular he came in later years to recognize as untenable his assertion that Berlioz had burnt himself out by the age of 40, that the last twenty-five years of his life (during which, among other things *L'Enfance du Christ*, the *Te Deum*, *Les Troyens* and at any rate parts of *La Damnation de Faust* were written) was a period of uninterrupted physical and intellectual decline, or, as he put it even more drastically in 1901 in an essay in *The Contemporary Review* that I have not included here, "the decline of his [Berlioz's] powers . . . is too pathetic for criticism."

If that makes strange reading today, it must be remembered that at the turn of the century, when Newman first began to concern himself with Berlioz and wrote a number of essays that he subsequently compounded into the study of 1905, he was writing, as any critic may from time to time be forced to do, from an incomplete knowledge of his subject. It is not possible to determine what works he had heard in the flesh by 1905. But a glance through his cuttings during the fifteen years (1904 to 1919) he was critic of the *Birmingham Post*, reveals that he wrote only about *Romeo and Juliet*, the *Symphonie fantastique*, *La Damnation de Faust* and an occasional overture, and it is hardly likely that he would have failed to cover less-known works by a composer who so exercised his mind and imagination, had the occasion presented itself. As comparatively recently as 1919 Newman wrote that the fiftieth anniversary of Berlioz's death had passed "almost unnoticed in the English musical press".

It is even more important to bear in mind that, as indeed he mentions in his study of 1905, it was only towards the end of the last century that Breitkopf and Härtel started to publish an edition, which was destined to remain incomplete, of the major scores, and a handful of the overtures and one or two of the best-known works appeared in miniature score. Nor did Newman have much chance to travel at a time when that was a prerogative of the rich, not extended to critics. (It is amazing to reflect today on the rarity of his visits to the Continent, apart from an annual pilgrimage to the gaming tables of Monte Carlo.)

By 1919 Newman had already begun to modify some of his more sweeping dismissals of Berlioz's later music. Now Berlioz was "a tired and broken man" only in the last decade of his life, though *Les Troyens* was still rejected as a lost cause. If ten years later, he saluted it as Berlioz's "latest and greatest work" (it was in fact composed before *Béatrice et Bénédict*, though only performed subsequently), that was because in 1921 in Paris for the first time in his life he had experienced the work on the stage. An amateur performance—the first in this country—followed in Glasgow in 1935, and in 1947 Beecham conducted a memorable BBC studio performance, which struck the present writer with the force of a revelation.

At each rehearing Newman's understanding of the work grew deeper and his enthusiasm for it more intense, so that by 1949 he is found rebuking a colleague, who had been rash enough to assert that *Les Troyens* and *Béatrice et Bénédict* (alas, Newman did not live to see the latter on the stage, in which case he might have felt less sure of his ground in this particular instance) contained nothing but a few fine passages. Finally, towards the end of his life, in 1957, he claimed that, in the years in which Berlioz was composing *Les Troyens*, he "was at the very height not only of his musical but of his intellectual powers". Indeed, by the time he came to the performance at Covent Garden the work had become such a sacred cause that Newman could hardly bear the prospect of once again encountering the beloved in the flesh.

Far from trying to eliminate these discrepancies, I have given them emphasis by including a larger number of articles on *Les Troyens* than on any other work. My immediate reason is simply that from the moment he first heard this opera in Paris in 1921 to his death thirty-eight years later, it was a work that exercised his mind more than any other. But this emphasis will also, I hope, serve to illustrate the development of his understanding of Berlioz's genius, for it was through *Les Troyens* that he found his way to a more complete assessment of Berlioz's genius than is apparent in the study of 1905. And where he led, others have followed, so much so that many attitudes to Berlioz we today take for granted are due to his pioneering work.

But though Newman's sympathies for Berlioz broadened and ripened like fruit under an autumnal sun, he never lost that sense of critical perspective that so many of the composer's latter-day admirers find hard to preserve. The centenary orations of 1969 would certainly have struck him as a welcome contrast to the reception that the centenary of the composer's birth received in 1903, when he was obliged to seek rueful consolation in the fact that there were at any rate "no passionate admirers, no over-zealous enthusiasts to damage his cause". That was not the case in 1969, when I fancy that his pen would have been kept busy, puncturing some of the more uncritical effusions occasioned by the widespread celebrations that took place in Britain in that year.

For Newman was never a fan. As in the case of Wagner and Strauss, he never lost sight of the failings of the composers he was particularly drawn to. No doubt it was because he already sensed an over-drastic change of prevailing winds that he sought to let restrain them towards the end of his life. In 1955, in a generous review of Barzun's huge study, he warned against the dangers of uncritical over-estimation of a composer, who for all his genius remains in many ways as problematic as Berlioz, and proceeded gently to ease a few pins into Professor Barzun's more exalted claims for his hero. Indeed, one of the aspects of Newman's writings on Berlioz I have come particularly to admire in the course of preparing them for publication is his critical equilibrium, his refusal to hush up Berlioz's shortcomings, his readiness to examine criticism and to admit that it is not always based on error or ignorance. On the other hand, when he encountered what he took to be *a priori* condemnation, as in the notorious case of Ravel (see p. 117), he was never backward in defending a composer whose genius he revered.

In selecting these essays and articles I have naturally tried to keep the repetition which is an inescapable committent of regular journalism to a minimum. That is why I have, for example, omitted a number of quite substantial early pieces that were subsequently used in "Berlioz, Romantic and Classic". The other reason is that in this case, of course, Newman himself had in effect decided what he wished to be preserved.

Elsewhere, however, identical points are often raised with others that seem to warrant inclusion and in these instances it has not been possible to avoid a degree of overlapping. Where it occurs, I hope the reader will bear with it. In some cases, during and after the last war, Newman was obliged by shortage of space to cast what he had to say in serial form, and here I have done away with the opening and closing paragraphs that served no purpose other than that of linking articles that were read at a week's interval. Exceptionally, and with Mrs. Newman's agreement, I have taken the liberty of telescoping articles in which he raises subsidiary points that he has dealt with more thoroughly and convincingly elsewhere. In a small section that I have called "Miscellaneous Comments" I have assembled a few isolated excerpts that touch on matters not referred to elsewhere; and in one or two cases I have attached an excerpt to a complete article, where it can be distinguished by the presence of a separate date and the absence of a heading. In this connection I should add that, in a few instances, I have provided suitable headings where these did not exist.

In these matters I hope that I have not exceeded editorial licence.

It is in the nature of the beast that journalism should bear the hall-mark of its time. Had Newman written his projected study he would naturally have revised some of the judgements and assertions that occur in these articles and in this process have taken recent research into account. On reflection, I have preferred not to pepper the text with notes and amendments, but to let Newman's writing stand as an historic bridge between the dismissive view of Berlioz current in his youth and present-day attitudes. Accordingly, I have only in isolated instances added footnotes to correct errors of fact that might prove misleading. Here and elsewhere, my principle has been to reduce all tampering to a minimum. Except where otherwise stated, all excerpts are from the *Sunday Times*, to whom I would like to express my appreciation for permission to reprint them here.

With some hesitation I have ventured to include a revised version of a memoir of Ernest Newman that I wrote for *High Fidelity* immediately after his death. I have done so in part as a small act of homage to a man I admired immensely and at whose feet I was occasionally privileged to sit. But beyond that it may serve a practical purpose. In the years since Newman's death there has already grown up a half-generation, for whom he is no more than an august name on a library shelf. Yet he was more than an outstanding scholar and critic; he was also a substantial and formative figure in English musical life in the first half of this century. Accordingly, some brief sketch of his career and character will not, I trust, be found out of place.

I would like to express my gratitude first and foremost to Mrs. Vera Newman, who not only made available her husband's books of cuttings and indicated where suitable material might lie, but also responded unstintingly to my request for more. I am indebted to Professor Jacques Barzun, Mr. Herbert van Thal, Mr. Robert Ponsonby and Mr. Herbert Weinstock, who most generously gave their time in locating articles. I am also deeply obliged to Mr. R. F. Dignum of Victor Gollancz Ltd., who on repeated occasions uncomplainingly conveyed substantial cartons of books and cuttings to and from London.

PETER HEYWORTH

LONDON, APRIL 1971

I

Berlioz, Romantic and Classic

1

Berlioz, Romantic and Classic

I

IT IS FAIRLY safe to say that—with the possible exception of Liszt—there is no musician about whom people differ so strongly as about Berlioz. His case is, indeed, unique. We are pretty well agreed as to the relative positions of the other men; roughly speaking, all cultivated musicians would put Wagner and Brahms and Beethoven in the first rank of composers, and Mendelssohn, Grieg, and Dvořák in the second or third. Even in the case of a disputed problem like Strauss, the argument among those who know his work is not, I take it, as to his being a musician of the first rank, but as to the precise position he occupies among the others of that limited regiment. Upon Berlioz, however, the world seems unable to make up its mind. The dispute here is not as to where he stands among the great ones, but whether he really belongs to the great ones at all. Though there is no absolute unanimity of opinion upon the total work of, say, Wagner or Beethoven—no complete agreement as to the amount of weakness that is bound up with their strength—there is at all events perfect unanimity of opinon that Wagner and Beethoven are of the royal line. But we have Berlioz extolled to the skies by one section of competent musicians, while another section can scarcely speak of him politely; he really seems to create a kind of physical nausea in them; and some of them even deny his temperament to have been really musical. There is surely nothing in the history of music to parallel the situation. The difference of opinion upon him, be it observed, is quite another thing from the frequent and quite excusable perplexity that men feel over a *contemporary* composer. Men drift widely apart over Wagner while he is alive; but the next generation, at all events, sees him practically through the same eyes. The quarrel over Berlioz is not a contemporary quarrel; the bulk of his most significant work had all appeared before 1850, and yet here we are, half a century after that time, still debating whether he is really one of the immortals. For many people Schumann's old question, "Are we to regard him as a genius, or only a musical adventurer?" still remains unanswered.

On the whole—looking for a moment only at the external aspect of the case—the current is now flowing not from but towards him. Even putting aside the exceptional spasm of 1903, the centenary of his birth, he probably gets more performances now than he ever did. Messrs. Breitkopf and Härtel are bringing out a magnificent complete edition of his works in score, superbly edited by Weingartner, the great conductor, and Charles Malherbe, Archivist of the Paris Opera; while in the admirable little Donajowski editions the full scores of the *Symphonie fantastique, Harold en Italie, Roméo et Juliette*, and half-a-dozen of the overtures, can now be had for a total expenditure of a few shillings. Publishers do not generally take to bringing out full scores, particularly at very low prices, unless there is some demand for the works; and I think we may take it that just now there is a quickening interest in Berlioz. Yet all the while the critical war goes on, without signs of compromise on either side. The attitude of a great many people is of course to be explained partly by imperfect acquaintance with Berlioz's work, partly by their having revolted against him at the outset and never settled down to ask themselves whether their first impressions did not need revising. It is not every one who has either the candour or the capacity for hard and patient work of Weingartner, who has placed on record his own progress from the traditional view of Berlioz as "a great colourist, the founder of modern orchestration, a brilliant writer, and, in fact, almost everything else except a composer of inspiration and melody", to the view that Berlioz is one of the great masters, rich in feeling, in beauty, in inventiveness. Many worthy people no doubt took their cue from Wagner, who, besides giving a nonsensical pseudo-analysis of Berlioz in *Opera and Drama*, referred to him disparagingly in a well-known letter to Liszt. It is tolerably clear, however, that Wagner knew comparatively little of Berlioz at that time, and that in running down *Benvenuto Cellini* and *La Damnation de Faust* he was only indulging that unfortunate habit of his of expressing himself very positively upon subjects he knew nothing about.* But put aside all the criticism of him that comes from imperfect knowledge—and it must be remembered that up to quite recently it was not easy to get a perfect knowledge of him, for his scores were rather scarce, and so badly printed as to make the reading of them a trial —and we are still left face to face with a certain amount of good critical intelligence that cannot, do what it will, take to Berlioz's

* The reader who is interested in the matter may turn to Wagner's letters to Liszt of 1852. Here he speaks slightingly of Berlioz's *Cellini*, and alludes to "the platitudes of his Faust *Symphony* (!)" The last phrase alone is sufficient to show that Wagner was completely ignorant of the work he had the impertinence to decry—for every one knows that Berlioz's *Faust* is not a symphony. In a recent article in *The Speaker*, "The Relations of Wagner and Berlioz", I have, I think, shown that Wagner could not have known a note either of the *Faust* or the *Cellini*; the dates of performance and of publication put any such knowledge on his part out of the question. It is necessary, however, to warn the reader that in both the English translation of the Wagner-Liszt letters (by Dr. Hueffer, revised by Mr. Ashton Ellis), and the big Glasenapp-Ellis *Life of Wagner*, the real facts are kept from the English public. The incriminating phrase, "Faust Symphony," is quietly abbreviated to "Faust", so that there is nothing to rouse the reader's suspicions and make him look further into the matter. In the big *Life*, again, now in course of publication, Mr. Ellis, though he has thousands of pages at his disposal—though, indeed, he can devote a whole volume of five hundred pages to two years of Wagner's life —still cannot find room for the brief line or two from the 1852 letter that would put the real facts before the reader; discreet and silent dots take their place. The British public is apparently to be treated like a child, and told only so much of the truth about Wagner as is thought to be good for it—or at any rate good for Wagner.

music. And since criticism is, or ought to be, concerned not only with the psychological processes that go to make a work of art, but also with the psychological processes that make us judge it in this way or that—it is worth while trying to discover what it is in Berlioz that makes so many worthy people quite unsympathetic towards him.

II

Let us first of all look at him biographically and historically, as he was in himself and in his relations to his contemporaries. His is perhaps the strangest story in all the records of music. In contrast to musicians like Bach, Beethoven, Mozart, Wagner, and a score of others, who grew up from childhood in an atmosphere saturated with music, Berlioz is born in a country town that is practically destitute of musical life. Even the piano is not cultivated there, the harp and guitar being almost the sole instruments known; in 1808—five years after the birth of Berlioz —there is still only one piano in the Department. There is no teacher of music in the place; Berlioz's father ultimately combines with other residents to bring over for this purpose a second violinist from the theatre at Lyons. Although the music in the boy cannot quite be kept down, for nearly the first twenty years of his life he is, to all intents and purposes, ignorant of the elements of technique, and never hears a bar of first-rate music. "When I arrived in Paris in 1820,"* he says, "I had never yet set foot in a theatre; all I knew of instrumental music was the quartets of Pleyel with which the four amateurs composing the Philharmonic Society of my native town used to regale me each Sunday after mass; and I had no other idea of dramatic music than what I had been able to get in running through a collection of old operatic airs arranged with an accompaniment for the guitar." Yet, untutored as he was, and practically ignorant of even the elements of harmony, he had from his boyhood been writing music. The opening melody of the *Symphonie fantastique*

* This is an error; he arrived in Paris in 1821. (Actually 1822 [P.H.].)

was really written by Berlioz in his twelfth year, to some verses from Florian's *Estelle*;* and we know of other boyish compositions, fragments of which have been conserved in some of his later works. It may not be absolutely true, as M. Edmond Hippeau says, that until the age of twenty-three he was "ignorant of the most elementary principles of music"; but at all events he was just beginning to learn these principles at an age when nine other composers out of ten have left far behind them all the drudgery of the apprentice. In Paris he does indeed study after a fashion; but it is characteristic of him that he gets most of his musical experience from the performances at the Opera, and from a diligent reading of the scores of Gluck in the library of the Conservatoire.

Even in Paris, at that time, there was little to call out the best there was in such a man as Berlioz—little that could teach him the proper use of his own strange faculties, or by whose standard he could test the worth of his own inspiration. He did indeed hear a little Gluck occasionally, and a travesty of Weber; but it was not until 1828 that Beethoven made any impression on Paris. Orchestras were generally incompetent and audiences ignorant. The calibre of the average French orchestra of the time may be gauged from the fact that even the more reputable bands found Mozart's symphonies by no means easy. One shudders to think what the ordinary orchestras must have been like, and what was the quality of music to which they had grown accustomed. As for the audiences, where they were not extremely uneducated they were extremely prejudiced, clinging blindly to the remains of the pseudo-classical principles that had been bequeathed to them by their fathers. An audience that could be worked into a perfect frenzy of rage because an actor, outraging all the proprieties of the time, actually referred in *Othello* to something so vulgar as a handkerchief, would hardly look with favour on anything revolutionary either in idea or technique. At the opera the Italians were most in vogue. The French public knew little of

* See Julien Tiersot's *Hector Berlioz et la société de son temps* (1904)—an excellent book that is indispenable to every student of Berlioz.

instrumental music pure and simple, and were almost entirely ignorant of the huge developments of German music. Cherubini, of course, was a stately and impressive figure, a serious thinker of the same breed as the great Germans; but apart from him, there were no Parisian composers who could by any stretch of the imagination be called modern, or could do anything to teach a man like Berlioz. Lesueur, the favourite master of Berlioz, seems to have been progressive—indeed, revolutionary—in some of his theories of music and poetry; but his theory was better than his practice. From such a type as the amiable and ineffectual Boïeldieu nothing new could possibly come. He frankly avowed his inability to understand Beethoven, and declared to Berlioz his preference for "la musique qui me berce". Yet this young musician from the country, with years of lost time to regret, with little musical education, with the very slightest of stimuli from the great music of the past, and with little encouragement in his own surroundings, produces in quick succession a number of works of the most startling originality—original in every way, in the turn of their melodies, in their harmonic *facture*, in their orchestration, in their rhythm, in their view of men and things. Now that the complete Berlioz is being printed, we know a good deal more of him than was possible even a few years ago. We do not now commence our study of him with the *Symphonie fantastique*; we can watch the workings of his brain in the two early cantatas—*Herminie* and *Cléopâtre*—that in the eyes of two sapient juries of the time were insufficient to win him the *Prix de Rome*. Here we see a freshness of outlook and of style—particularly in the matter of rhythm—that is one of the most remarkable phenomena in the history of music. In his earliest years, as in his latest, Berlioz was himself, a solitary figure owing practically nothing to other people's music, an artist, we may almost say, without ancestry and without posterity. Mozart builds upon Haydn and influences Beethoven; Beethoven imitates Mozart and in turn influences the practice of all later symphonists; Wagner learns from Weber and gives birth to a host of imitators. But with Berlioz—and it is a point to be insisted on—there is no one whose speech he tried to copy in his early years, and there is no one since who speaks with *his* voice. How many things in the early Beethoven were made in the factory of Mozart; how many times does the early Wagner speak with the voice of Weber! But who can turn over the scores of Berlioz's early works and find a single phrase that can be fathered upon any previous or contemporary writer? There was never any one, before his time or since, who thought and wrote just like him; his musical style especially is absolutely his own. Now and then in *L'Enfance du Christ* he suggests Gluck—not in the turn of his phrases but in the general atmosphere of an aria; but apart from this it is the rarest thing for him to remind us of any other composer. His melody, his harmony, his rhythm, are absolutely his own.

III

We are face to face, then, with a personality which, whether we like it or not, is of extraordinary strength and originality. If we are to realise what kind of force he was, and how he came to do the work he did, we must study him both from the standpoint of history and from that of physiological and psychological science. Musical criticism is apt to become too much a mere matter of wine-tasting, a bare statement of a preference of this vintage or a decided dislike for that. We need to study musicians as a whole, as complete organisms hanging together by virtue of certain peculiarities of structure. If a man does not like Liszt's music he compares it disparagingly with Wagner's—as if this placing of people on the higher or lower rungs of a ladder were the be-all and the end-all of criticism. Shakespeare is the greatest figure of the Elizabethan literary world; but what critic thinks of disposing of Ford and Massinger and Jonson and Webster and Marlowe and Tourneur with the off-hand remark that not one of them was a Shakespeare? In the same way it is not sufficient to write down Berlioz as a purveyor of extravagant ideas clothed sometimes in ugly and unpleasing forms; it is much more profitable to set ourselves to find out why he came to have such a bias in art, and what were his relations to the general intellectual movements of his time. It is only when we study him from the historical standpoint that we can understand many of his ideals; and to understand them is more important than to rail at them. The criticism that rejects the less beautiful specimens of an art because they are not perfect is like the natural history that would take account only of the typical organisms, passing over the many instructive variations from the type. In the long run human folly and human failure are just as interesting to the student of humanity as its wisdom and its triumphs; and the critic should always aim at being an impartial student of humanity, not a mere wine-taster or a magistrate.

As we have seen, whatever other qualities we may deny to Berlioz, we cannot at any rate refuse his claim to originality. Readers of Théophile Gautier's *Histoire du Romantisme*, in which the cool, objective poet and critic reviews all the leading figures of the Romantic movement—Victor Hugo, Gérard de Nerval, Alfred de Vigny, Delacroix, and a score or so of lesser lights— will remember that Berlioz is the only musician admitted to that brilliant company. It was not due to any personal preference on Gautier's part, or to his ignorance of the other Romantic musicians; there simply were no others. So far as music was concerned, the whole Romantic movement began and ended with Berlioz. When we are tempted to feel annoyed at some of his extravagances or banalities we should remember that he had to conquer a new world unaided. He was not only without colleagues but without progenitors. When he arrived in Paris in 1821, at the age of eighteen, what was the position of music in France? Gluck's epoch-making work had terminated in 1779 with *Iphigenia in Taurus*; the dramatic school of which he was the leader made something like its last effort in Sacchini's *Œdipe à Cologne* in 1789. The often charming but flimsy work of Dauvergne, Duni, Monsigny, Dalayrac and Grétry was without any importance for the opera of the future. Two musicians alone commanded serious respect—the great Cherubini, who, however, was neither typically French nor very revolutionary, and Méhul, whose *Joseph* appeared in 1807. Lesueur and Berton do not count; while Hérold, strong man as he was in some ways, was not strikingly original either in form or in expression. The French music produced during the years of Berlioz's early manhood was of the type of Boïeldieu's *La Dame Blanche* (1828), Auber's *Masaniello* (1828) and *Fra Diavolo* (1830), or Adam's *Postillon de Longjumeau* (1836). Neither Spontini in the first decade of the century, nor Rossini in later years, was a necessary link in the chain of development of French music. In fact, of almost all the music heard in Paris between 1790 and 1830 we may say that whenever it was great it was not French, and whenever it was French it was not great. Above all it was scarcely ever *contemporary* music; it rarely showed any trace of having assimilated the life and art of its own day. Especially was it unaffected by the hot young Romantic blood that in the second and third decades of the century was transforming both French poetry and French painting. Think of the artists and poets, and then think of the musicians, and you seem to enter another and inferior world of thought.

It was Berlioz, and Berlioz alone, who brought French music into line with the activities of intelligent men in other departments. He put into it a ferocity and turbulence of imagination and an audacity of style to which it had hitherto been a stranger. Often when I listen to him now I feel that we do not even yet quite appreciate his originality. Even after the lapse of so many years the music sometimes strikes us, in spite of all the enormous development of the art between his day and ours, as startlingly new and unconventional. What then must it have sounded like in the ears of those who heard it for the first time? Imagine the bourgeois audience of those days suddenly assailed by the March to the Scaffold, or the Witches' Sabbath, in the *Symphonie fantastique*! There was here as violent a rupture with the staid formulas of the classic and the pseudo-classic as anything achieved by Victor Hugo or Delacroix or Gros or Géricault.

The springs that moved Berlioz, in fact, were just the springs that moved his great contemporaries. The essence of their revolt was an insistence upon the truth that beauty is co-extensive almost with life itself. The nerves of the younger men were sharper than their fathers'; their ears were more acute, their eyes more observant. They saw and felt more of life, and tried to express in art what they had seen and felt; which could not be done without not only breaking the mould of the pseudo-classic technique, but also finding voice for a lot of sensations and ideas to which the men of the previous generation had been impervious. Recent French critics have noticed, as one evidence of the more sensitive nerves of the early Romanticists, the fineness and variety of their perceptions of colour. To the literary man of the eighteenth century an object is merely blue or red; the new writers perceive a dozen shades of blue and red, and ransack the whole vocabulary to find the right discriminating word.* There was a general effort to escape from the conventions that had fast-bound poetry, painting, the drama, and the opera. The dress of the actors and singers now aimed at some correspondence with that of the epoch of the play, instead of making the vain attempt to produce an historical illusion with the costume of their own time. The subjects of dramas, novels, poems, and operas, instead of being exclusively classic, were now sought in contemporary manners or in earlier European history; and with the change of matter there necessarily came a change of style. At the same time there sprang up an intellectual intimacy, previously unknown, between all classes of artists. The poet and the musician hung about the studio of the painter; the painter and the poet sang the songs of the musician, or attended the performances of his opera, to criticise it from the point of view of men who themselves were used to thinking in art. The imagination of each was stimulated and enriched by the ideas and sensations of the others. The new achievements of line or colour or language or sound prompted

* It is interesting to note that Alfred de Musset anticipated Arthur Rimbaud and the modern symbolists in having coloured audition. He once maintained that the note F was yellow, G red, a soprano voice blond, a contralto voice brown. See Arvède Barine's *Alfred de Musset* (in *Les Grands Écrivains Français*), p. 115.

the devotee of each art to fresh experiments in his own medium. This in turn led to another new phenomenon, of particular importance in the history of music. There came to the front an original type—the literary musician, who made a practice, and sometimes a profession, of writing about his art, of educating the public at the same time as he clarified his own ideas and tested his own powers. This type was accompanied by yet another new product—the literary man or poet who wrote on music, not as a professor or a pedant, and not after the manner of the Rousseaus and Suards of the eighteenth century, but with dynamic force and directness, correlating music with life and thought, estimating it by its actual meaning to living men. There was nothing in the eighteenth century to correspond to the prose writings of musicians like Berlioz and Schumann, nothing to compare with the treatment of musical subjects by literary men such as Hoffmann and Baudelaire.* And yet, while there was in this way a greater actual expenditure of brain-power upon music and art generally, the men themselves were not such solid types as the men of the eighteenth century. Neither Hugo, nor Gautier, nor Delacroix, nor Berlioz had the intellectual weight and fixity of Diderot, or Condorcet, or David, or Gluck. The reason of the eighteenth century was transformed into sentiment, its activity into reflection, its repose into enthusiasm, its sobriety into passion.

Against this spirit the now anæmic idealism of pseudo-classical art could not stand for long. If artists had taught the public to believe that whatever tasted of real life was vulgar or barbaric, the public must now be disabused of that notion. All life was claimed as the province of the artist; he claimed also the right to draw it as he had seen it. "There are no good subjects or bad subjects," said Victor Hugo; "there are only good poets and bad poets." Expression—vital expression, biting to the very heart of the theme —was now the ideal; beauty, in the limited sense that had been given to it by the false classics, was only a formula more or less

---

* Hoffmann was, of course, a musician as well; but he is more truly the novelist who wrote about music than the musician who wrote fiction.

platitudinous. "The realisation of beauty by the expression of character" was the avowed purpose of the Romanticists. M. Brunetière aptly contrasts with this the classic theorem of Winckelmann, that the ideal beauty was "like pure water, having no particular savour". "We must say it and repeat it", cries Hugo in the preface of 1824 to the *Odes et Ballades*; "it is not the need for novelty that torments our minds; it is the need for truth—and that need is immense." Delacroix summed up the general falsity of the conventional attitude towards art when he wrote: "In order to make an ideal head of a negro, our teachers make him resemble as far as possible the profile of Antinous, and then say, 'We have done our utmost; if he is, nevertheless, not beautiful, we must abstain altogether from this freak of nature, this squat nose and thick lips, which are so unendurable to the eyes.'" A journalist of 1826 (cited by M. Gustave Lanson in his admirable *Histoire de la Littérature française*) cried, "Vive la nature *brute et sauvage* qui revit si bien dans les vers de M. de Vigny, Jules Lefèvre, Victor Hugo!" It was not that they worshipped ugliness and violence in themselves, but that they felt there are certain occasions when truth can be reached only through the repellent and the extravagant, which, however, may be bent by a wise eclecticism to the purposes of the ideal. There is scarcaly anything in the imagination of Berlioz that is not paralleled in the imaginations of the contemporary poets and painters; there is no leap of theirs towards freer verse or more expressive colour that was not also taken by the musician. Only while they had at least some roots in the past, not only in their own country but in England and Germany, and while they were many and could support and purify each other by mutual criticism, Berlioz stood by himself, without any musician, dead or living, being of any practical value to him in the course he took.

IV

Few literary and artistic movements have their social and physical roots laid as clearly open to us as the Romantic. The most astonishing thing in connection with this chain of causes and results is that there should be only the solitary figure of Berlioz to represent the musical side of it. One would have thought that the vast liberation of nervous energy effected by the Revolution and the Napoleonic period would have been too great to be confined to literature and the plastic arts—that a really French school of music would have arisen, interwoven with the past and the present of French history and social life, and as typical of contemporary French culture in its own way as the poetry, drama, and painting of the time were in theirs. That this did not happen was in all probability due to the confirmed hold which the theatre had upon music-lovers in France. To nine men out of ten there music was synonymous with opera; and opera meant a spectacle in which only the greatest pleasure of the greatest number had to be consulted. It was an art-form in which compromise was carried to its highest points; the audience was cosmopolitan and not too critical, and the composers, whether native or foreign, had to think only in the second place of art, and in the first place of speaking a musical language that would be intelligible and acceptable to all. No independent, contemporary expression of culture could be expected in opera, for no one, composer or spectator, took it quite seriously enough for that.

On the other hand, there was no purely instrumental form existing that could serve as a vehicle for such revolutionary modes of feeling as found expression in the literature and painting of the day. Finally, there was no public with sufficient musical training to demand a new revelation in music, or to comprehend it if it came. The French orchestras of the time, as we have seen, were almost uniformly inefficient, incapable of playing great music with any intelligence. It was impossible, then, for the public to be as alive, as up-to-date, in music as it was in other things; and music, more than any other art, is dependent upon collective as distinguished from individual patronage. Perhaps, also, the language of French music was as yet not sufficiently developed to fit it to answer the needs of the young generation of Romanticists. It was not real enough, not close enough to actual life to spur the energies of men either into approval or disgust. There was no mistaking the angry flare of the new spirit in other fields. The realism of Gros or of Delacroix was patent to every eye; the mere change in the choice of subjects was a challenge and a provocation. So again in poetry, one could not fail to be agitated by the incessant whipping of the language to new feats of technique, the perpetual evocation of new forms of expression, new vibrations of verbal colour. All this was on very much the same plane as the everyday life of men. It was something they could feel a fighting interest in. But no one took music so seriously. It was long before it lost the grand manner, the trick of wig and sword, of the eighteenth century; and when it did there was nothing of equal grandeur to take its place. Where it was great, and had the large stride and the flowing cloak, it breathed of the psychology of the past; where it took part in the lives of the men of its own day it attacked them only on their more sensuous, more frankly epicurean side. It was a mistress, not a wife.

In Berlioz alone, then, the Romantic movement expended its musical energies. He alone among French musicians of the time shows the same characteristics of body and mind as went to the making of the art or literature of his contemporaries. With him, as with them, the physiological structure counts for very much. No doubt a good deal of the motive-power came from the great awakening of the Napoleonic era. The nation that had been wrestling for a generation with every country in Europe necessarily touched life on more sides than it had ever done before. The old formalities no longer sufficed; indeed, the mere antiquity of any thought or any practice was no recommendation of it in the eyes of this people, to whom the strange kaleidoscopic present was a spectacle of ever-changing interest. It was this aspect of the situation to which Stendhal gave expression when he compared his own century with the eighteenth, the classic nutriment with the romantic. "The classic pieces are like religions—the time for creating them has gone by. They are like a clock that points to midday when it is four in the afternoon. This kind of poetry was all right for the people who, at Fontenoy, raised their hats and said to the English column, 'Gentlemen, be good enough to fire first.' And it is expected that this poetry should satisfy a Frenchman who took part in the retreat from Moscow!" When the Napoleonic empire had fallen, a new motive-power of great literary value was discovered in the intense melancholy which, according to Musset, seized upon the younger spirits at the sudden limitation of the nation's activities. "A feeling of inexpressible *malaise* commenced to ferment in every young heart. Condemned to inaction by the sovereigns of the world, given up to indolence, to *ennui*, the young men . . . experienced, at the foundation of their souls, a misery that was insupportable."

The physiological causes, however, of this nervous irritability, this dissatisfaction with existing things, which is as strongly marked in Berlioz as in Musset or Delacroix, were probably more important than the moral ones. The majority of the artists and literary men of this epoch had a poor, neurotic physique. In almost all of them there was a tendency to nervous derangement, or some weakness of the heart or lungs that would predispose them to melancholy. Maxime du Camp bore strong testimony to the physical lassitude that characterised this epoch. "The artistic and literary generation that preceded me," he wrote, "that to which I belonged, had a youth of artistic sadness, inherent in the constitution of men or in the epoch." Again, speaking of the proclivity to suicide among the young men of the time, he says, "It was not merely a fashion, as one might believe; it was a kind of general debility that made the heart sad and the mind gloomy, and caused death to be looked upon as a deliverance."

This *défaillance générale*, this *tristesse sans cause comme sans objet, tristesse abstraite*, must have had its roots in something deeper than the mere psychological outlook of the youth of the period. It seems probable that there was a general physical exhaustion, a widespread undermining of physique. The children born about the beginning of the century must have had for their parents, in many cases, people who had lived in an atmosphere of intense social and political excitement, and had probably undergone a considerable amount of actual physical hardship. The Napoleonic wars can hardly have failed to leave their mark upon the physiological constitution of the French race. If it be true that the fine nervous quality of the Irish comes in part from the centuries of troubled life through which the race has passed, there must certainly have been some impression left upon the physique of France by the lurid, swiftly changing episodes of the Revolution and the Empire. The mere loss of young blood must have counted for a good deal. De Musset, indeed, in his *Confession d'un enfant du siècle*, bears testimony to the melancholy of the young generation—"une génération ardente, pâle, nerveuse", "conceived between two battles", and born of "les mères inquiètes".★ Maxime Du Camp too suggests this explanation of the morbidity of the time, and adds to it another. "Often I have asked myself whether this depression may not have been the outcome of physiological causes. The nation was exhausted by the wars of the empire, and the children had inherited their fathers' weakness. Besides, the system of medicine and hygiene then prevalent was disastrous. Broussais was the leader of thought, and doctors went everywhere lancet in hand. At school they bled us for a headache. When I had typhoid fever I was bled three times in one week, sixty leeches were applied, and I could only have recovered by a miracle. The doctrines preached by Molière's Diafoiruses had lasted on to our day, and resulted in the anæmic constitution so frequently met with. Poverty of blood combined with the nervous temperament makes a man melancholy and depressed."

One consequence of this flawed physique was that the young men of the time not only had extravagant conceptions, but that they took these and themselves with enormous seriousness. The

★ Buckle (note 316 to Chap. VII of the *History of Civilisation*) remarks that "All great revolutions have a direct tendency to increase insanity, as long as they last, and probably for some time afterwards, but in this as in other respects the French Revolution stands alone in the number of its victims." See the references he gives, bearing upon "the horrible but curious subject of madness caused by the excitement of the events which occurred in France late in the eighteenth century". Buckle speaks only of the Revolution, but of course the subsequent wars must have operated in much the same way.

majority of them posed unconscionably at times. They could not be unhappy without playing upon their own sensations for the benefit of an audience; there was something of the actor in almost all of them. Each was a Werther in his own eyes, a person towards whom the cosmos had behaved with a special and quite unpardonable malevolence. Listen, for example, to the declamation of Chateaubriand: "I have never been happy, I have never attained happiness though I have pursued it with a perseverance corresponding with the natural ardour of my soul; no one knows what the happiness was that I sought, no one has fully known the depths of my heart; the majority of my sentiments have remained immured there, or have only appeared in my works as applied to imaginary beings. Today, when I still regret my chimæras without however pursuing them, when, having reached the summit of life, I descend towards the tomb, I wish, before dying, to revert to those precious years, *to explain my inexplicable heart*, to see, in short, what I can say when my pen abandons itself unconstrainedly to all my recollections."* One detects a little note of insincerity in it all. The gentleman doth protest too much; he is wearing his heart too visibly on his coat-sleeve, trafficking in melancholy as a man traffics in cotton or steel, simply because there is a market for that kind of thing. We need to read Berlioz's letters with this suspicion always before us if we are to take them at their real value. A fair summary of the half-sincere, half-posing mood that was prevalent among the young men of genius of the time is to be had in Géricault's portrait of himself, in the Louvre, with the forced melodrama of the skull on the shelf intruding itself upon the real earnestness of the picture as a whole. We get plenty of this somewhat far-fetched and too conscious *diablerie* in some of the early work of Berlioz; and there is no need to be more contemptuous of it there than when we meet with it in the poets or the painters who were his contemporaries. To say nothing of the grandiloquent Hugo and his youthful followers, even so strong and philosophical a type as Flaubert was decoyed now and then into the same kind of pose of exaggeration. His

* Chateaubriand, *Souvenirs d'enfance et de jeunesse*, p. 2.

early letters have their full share of sentimentality, of talk about man being as a frail skiff in the tempest, and all the other formulas of the school,* although Flaubert expressly dissociated himself from the more lymphatic specimens of Romanticism. "Do you know", he wrote, "that the new generation of the schools is extremely stupid; formerly it had more sense; it occupied itself with women, sword-thrusts, orgies; now it apes Byron. . . . It is who shall have the palest face and say in the best manner 'I am *blasé, blasé*!' What a pity! *blasé* at eighteen!"

V

If ever the physiological structure of a man had to be taken into account in trying to explain the nature of his work, it is surely when we are dealing with Berlioz. We have only to look at his portrait to see how highly strung he was, how prone he must have been to disorders of the nervous system. There is a passage in one of his letters that seems to indicate an anxiety for his health on the part of his father, who, being a doctor, would probably understand his son's bias towards nervous troubles: "Je suis vos instructions quant au régime," writes Hector; "je mange ordinairement peu et ne bois presque plus de thé." His early life, after he left the paternal home, was certainly one of great privation. He moreover seems to have been exceedingly careless of his health, indulging in long walks without a proper supply of food—presuming upon a nervous energy that to him no doubt seemed like a solid physical constitution. Worse even than this was his occasional deliberate resort to starvation, as one of his friends tells us, "pour connaître les maux par lesquels le génie pouvait passer." The wonder is not that he should always have been a prey to some trouble or other of the nerves, or that in middle age he should have been attacked by a frightful intestinal disorder, but that he should have lived as long as he did, and

* In his letter of March 18, 1839, he gives Ernest Chevalier the plan of a work that is curiously like that of Berlioz mentioned on page 45, in its preposterous fantasies and its over-emphasis of form and colour.

found strength enough for such work as he has bequeathed to us. "How unhappily I am put together," he once wrote to his friend Ferrand—"a veritable barometer, now up, now down, always susceptible to the changes of the atmosphere—bright or sombre —of my consuming thoughts." As it was, the nerves plainly underwent a gradual deterioration. There are the same general mental characteristics in his later work as in his earlier, but the music of the last fifteen years of his life will as a whole hardly bear comparison with that written between the ages of twenty-five and forty. The fine bloom seemed to have been rubbed off his spirit; even where the music still has the nervous energy of former years it is almost entirely an external thing—a mere tendency to break out into the unexpected because of the impossibility of continuing for long on the one level path; while too often there is a sheer dulness that evidently comes from the long-continued stilling of his pains with opium. But until his system wore itself out in this way through every kind of over-strain, it was clearly one of extraordinary sensitivity, susceptible to a hundred impressions that must have remained a sealed book to every other French musician of the time.

This was the keynote to his mental life and to the world which he tried to reproduce in art; and if we study his physical organisation he becomes far more typical of the Romantic movement than the most brilliant of his contemporaries. If their distinguishing mark was the extraordinary seriousness with which they took their artistic impressions, the strange convulsions produced in them by the sight of a beautiful thing or by the mere rapturous act of composition, it must be said that not one of them can compare with Berlioz in this respect. A hundred passages, in his *Memoirs*, his letters, and his prose works, reveal his temperament as perhaps the most extraordinarily volcanic thing in the history of music. Musicians as a whole have an unenviable notoriety for not being as other men are; they surpass even the poets in the fineness of their nerves and the tendency of these to evade the control of the higher centres. But surely, outside the history of religious mania or the ecstasy of the mystics, there is nothing to parallel the abnormal state into which Berlioz was thrown by music. "When I hear certain pieces of music, my vital forces at first seem to be doubled. I feel a delicious pleasure, in which reason has no part; the habit of analysis comes afterwards to give birth to admiration; the emotion, increasing in proportion to the energy or the grandeur of the ideas of the composer, soon produces a strange agitation in the circulation of the blood; tears, which generally indicate the end of the paroxysm, often indicate only a progressive state of it, leading to something still more intense. In this case I have spasmodic contractions of the muscles, a trembling in all my limbs, a complete torpor of the feet and the hands, a partial paralysis of the nerves of sight and hearing; I no longer see, I scarcely hear: vertigo . . . a semi-swoon." Still more curious is the effect created on him by music he does not like. "One can imagine", he says, "that sensations carried to this degree of violence are rather rare, and that there is a vigorous contrast to them, namely *the painful musical effect*, producing the contrary of admiration and pleasure. No music acts more strongly in this respect than that whose principal fault seems to me to be platitude plus falsity of expression. Then I redden as if with shame; a veritable anger takes possession of me; to look at me, you would think I had just received an unpardonable insult; to get rid of the impression I have received, there is a general upheaval of my being, an effort of expulsion in the whole organism, analogous to the effort of vomiting, when the stomach wishes to reject a nauseous liquor. It is disgust and hatred carried to their extreme limit; this music exasperates me, and I vomit it through all my pores."

This is not a piece of merely literary exaggeration, for time after time in his letters we come across corroborative evidence that Berlioz was really affected by music in this way. He thus surpasses in nervous extravagance the most abnormal of the young poets and painters of his time. And as with them the susceptibility of their physical organisms led to a new sympathy with things, a new tenderness, a new pity, so did the weakness of Berlioz lead him to the discovery of shades of emotion that had never before found expression in music. Madame de Staël's remark, that "la littérature romantique . . . se sert de nos impressions personnelles pour nous émouvoir", had a wider application than she imagined. The French Romantic was a new type in art; in most cases a nervous sufferer himself, he had glimpses of a whole world of human pain and pathos that were denied his forerunners. The great figures of the eighteenth century are for the most part objective, travelling by the way of reason rather than that of emotion, philosophers rather than artists, living in the central stream of things, and with a broad, clear outlook on the actual affairs of their own day. Their very sentiment is a different thing from the sentiment of the later generation; it is more under control, has less heart and more brain in it, is less suggestive of an overwhelming surge along the nerves. Only now and again in the literature of the eighteenth century do we catch a fore-shadowing of that species of quivering emotion which found, sometimes only too easily, expression in the Romantics. We have it in a noteworthy passage of Diderot: "Le premier serment que se firent deux êtres de chair, ce fut au pied d'un rocher qui tombait en poussière; ils attestèrent de leur constance un ciel qui n'est pas un instant le même; tout passait en eux, autour d'eux, et ils croyaient leurs cœurs affranchis de vicissitudes. O enfants! toujours enfants!" This, in the literature of its time, is like a lyric of Heine appearing among the pages of Lessing, a song of Schumann in the middle of a score of Gluck. We have something of the same tone again, a similar adumbration of the romantic spirit, here and there in the *Rêveries* of Rousseau. But it is in the Romantics that we first find the full expression of that new tremor of feeling that comes from the sense of the weakness of our poor flesh, the sense of the mortality of our clay, our hourly nearness to corruption, our community with everything that suffers and perishes.

VI

Before coming to consider his music, let us complete the study of Berlioz as an organism by examining his prose, where we shall find many things that throw light on his structure. The assistance given to the student of musical psychology by the prose writings of musicians is so great, that one could almost wish that every composer of any note had left the world a volume or two of criticism or of autobiography. They would not necessarily have added very much to our positive knowledge of life or art; but a book is such an unconscious revelation of its writer, he shows himself in it so faithfully and so completely, no matter how much he may desire to pose or deceive, that the psychologist is able to reconstruct the man's mind from it as the scientist can reconstruct in imagination the body of an animal from a few of its bones. One does not lay much store, for example, by the actual contents of the volumes of prose which Wagner was unkind enough to bequeath to us; but after all one would not willingly let them die, for they are of the utmost help to the study of Wagner, indirectly, if not directly, throwing sidelights on him of which he was quite un-conscious. The prose of Berlioz has greater intrinsic interest. Deeply as he said he loathed his journalistic work, he was after all a born journalist, a fluent writer, a cynical wit, an accomplished story-teller in certain *genres*, a master of polished and mordant irony. My present purpose, however, is not to attempt an appreciation of Berlioz's prose as a whole, but to call attention to certain curious elements in it that have not, so far as I am aware, been pointed out before, and that are extremely interesting to the student of so strange and complex a personality as Berlioz.

Readers of Hennequin's fine, if not quite convincing, essay on Flaubert in *Quelques Ecrivains Français*, will remember the attempt to exhibit the structure and functioning of the novelist's brain by dissection of his prose. Flaubert, he shows, tends always to write thus and thus; he has a vocabulary of such and such a kind, and he tends to build up words in such and such a way. Proceeding from this basis, Hennequin goes on to examine Flaubert's construction of his sentences, then of his paragraphs, then of his chapters, then of his novels, and thus to explain the final form of the books in terms of a fundamental intellectual structure that has been conditioned by a certain verbal faculty.

Hennequin, I think, pushes his method rather too far here, making blindly for his thesis regardless of all that may be urged against it; but on the whole the essay is a novel and valuable contribution to a neglected science—the study of a man's brain through the medium of his forms of expression. Now any one who reads critically through the prose works of Berlioz must be struck by certain elements in the prose that seem to give the key to much that is almost inexplicable in his music and his character. "Extravagant", "theatrical", "bizarre"—these are the terms that have always been used of Berlioz. Sir Hubert Parry takes the easy course of attributing his theatricalism to his being a Frenchman, oblivious of the fact that the French disliked it and ridiculed it more than any other nation. The early prose of Berlioz indicates that he was a man of a cerebral structure that tended always to express itself extravagantly; a man who did not see things upon the ordinary level of earth quite so clearly as shapes in cloud and on mountain-top.

The big effects at which he aimed in music were, indeed, only one form of manifestation of a curious faculty that was always leading him to the grandiose. The ordinary orchestra, the ordinary chorus, the ordinary concert-room would never do for him; everything must be magnified, as it were, beyond life-size. Similarly in his prose, the ordinary similes, the ordinary metaphors rarely occur to him; the dilated brain can only express itself in a dilation of language. Thus one adjective is rarely enough for Berlioz; there must generally be at least three, and these of the most exaggerated kind. A thing is never beautiful or ugly for Berlioz; it is either divine or horrible. A scene in his early work, where Cleopatra reflects on the welcome to be given her by the Pharaohs entombed in the pyramids, is "terrible, frightful". His *Francs Juges* overture in one place is described as "monstrous, colossal, horrible". On another occasion he writes, "There is nothing so terribly frightful as my overture. . . . It is a hymn to despair, but the most despairing despair one can imagine —horrible and tender." Everywhere there is the same tumefaction of language. When he ponders over the memory of his first wife and her sufferings, he is overcome by "an immense, frightful, incommensurable, infinite pity". Towards the end of his life he is seized by "the furious desire for immense affections". He can hardly speak of anything that has moved him without this piling-up of the most tremendous adjectives in the language.

As might be expected, his imagery is of the same order; the very largest things in the universe are impressed into the service of his similes and metaphors. He speaks in one place of "those superhuman adagios, where the genius of Beethoven soars aloft, immense and solitary, like the colossal bird above the snowy summit of Chimborazo". He had never seen the bird above the summit of Chimborazo, but his brain reverts spontaneously to this conception in the effort to express the sensation of immensity and solitude given him by Beethoven's music. The pyramids, being conveniently large, frequently enter into his similes. "It needs a very rare order of genius to create the things that both artists and public can take to at once—things whose simplicity is in direct proportion to their mass, like the pyramids of Djizeh." "Yesterday", he writes after a certain performance of his works, "I had a pyramidal success." When the pyramids fail him he falls back on Ossian, or on Babylon and Nineveh. After having heard 6500 children's voices in St. Paul's, he writes, "It was, without comparison, the most imposing, the most Babylonian ceremony I had ever beheld." The "Tibi omnes" and the "Judex" of his *Te Deum* are "Babylonian, Ninivitish pieces". One night he hears the north wind "lament, moan, and howl like several generations in agony. My chimney resounds cavernously like a sixty-four feet organ-pipe. I have never been able to resist these Ossianic noises."

Occasionally the heaping of Pelion on Ossa becomes necessary in order to enable him to give the reader a faint impression of what he feels. Beethoven is "a Titan, an Archangel, a Throne, a Domination". When he is writing his hated feuilletons, "the lobes of my brain seem ready to crack asunder. I seem to have burning cinders in my veins." The scene of the benediction of the poniards in the *Huguenots* is a terrible piece, "written as it were in

44

electric fluid by a gigantic Voltaic pile; it seems to be accompanied by the bursting of thunderbolts and sung by the tempests". A reminiscence of some incident in his career brings out this ejaculation—"Destruction, fire and thunder, blood and tears! my brain shrivels up in my skull as I think of these horrors!" His second love, he tells us, "appeared to me with Shakespeare, in the age of my virility, in the burning bush of a Sinai, in the midst of the clouds, the thunders, the lightnings of a poetry that was new to me".

All his youthful conceptions and desires were of this extravagant order. He writes in a letter of 1831, from Florence, "I should like to have gone into Calabria or Sicily, and enlisted in the ranks of some chief of *bravi*, even if I were to be no more than a mere brigand. Then at least I should have seen magnificent crimes, robberies, assassinations, rapes, conflagrations, instead of all these miserable little crimes, these mean perfidies that make one sick at heart. Yes, yes, that is the world for me: a volcano, rocks, rich spoils heaped up in caverns, a concert of cries of horror accompanied by an orchestra of pistols and carbines; blood and lacryma christi: a bed of lava rocked by earthquakes; come now, that's life!"* In the same year he has the idea of a colossal oratorio on the subject of "The Last Day of the World". There are to be three or four soloists, choruses, and two orchestras, one of sixty, the other of two or three hundred executants. This is the plan of the work: "Mankind having reached the ultimate degree of corruption, give themselves up to every kind of infamy; a sort of Antichrist governs them despotically. A few just men, directed by a prophet, are found amid the general depravation. The despot tortures them, steals their virgins, insults their beliefs, and commands their sacred books to be burnt in the midst of an orgy. The prophet comes to reproach him for his crimes, and announces the end of the world and the Last Judgment. The irritated despot has him thrown into prison, and, delivering himself up again to his impious pleasures, is surprised in the midst of a feast by the terrible trumpets of the Resurrection; the dead come out of their

* He puts the same rhodomontade into the mouth of his Lélio.

graves, the doomed living utter cries of horror, the worlds are shattered, the angels thunder in the clouds—that is the end of this musical drama."

These examples will be sufficient to show the peculiarity of mind to which I have referred. The early ideas of Berlioz seem to bear the same relation to those of ordinary men as a gas does to a solid or a liquid; the moment they are liberated they try to diffuse themselves through as much space as they can. In this connection it is interesting to note that from his earliest years he had a love for books of travel and for pondering dreamily over maps of the world; he sought the remoter conceptions that were not limited by any narrow boundary. One gets a curious sensation, after reading much of his prose, that the things of the world have lost their ordinary proportions and perspectives; the adjectives are so big and so numerous that one begins to take this inflated diction as the normal speech of men. Occasionally a truly superb effect of vastness, of distance, is produced, an effect we also get sometimes in Berlioz's music. It has always seemed to me, for example, that the opening of his song "Reviens, reviens", gave the most perfect suggestion of some one being recalled from a great distance; the whole atmosphere seems to be attenuated, rarefied almost away; the melancholy is the melancholy of a regret that sweeps the ocean to the horizon and fails to find what the eyes hunger for.

VII

It is time, however, to remind ourselves that the picture painted so far does not represent the complete Berlioz. It is all the more necessary to give ourselves this reminder because the only Berlioz known to most people is this being of wild excitement and frenzied exaggeration, with a dash in him here and there of pose. There is a "legend" of each great composer—a kind of half-true, half-false conception of him that gradually settles into people's minds and prevents them, as a rule, from thinking out the man's character and achievement for themselves. There is the Mozart legend, the Beethoven legend, the Liszt legend, the authenticity of which not one amateur in a thousand thinks of questioning. There is the Berlioz legend, too, the causes of the growth of which, in this country especially, are not far to seek. We really know very little of him over here. The *Carnaval romain* overture and the *Faust* are heard occasionally; but the average English amateur, when he thinks of Berlioz, has chiefly in mind the *Symphonie fantastique* and the *Harold en Italie*—particularly the final movements with their orgies of brigands, witches, and what not. Industrious compilers of biographies and of programme notes do their best to keep this side of Berlioz uppermost in the public mind, by always harping upon the eccentricities of his youth. One needs to remember that Berlioz died in 1869, and that from, say, 1835 to 1869 he was a very different man, both in his music and in his prose, from what he was between 1821 and 1835. His letters to the Princess Sayn-Wittgenstein hardly suggest for a moment the Berlioz of the earlier letters to Humbert Ferrand and others. And as for his music, the British public that winks and leers knowingly at the mention of his name, thinking all the time of the *Symphonie fantastique* and the *Harold en Italie*, would do well to reflect that it knows nothing, or next to nothing, of the *Waverley*, *Francs Juges*, *Le Roi Lear* and other overtures, of *Lélio*, of the *Tristia*, of *Le Cinq Mai*, of the *Messe des Morts*, of the operas—*Benvenuto Cellini*, *Béatrice et Bénédict*, *La Prise de Troie*, and *Les Troyens à Carthage*—of the *Symphonie funèbre et triomphale*, of the *Roméo et Juliette*, of *L'Enfance du Christ*, of the *Te Deum*, and of other works, to say nothing of the score or so of songs. In the whole history of music, there is probably no musician about whose merit the average man is so sublimely confident on the basis of so sublime an ignorance of his work.

VIII

Bearing in mind, then, that the Berlioz whom we have hitherto been discussing is mostly the youthful Berlioz—the writer of mad letters, the actor of extravagant parts, the composer of the *Symphonie fantastique* (1829-1830), and *Lélio* (1831-1832)—let us look for a moment at his art as it was then, and afterwards trace it through its later and more sober manifestations.

In trying to follow him historically we meet with this difficulty, that it is impossible to say exactly when some of his conceptions first saw the light. He was in the habit of using up an early piece of material in a later work, especially if the early work was one that had been tried and had failed. We know, as I have already said, that the theme of the opening of the *Symphonie fantastique* is taken from a boyish composition. A phrase from another boyish work—a quintet—is used again in the *Francs Juges* overture. Parts of the early cantata *La Mort d'Orphée* become the *Chant d'amour* and *La harpe éolienne* in *Lélio*. The *Chœur d'ombres* in *Lélio* is a reproduction of an aria in the scena *Cléopâtre*—one of his unsuccessful *Prix de Rome* essays. Part of the *Messe solennelle* (1824) goes into *Benvenuto Cellini* (1835–1837). The *Marche au supplice* in the *Symphonie fantastique* is taken from his youthful opera *Les Francs Juges*. The fantasia on *The Tempest* goes into *Lélio*. I strongly suspect, indeed, that more of his work dates from the first ten years of his artistic life (1824–1834) than we have ever imagined. My theory is that he was overflowing with ideas in his younger days, and that there was a gradual failure of them in his latest years, owing to the terrible physical tortures he endured, and the large quantities of morphia he had to take to still his pangs. At first he turns out work after work with great rapidity. Taking the larger ones alone, we have in 1826* *La révolution grecque*, in 1827 or 1828 the *Waverley* and *Francs Juges* overtures, in 1828–1829 the eight *Faust* scenes, in 1829 the *Irish Melodies*, in 1829–1830 the *Symphonie fantastique*, in 1830 the *Sardanapalus* and the *Tempête*, in 1831 the *Corsair* and *Le Roi Lear* overtures, in 1831–1832 the *Rob Roy* overture, *Le Cinq Mai*, *Lélio* and part of the *Tristia*, in 1832–1833 various songs, in 1834 the *Harold en Italie*, and the *Nuits d'Eté*, in 1835–1837 *Benvenuto Cellini* and the *Messe des Morts*, in 1838 the *Roméo et Juliette*.

* One or two of these dates can only be looked upon as approximative, but if wrong at all, they are so only to the extent of a year or two, which does not affect the question.

This is a good output for some twelve years of a busy and struggling man's life, during the earlier part of which he was little more than an apprentice in his art. Berlioz lived another thirty-one years, but in that time did surprisingly little. Again keeping to the larger works, we have in 1840 the *Symphonie funèbre et triomphale*, in 1843 the *Carnaval romain* overture, in 1844 the *Hymne à la France*, in 1846 the completion of *Faust*, in 1848 the remainder of the *Tristia*, in 1851 *La Menace des Francs*, in 1850–1854 the *Enfance du Christ*, in 1849–1854 the *Te Deum*, in 1855 *L'Impériale*, in 1860–1862 *Béatrice et Bénédict*, in 1856–1863 the double opera *La Prise de Troie* and *Les Troyens à Carthage*. Even allowing for the facts that in his middle and later periods he spent a good deal of time in foreign tours and in literary work, we shall still, I think, be forced to conclude that his ideas flowed more slowly in his later days, while they were certainly of an inferior quality at times. We must remember, too, that some of his works were written long before their production, and that there is sometimes reason to believe this to have been the case even where we have no positive testimony on the point. The *idée fixe* theme of the *Symphonie fantastique* first appeared in *Herminie* (1828); the "Harold" theme in the *Harold en Italie* had already figured on the *cor anglais* in the *Rob Roy* overture. It is probable that the *Roméo et Juliette* was not all written in 1838 as a consequence of Paganini's gift, as every one was led to believe; Berlioz had the idea of the work in 1829, and perhaps conceived some of the music then.* The *Symphonie funèbre et triomphale*, produced in 1840, was to a great extent written in 1835. The stirring phrases that are the life and soul of the *Carnaval romain* overture (1843) are taken from *Benvenuto Cellini* (1835–1837); while the theme of the love-episode in the overture had already appeared in *Cléopâtre* (1829). It is, indeed, impossible to say how much of the music

---

* It appears from the Sayn-Wittgenstein letters that the beautiful theme of the love-scene in *Roméo et Juliette* was inspired by the youthful love for Estelle that also produced the opening theme of the *Symphonie fantastique*. It must, therefore, have been quite a boyish invention, though no doubt its development and general treatment really belong to 1838.

of what I have called Berlioz's second epoch really dates from his first, thus still further diminishing the quantity belonging to the years after 1838. I think, if the truth were known, it would be found that one or two of the themes of *Béatrice et Bénédict*, ostensibly written between 1860 and 1862, belong to 1828,* when Berlioz first resolved to make an opera out of Shakespeare's play. It is incontestable that the ten years from 1828 to 1838 were years of inexhaustible musical inspiration. At times, he himself has told us, he thought his head would have burst under the peremptory pressure of his ideas; so rapidly did they flow, indeed, that he had to invent a kind of musical shorthand to help his pen to keep pace with them. There was, I take it, very little of this in the last two or three decades of his life. Make what allowances we will for other demands upon his time, it seems undeniable that his brain then worked less eagerly and less easily in musical things. Had the ideas been there in full vigour they would have come out in spite of all other occupations; and that they were not there as they were in his youth can only be explained, I think, on physiological grounds.†

* 1833 (P.H.).

† M. Julien Tiersot, in his admirable *Berlioz et la société de son temps*, divides the life of Berlioz into five epochs—1803–1827 (his childhood, youth, and apprenticeship), 1827–1842 (the epoch of his greatest activity), 1843–1854 (in which he does little except *Faust*, which in reality, perhaps, dates from an earlier time), 1854–1865 (the epoch of *L'Enfance du Christ*, *Béatrice et Bénédict*, and *Les Troyens*), and 1865–1869 (barren of works). The discussion in the text will make it clear why I have substituted my own classification for that of M. Tiersot, and will, I hope, be convincing. One other point deserves noting. Towards the end of his *Mémoires* Berlioz tells us that he had dreamed a symphony one night, but deliberately refrained from writing it because of the expense of producing and printing it. Such a reason may have weighed a little with him; but no one who knows anything of artistic psychology can regard it as the total explanation. If the dream-work had really sunk into Berlioz's soul and he had felt that he had full command of it, he could not have rested until he had it down on paper, if only for his own gratification. It is far more probable that he felt himself unequal to the mental strain of thinking out his vision and forcing the stubborn material into a plastic piece of art. There was, I take it, a lassitude of tissue in him at this time that made protacted musical thinking a burden to him.

The latter aspect of the case, however, will be dealt with more fully later on. Here we may just note that Berlioz's early life was in every way calculated to produce both the inflation of the prose style that we see in his letters and the eccentricity and exaggeration that we see in some of his early music. His friend Daniel Bertrand tells us that "in his youth he sometimes amused himself by deliberately starving, in order to know what evils genius could surmount; later on his stomach had to pay for these expensive fantasies". At the time of his infatuation with Henrietta Smithson, he used to play the maddest pranks with his already over-excited brain and body; he would take long night-walks without food, and sink into the sleep of utter exhaustion in the fields. His body, like his brain, could not be kept at rest; he had a mania for tramping and climbing that invariably carried him far beyond his powers of endurance.* In 1830 the veteran Rouget de l'Isle, without having seen the youthful musician, diagnosed him excellently from his correspondence—"Your head", he wrote, "seems to be a volcano perpetually in eruption." We may smile at his antics all through this epoch, especially in *l'affaire Smithson*. But though there may have been a little conscious pose in it all, it is unquestionable that in the bulk of it he was in deadly earnest. Twice he tried to commit suicide—once at Genoa, and again in the presence of Henrietta. Nor were they merely stage performances, mere efforts at effect; it was not his fault that they did not turn out successfully.

IX

Roughly speaking, it will be found that the Berlioz I have so far depicted comes into view about 1827. It was about that date, apparently, that youthful enthusiasm, combined with starvation and folly, gave his system that lurid incandescence that people always think of when they hear the name of Berlioz. It is about that date that his letters begin to show the inflation of style to

* On the whole question see the chapter on "Le Tempérament" in Edmond Hippeau's *Berlioz Intime*.

which I have referred, and his music begins to acquire force and penetration and expressiveness, together with a tincture of the abnormal. Previously to 1827 he had presumably not written very much, or if he had it has not survived. What has remained is now accessible to us in the new complete edition of his works. There we can see some songs that, whatever their precise date may be, clearly belong to his earliest period. One of the very earliest—*Le Dépit de la Bergère*—shows a quite inexperienced brain and hand. *Amitié, reprends ton empire* is of much the same order; it looks, indeed, like a pot-boiler, an attempt to meet the contemporary demand for this kind of thing. Nor does the little cantata *La Révolution grecque* come to anything. But negative and futile as much of this early work is, it shows one thing quite clearly—that individuality of manner that accounts at once for the successes and the failures of Berlioz. As I have already pointed out, his type of melody is something peculiarly his own. The same may be said of his harmony, which moves about in a way so different from everything we are accustomed to that often we are quite unable to see the *raison d'être* of it. The popular judgment is that his melody is ugly and his harmony shows a want of musical education. This, however, is rather a hasty verdict. Nothing is more certain than that our first impression of many a Berlioz melody is one of disgust—unless it be that the second impression is one of pleasure. What Schumann noticed long ago in connection with the *Waverley* overture is still quite true, that closer acquaintance with a Berlioz melody shows a beauty in it that was unsuspected at first. I can answer for it in my own experience, for some of the things that move me most deeply now were simply inexpressive or repellent to me at one time; and I fancy every one who will not be satisfied with the first impression of his palate, but will work patiently at Berlioz, will have the same experience. The truth seems to be that many of his conceptions were of an order quite unlike anything else we meet with in music, and hence we have some difficulty in putting ourselves at his point of view and seeing the world as he saw it. And occasionally this individuality of thought degenerates into sheer incomprehensibility. Some of his melodies, play and sing them as often as we will, never come to mean anything to us. It is not that they are ugly or commonplace, not that they are cheap or platitudinous, but simply that they convey nothing; they stand like something opaque between us and the emotion that prompted them; instead of being the medium for the revelation of the composer's thought they are a medium for the concealment of it. In cases like these the explanation seems to be that his mental processes, always rather different from ours, are here so very different that the chain of communication snaps between us; what was a difference of degree now becomes a difference of kind; he speaks another language than ours; the thought, as it were, lives in a space of other dimensions than ours. We may find a rough-and-ready analogy in a writer like Mallarmé, where the general strangeness of thought and style becomes now and then downright unintelligibility. In the one case as in the other, we are dealing with a type of brain so far removed from the normal that the normal brain occasionally finds it simply impossible to follow it.

So again with the harmony of Berlioz. Here the peculiarity of his style has often been commented on, with its odd way of getting from one chord to another, its curious trick of conceiving the harmony in solid blocks, that succeed one another without flowing into one another—much as in certain modern Dutch pictures the colours stand away from each other as if a rigid line always lay between them and prevented their being blended by the atmosphere. The general explanation of this peculiarity of Berlioz's harmony is the easiest one—that it comes from his imperfect technical education. There may be something in this, but a little reflection will show that it is a long way from being the complete explanation. In the first place, one needs scarcely any "training" to avoid some of the progressions that Berlioz constantly uses; the mere hearing of other music would be sufficient to establish unconsciously the routine way of getting from one chord to another; and if Berlioz always takes another way, it can only be because the peculiarity of his diction has its root in a peculiarity of thought. In the second place, the harmonic oddities are really not so numerous in his earliest as in his later works. The melodies of the *Waverley*, *Francs Juges*, and *King Lear* over-tures and of many of the earlier songs are usually harmonised more in the ordinary manner than the melodies of the works of his middle and last epochs; which seems to show again that his harmonic style was rooted in his way of thinking, and became more pronounced as he grew older and more individual. In the third place, if the peculiarities of his harmony had been due to lack of education, one would have expected him, when in more mature years he revised an early work, to correct some of the so-called faults to which a wider experience must have opened his eyes. But it is quite clear that the matter never struck him in this way. In the new edition of his works we have some instructive examples. In 1850, for example, he revised one of his songs, *Adieu, Bessy*, which he had written in 1830. He has altered it in many ways, and made many improvements in the melody, in the phrasing, and in the accompaniment; but the sometimes odd harmonic sequences of the original version remain unchanged in the later. It clearly never struck him that there was anything odd about them; he had really seen his picture in that particular way; it was a question not so much of mere technique as of fundamental conception. In the fourth place, we must always remember that whatever Berlioz thought he thought in terms of the orchestra. He neither played nor understood the piano, and his writing is not piano writing. Now every one knows that many effects that seem strange or ugly on the piano are perfectly pleasurable on the orchestra, where they are set not in the one plane, as it were, but in different planes and different focuses. I fancy that when Berlioz imagined a melodic line or a harmonic combination he saw it not merely as a melody or a harmony but as a piece of colour as well; and the movement of the parts was not only a shifting of lines but a weaving of colours. Many things of his that are ugly or meaningless on the piano have a beauty of their own when heard, as he conceived them, on the orchestra, set in differ-ent depths, as it were, with the toning effect of atmosphere between them; not all standing in the same line in the foreground, with the one white light of the piano making confusion among their colour-values.

There is good reason for believing, then, that much of Berlioz's peculiarity of style is far less the result of lack of education than is generally believed, and that more of it must be attributed to a peculiar constitution of brain that made him really see things just in the way he has depicted them.

Among these early songs and other works there are some that show great strength and charm and originality of expression, such as *Toi qui l'aimas, verse des pleurs*, *La belle voyageuse*, *Le coucher du soleil*, and *Le pêcheur* (that was afterwards incorporated in *Lélio*). His two youthful overtures, the *Waverley* and the *Francs Juges*, though relatively unsubtle in their working-out—for he had little feeling for the symphonic form pure and simple—are yet very individual, while parts of the *Francs Juges* in particular are exceedingly strong. Then the apprentice makes rapid strides on to mastery. The year 1828 may be taken as the turning-point in his career. His unsuccessful scena for the *Prix de Rome*—*Herminie*—exhibits remarkable ardour of conception. There is much that is very youthful in it; but it is decidedly individual, and above all it shows a feeling for rhythm to which there had been no parallel in French music up to that date. The next year saw another *Prix de Rome* scena—*Cléopâtre*—of which the same description will mostly hold good. The rhythmic sense is just as delicate, the melody is becoming purer and stronger, and we have in the aria *Grands Pharaons* a really fine piece of dramatic writing. About the same time he wrote the original eight scenes from *Faust*, containing such gems as the chorus of sylphs, the song of the rat, the song of the flea, Margaret's ballad of the King of Thule, her "Romance", and the serenade of Mephistopheles. Berlioz's musical genius was now entering upon its happiest phase; never, perhaps, did it work so easily and so joyously as in 1829 and the next seven or eight years. It was about 1829, too, that his orchestration began to be so distinctive; one can see him reaching out to new effects in the *Cléopâtre*, the chorus of the sylphs, the ballad of the King of Thule, the *Ballet des Ombres*★ and the fantasia on *The Tempest*.

This increasing mastery of his thoughts coincided with the epoch of his most intense nervous excitement, in which Henrietta Smithson played the part of the match to the gunpowder. So there came about the typical Romantic Berlioz of the *Symphonie fantastique* and *Lélio*, moving about in the world with abnormally heightened senses, his brain on fire, turning waking life into a nightmare, dreaming of blood and fantastic horrors. He exploited this mad psychology to its fullest in the last two movements of the symphony; after that the volcano lost a good deal of its lurid grandeur, and in *Lélio* we get rather less molten lava and rather more ashes than we want. Some of the music of *Lélio*—the ballad of the fisher, the *Chœur des ombres*, the *Chant de bonheur*, the *Harpe éolienne*—is among the finest Berlioz ever wrote; but the scheme as a whole, with its extraordinary prose tirades, is surely the maddest thing ever projected by a musician. Here was the young Romantic in all his imbecile, flamboyant glory, longing to be a brigand, to indulge in orgies of blood and tears, to drink his mistress' health out of the skull of his rival, and all the rest of it. But after all there is very little of this in Berlioz's music. We meet with it again in the "orgy of brigands" in the *Harold en Italie*; and whether that really belongs to 1834 or was written two or three years earlier, at the time when the hyperæmic brain was working at its wildest in the *Symphonie fantastique* and *Lélio*,† matters comparatively little. In any case, the madness ends in 1834 with *Harold*.

And then, with almost startling suddenness, a new Berlioz comes into view. We first see the change in the scena *Le Cinq Mai*—a song on the death of the Emperor Napoleon, to words by

★ Not an orchestral work (P.H.).

† The date of *Lélio* is 1831–1832, but the most absurd thing in it, the *Chanson de brigands*, was written in January 1830—at the same epoch, therefore, as the *Symphonie fantastique*. It is fairly clear that 1829–1830 marked the climax of Berlioz's eccentricity, and that his passion for Henrietta Smithson had much to do with it.

Béranger—which is dated 1834 by M. Adolphe Jullien and 1832 by Herr Weingartner and M. Malherbe. The precise date is unimportant. The essential fact is that Berlioz's brain was now acquiring what it had hitherto lacked—it was beginning to be touched with a philosophic sense of the reality of things. He had, of course, in much of his earlier work, written seriously and beautifully; but *Le Cinq Mai* has qualities beyond these. His songs *La captive* (1832) and *Sara la baigneuse* (1833?) carry on the line from the earlier songs and overtures; what we get in addition, in *Le Cinq Mai*, is a gravity and ordered intensity of conception that as a whole are absent from the earlier works. He is becoming less of an egoist, more capable of voicing the thought of humanity as a whole; the Romanticist is making way for the complete human being. In the *Nuits d'Eté* (1834) there is a larger spirit than in any of his previous songs. Between 1835 and 1838* we have three noble works—*Benvenuto Cellini*, the *Requiem*, and *Roméo et Juliette*; and to no previous work of Berlioz would the epithet "noble" be really applicable. The change is not so much a musical as an intellectual—we may almost say ethical—one. Look at him, for example, in the opening of the *Requiem*. All the madness, the pose, the egoism of the *Symphonie fantastique* and its brethren have disappeared. Berlioz now has an eye for something more in life than his own unshorn locks and his sultry amours. He no longer thinks himself the centre of the universe; he no longer believes in the Berliozcentric theory, and does not write with one eye on the mirror half the time. In place of all this we have a Berlioz who has sunk his aggressive subjectivity and learned to regard life objectively. His spirit touched to finer issues, he sings, not Berlioz, but humanity as a whole. He is now what every great artist is instinctively—a philosopher as well as a singer; by the *Requiem* he earns his right to stand among the serious, brooding spirits of the earth. So again in the final scene of *Roméo et Juliette*, where he rises to loftier heights than he could ever have attained while he was in the throes of his egoistic Romanticism. Here again, as in the *Requiem*, he speaks with the authority of the

* 1839 (P.H.).

seer as well as the voice of the orator; there is the thrill of profound conviction in the music, the note of inspired comprehension of men and nature as a whole. In a word, the old Berlioz has gone; a new Berlioz stands in his place, wiser than of old, purified and chastened by his experiences, artist and thinker in one.

x

In 1838, then, everything seemed of the happiest promise for his art. But that promise, alas, was not fulfilled so amply as might have been hoped for. Whatever the real cause may have been, Berlioz, as we have seen, now slackened greatly in his musical production. It could not have been wholly due to his *feuilleton* writing, for he was never so busy with this as in the seven years onward from 1833 (the year in which he married Henrietta Smithson, and had to earn money in some way or other). He complains to Humbert Ferrand that his journalism leaves him little time to write music, but the facts are that he was really keeping up a very good output. At the end of what I have called his first epoch he received some large sums of money—4,000 francs for the *Requiem* (1837), 20,000 francs from Paganini for *Harold en Italie* (1838), and 10,000 francs for the *Symphonie funèbre et triomphale* (1840)—enabling him to give up journalism and to travel. He was away frequently between 1841 and 1855, but not enough to account for the singularly small amount of music he wrote—an amount that becomes still smaller in the later years.

We cannot, I think, resist the conclusion that even between 1840 and 1855 the seeds of his illness were in him and affecting his powers of work. So far as can be ascertained from his letters, he became aware of his malady about 1855, but there is no warrant for thinking it actually began then; his father had suffered from the same complaint, and the son was evidently a doomed man. It is about 1855 that his letters begin to show what ravages his awful malady—a neuralgia of the intestines, he calls it—was making in him. The atrocious pain weakened him through and through; then the springs of energy within him were still further relaxed by the quantities of opium he had to take. He lost, at times, even his interest in art. In November 1856 he speaks to the Princess Sayn-Wittgenstein of "the horrible moments of disgust with which my illness inspires me", during which "I find everything I have written" (he is working at *Les Troyens*) "cold, dull, stupid, tasteless; I have a great mind to burn it all." A month later he writes that he has been so ill that he could not go on with his score. Thus the melancholy record continues in letter after letter: he is ill "in soul, in body, in heart, in head"; an access of his "damned neuralgia" keeps him on his back for sixteen hours; "I cannot walk, I only drag myself along; I cannot think, I only ruminate"; "I live in an absolute isolation of soul; I do nothing but suffer eight or nine hours a day, without hope of any kind, wanting only to sleep, and appreciating the truth of the Chinese proverb—it is better to be sitting than standing, lying than sitting, asleep than awake, and dead than asleep"; "my neurosis grows and has now settled in the head; sometimes I stagger like a drunken man and dare not go out alone"; "these obstinate sufferings enervate me, brutalise me; I become more and more like an animal, indifferent to everything, or almost everything"; his doctors tell him he has "a general inflammation of the nervous system", and that he must "live like an oyster, without thought and without sensation"; some days he has "attacks of hysteria like a young girl"; "Mon Dieu, que je suis triste!"; "I suffer each day so terribly, from seven in the morning till four in the afternoon, that during such crises my thoughts are completely confused"; he takes so long over the writing of *Béatrice et Bénédict* because, owing to his illness, his musical ideas come to him with extreme slowness—while after he has written it he forgets it, and when he hears it it sounds quite new to him. To his other correspondents it is always the same pitiful story: "On certain days I cannot write ten consecutive lines; it takes me sometimes four days to finish an article."

It is impossible to believe that so serious a disorder began only in 1855, when Berlioz first became fully conscious of it; it must have been in him years before, and must even then have affected his powers of work.* But such music as he did find energy to write is eloquent of the new condition of his being. Not only bodily but mentally Berlioz was a changed man—a point that should be insisted on in view of the traditional misunderstanding of him. I have already remarked upon the Berlioz "legend" that is generally accepted, a legend founded solely on the Berlioz of twenty-five or thirty. Heine gave perhaps the finest expression to this aspect of him in the passage in which he speaks of him as "a colossal nightingale, a lark the size of an eagle, such as once existed, they say, in the primitive world. Yes, the music of Berlioz, in general, has for me something primitive, almost antediluvian; it sets me dreaming of gigantic species of extinct animals, of mammoths, of fabulous empires with fabulous sins, of all kinds of impossibilities piled one on top of the other; these magic accents recall to us Babylon, the hanging gardens of Semiramis, the marvels of Nineveh, the audacious edifices of Mizraim, such as we see them in the pictures of the English painter Martin." That is not a bad description, in spite of its verbal fantasy, of the Berlioz of the last two movements of the *Symphonie fantastique*, the orgy of brigands in *Harold en Italie*, the ride to the abyss in *Faust*, and, let us even say, the "Tuba mirum" of the *Requiem*. But it is only a quarter, a tenth, of the real Berlioz. Yet the old legend still goes on; even so careful a student as Mr. W. H. Hadow has just said, in his article in the new "Grove's Dictionary", that "his imagination seems always at white heat; his eloquence pours forth in a turbid, impetuous torrent which levels all obstacles and overpowers all restraint. It is the fashion to compare him with Victor Hugo, and on one side at any rate the comparison is just. Both were artists of immense creative power, both were endowed with an exceptional gift of oratory, both ranged at will over the entire gamut of human passion. But here resemblance ends. Beside the extravagance of Berlioz, Hugo is reticent; beside the technical errors of the musician the verse of the poet is as faultless as a Greek statue."

* Jullien (p. 241) says "it was about this time that the neuralgia *to which he had always been subject* settled in the intestines. . . ."

One really gets rather tired of this perpetual harping upon the extravagance of Berlioz. The picture is pure caricature, not a portrait; one or two features in the physiognomy are selected and exaggerated, posed in the strongest light, and factitiously made to appear as the essential points of the man. Yet a baby with any knowledge of Berlioz could demonstrate the falsity of the picture. Where is the "extravagance", the want of "reticence", in the *Waverley* overture, the *Roi Lear* overture, the first three movements of the *Symphonie fantastique*, the twenty or thirty songs, the bulk of *Faust*, the bulk of *Harold en Italie*, the bulk of *Lélio*, the three fine pieces that make up the *Tristia*, the *Cinq Mai*, the bulk of the *Requiem, Benvenuto Cellini, Roméo et Juliette*, the noble *Symphonie funèbre et triomphale*, the *Carnaval romain* overture, the *Enfance du Christ, Béatrice et Bénédict*, or *Les Troyens*? Out of all these thousands of pages, how ridiculously few of them deserve the epithet of "extravagance"; of how many of them is it true that Berlioz's "eloquence pours forth in a turbid, impetuous torrent which levels all obstacles and overpowers all restraint"?

The truth is that even in the youthful Berlioz there was considerable "reticence," considerable power to sympathise with and express not only the flamboyant but the tender, the pathetic, the delicate. We have already seen that his intellectual and moral powers came to their climax about 1838, at which time he was singing with enormous passion, but also with perfect restraint and impressive nobility. Both the music and the prose of his later years show how greatly his character was altering; it is simply ludicrous to attempt to describe *this* Berlioz in the language that was applicable only to the worst of the Berlioz of twenty years before. Physical and mental suffering, trials in private and perpetual disappointment in public life, chastened the man's soul, brought out the finer elements of it. He fought the powers of evil calmly and steadily with that admirable weapon of irony of his. Once he forgot himself, in the Wagner affair of 1861; but one can forgive, or at any rate understand, the momentary wave of malevolence that surged up in him then, if one thinks of the grievous illness that racked the poor frame, and the unending insults that had been his own lot as an opera composer. Apart from this episode, Berlioz always commands our respect in his later years. Always the brain, the spirit, were uppermost; where other men would have become abusive he only became more mordantly witty; where the passion of defeat would have obscured the eyes of other men he only saw the more clearly and penetratingly. Look at him in his later portraits, with that fine intellectual mouth, full of a strength that is not contradicted, but reinforced, by the ironic humour that plays over it. Yes, he met the shocks of fortune well, and they were many and rude. If we want a summary contrast of the later and the earlier Berlioz, we have only to compare the ebullient letters of his youth with the letters written to the Princess Sayn-Wittgenstein between 1852 and 1867. The very style is altered; the later letters read easily and beautifully, without any of those abrupt distortions and exaggerations that pull us up with a shock in the earlier ones. When he has to castigate, he does it like a gentleman, with the rapier, not the bludgeon. And how perfectly does he maintain the essential dignity of the artist against this well-meaning but inquisitive and slightly vulgar aristocrat; with what fine breeding, what exquisite use of the iron hand within the glove, does he repel her interferences with matters that concern only himself, conveying to her that there are precincts within his soul to which neither her friendship nor her position give her the right of entry!

No, the cheap literary oleographs that do duty for the portraits of Berlioz are ludicrously insuggestive of what Berlioz really was. His fever had all died down even by 1846—supposing the ride to the abyss in *Faust* really to belong to that and not an earlier date; and everything after then speaks of a vastly altered being. Had he only kept his health up to this stage of his career, who knows to what sunlit heights he might not have attained? In spirit, in experience of life, in moral balance, in the technique of his art, he had now enormously improved; but set against all this was that insidious disease that so woefully hindered the free working of what had once been so eager and keen a brain. It diminished the quantity of work he could do; it spoiled some of it altogether—the cantata *L'Impériale*, for example, where the unimpressive writing is throughout that of a mentally exhausted man. Yet a sure instinct seems often to have guided him even in this epoch of distress and frustration. He could write only a few hours each week; but as a rule he seems to have chosen happily his times for work, seizing the rare and fleeting moments when the poor brain and body were held together in a temporary harmony. The best of his later work need not fear comparison with the best of his earlier periods. And how changed in mood and outlook it all is! All his old Romanticism is gone, not only from his music but from the basis of his music. Instead of the old violent literary themes, with their clangorous rhetoric and their purple colouring, he now loves to dwell among themes of classic purity of outline, and to lavish upon them an infinite delicacy of treatment. His musical style becomes at times extraordinarily beautiful and supple; without losing any of the essential strength of his earlier manner, he confutes, by the exquisite, pearly delicacy of *L'Enfance du Christ* and *Béatrice et Bénédict*, the ignoramuses who then, as now, saw nothing in him but a master of the *baroque* and grotesque. His subjects are simple; he draws and colours them, as in *Béatrice et Bénédict*, with the rarest and brightest grace,* or, as in *L'Enfance du Christ*, with a curiously engaging simplicity of manner that suggests Puvis de Chavannes or the *primitifs*. And his strength, where he chooses to let it show, is now so finely controlled, so thoroughly and masterfully bent to the creation of beauty. In the great *Te Deum* we see his style at something like its finest; all the coarseness and clumsiness that clung to his earlier strength have gone; the muscle shows none of the raw vigour of the early days, but plays easily and flexibly under the velvet skin; while in his softer moments there is a new and extraordinary sweetness, a honeying of the voice that yet sacrifices none of its old virility. And for his last work† he draws

---

* He himself describes it as "a caprice written with the point of a needle, and demanding excessive delicacy of execution". Yet this is the man for whom the world can find only the one epithet of "extravagant"!

† In fact Berlioz's last work was not *Les Troyens* but *Béatrice et Bénédict* (P.H.).

not upon any of the Romantic contemporaries of his youth, not even upon that other Romanticist—Shakespeare—to whom he was always so closely drawn, but upon his beloved Vergil; it is with a classic subject, set with classic sobriety of manner and amplitude of feeling, that he chooses to end his career. What that work meant for him only those can realise who study his letters during the seven years* in which he was engaged upon it. It was his refuge, his method of escape from the world; it was for him that "tower of ivory" of which Flaubert speaks, into which the artist can mount, there to dream of the ideal that is unrealisable in life. He was a dying man all these years, and in much of the music of *Les Troyens* there are only too many signs of physical and mental exhaustion. But it has its extraordinarily fine moments, and the general conception is grander than anything Berlioz had attempted since the *Requiem*. There is something strangely moving in this reversion of the old musician, in his latest years, to the passions and the ideals of his youth. Fiction could not invent anything more touchingly beautiful than that final meeting with the Estelle he had loved as a boy of ten or twelve, and the resurgence of all the old romantic feeling for his *Stella montis*—that curious blinding of the fleshly eye that permitted him to see in the woman of sixty-seven only the winsome girl he had loved half-a-century before. In his art there was a similar atavism; the old fighter puts away, with a sadly ironic smile, the red flag under which he had once fought so fiercely, and seeks companionship among the great calm figures of the past. There may have been a deliberate intention of separating himself quite pointedly from Wagner, which may account for something at least of his later clinging to Gluck and the classics. But on the whole it seems more probable that the reversion to these less fevered, more spacious spirits was just the spontaneous sinking of the weary soul into the arms that were most ready to receive it. He knew he was a beaten man; he knew that during his

* Seven years between inception and performance. The libretto and score were written in two years (1856–8) though Berlioz subsequently made extensive alterations (P.H.).

lifetime at any rate his star was doomed to suffer eclipse; whatever chance he might have had of fighting his way through the clouds again, of overcoming the Parisian ignorance of and prejudice against him, was shattered by the disease that broke him, body and soul. So he retired into himself and waited, as calmly and philosophically as might be, for the end.

To us his situation seems even more tragic than it must have seemed to himself. Knowing what extraordinary promise he was giving in 1838, we can only regard the last thirty years of his life as a failure to redeem that promise, at all events in its entirety. In both fields—the vocal and the instrumental—he seems to halt uncertainly, not quite knowing how to carry on the work he had begun. The later music, as I have tried to show, is generally beautiful enough; the fault does not lie there. But Berlioz failed to beat out for himself the new forms that might reasonably have been expected from him by those who had followed his career from the first. All his life he longed ardently to be an opera composer. But the failure of *Benvenuto Cellini* in 1837,* combined with the intrigues of his enemies, shuts him out of the Opera for twenty-five years; in 1846, again, the failure of *Faust* gives him another crushing blow. When he resumes his operatic writing, the capacity and the desire to strike out new forms seem to have gone; he is content to work within the limits of the frame that Gluck bequeathed to him. All this time he practically neglects purely instrumental music, thus failing to work out the conclusions towards which he seemed to have been feeling his way in his earlier works. Nothing in him comes to its full fruition; each branch is lopped off almost as soon as it leaves the trunk. He is a pathetic monument of incompleteness; his disease and the ignorant public between them slew his art. But the work he actually did seems on this account only the more wonderful. He was a genius of the first rank; and there is little doubt that the better his music is known the more respectful and the more sympathetic will be the tone of criticism towards him.

MUSICAL STUDIES 1905

* 1838 (P.H.).

II

General Essays

1

The Young Romantics

A CORRESPONDENT WHO evidently does not know that enough is as good as a feast reminds me that in some recent articles on Berlioz I left a thread untied, saying I would take up the loose end later. As well as I recollect, it had something to do with the mistaken popular view that artists in general are, and the French romantics in particular were, the same in their art as in their lives.

That the young romantics of the dangerous period—the 1830s —were a maladjusted crew, suffering from a "hypertrophy of the sensibilities", is beyond question. The trouble is generally put down to the excitement of the Napoleonic wars and their after-math of disillusion and exhaustion. Can you blame us for being what we are, Alfred de Musset cried in a passage that does duty in all the histories, conceived as we were between two battles? (Not, by the way, between two bottles, as a compositor, perhaps speaking more wisely than he knew, once made me say.) But the historians, I think, have not made enough distinction between the romantics as they were in the street and the café and what they were in their art, or between the stronger and the feebler members of the tribe.

If the reader wishes to realise the full extent of the emotional unbalance of these young people in general he should not be content with the specimens from their correspondence quoted in the biographies of those of them who later became famous.

He should turn to M. Louis Maigron's *Le Romantisme et les Mœurs*. M. Maigron had the good fortune to come into possession of a large number of unpublished letters from young Frenchmen who never achieved authorship but laid bare their tortured souls in their correspondence with their friends. On the surface the complaints are the same as those scattered about in the letters of the young Berlioz—complaints about the flatness and ugliness of the world around them, longings for more colourful worlds of sultans and odalisques and houris and hashish and pirates and brigands, worlds of magnificent rapes and assassinations and tortures, of wine drunk out of enemies' skulls, and so on.

Every one of these young would-be artists was the victim of the common delusion that to describe a thing in art one must have done it or suffered it. One poor fellow was confident he could have written a marvellous tragedy on illegitimacy if only he had not had the misfortune to be born in wedlock: why, he wailed, did not my parents create me a bastard?

M. Maigron swims with the stream in regarding Berlioz as "un exemplaire accompli" of this indiscipline of emotion, not only in his life but in his art, and not only in his youth but in his maturity:

> exaspérations, grincements de dents, pamoisons, rugissements, et tout l'attirail de la démence romantique. Rien de raisonnable, d'équilibré, d'harmonieux, de classique, au beau sens du mot. Il est toujours hors de lui, toujours dans un extrême. . . . Les jours de calme, de poésie, de rêve, sont de plus en plus rares, et c'est au contraire l'agitation, l'exaltation qui est bientôt dévenue son état normal.

All of which, I am afraid, merely proves that M. Maigron is not a musician. Berlioz talked a vast amount of laughable nonsense in his letters, but in his art he had himself on a tight rein from the beginning. So with Flaubert. As a young man he slept with a dagger under his pillow, did the regulation amount of talking about skulls, and lamented that his lot had been cast in bourgeois France. "I was born to be Emperor of Cochin-China, to smoke pipes six feet long, to have six thousand wives, scimitars to sweep off the heads of people whose looks I didn't like, Numidian mares, marble basins", and all the rest of it. But when it became a matter of artistic creation we find him slaving at his desk like a galley slave at his oar, labouring eight hours a day at polishing and filing his style—for expression, as he saw, is what finally matters in a work of art. In his creative hours there was no young-romantic rant about not being able to make literature of a subject unless and until you have lived it. "My dear fellow," he wrote to a friend, "you will depict wine, love, women, glory, only on condition that you are neither drunkard, nor lover, nor husband, nor swashbuckler."

Berlioz also was one thing in his talk and his letters and quite another in his art. As proof that he was the victim of an "imagination désordonnée, furieuse et toujours inassouvie", "un volcan sans cesse en éruption, un torrent de lave incandescente", M. Maigron cites the famous excursion of 1831 that had for its ostensible objects the murder of the fickle Marie Moke and Berlioz's suicide. Nothing, on paper, could be madder, sillier. But the fact is that at what should have been the critical moment Berlioz put love and jealousy out of his mind and settled down to the hard work of building up his *Lélio* out of material old and new; and that meant voluntary submission to the bridle and the bit.

The point I am labouring is of importance because it is still the careless way of even musical people who do not know the whole or the real Berlioz to write about him as if he were summed up in the macabre extravagances of the orgy of brigands in *Harold in Italy* and the Witches' Sabbath in the *Fantastique*. What do they know of the real Berlioz, the truly classic Berlioz who ranged from the *Eight Scenes from Faust* of the young man of twenty-five to the noble *Troyens* and the fine-fingered *Béatrice and Bénédict* of the last years? The farcical follies of his life are not to be found in his work. For art looks after her own: she may abandon her weaklings and bastards without remorse on the steps of the Foundling Hospital, but her strong and legitimate offspring she keeps and rules with a rod of iron.

7 September 1947

2

The Tragedy of Berlioz

SOME FRENCH ESSAYIST whom I was reading a little while ago (I cannot recall his name or the article at the moment), remarked very justly on the new facial type shown by some of the musicians of the Romantic period—the melancholy delicacy of Chopin's face, the nervous irony and half-concealed suffering of Berlioz's, the death-like thinness and pallor of Paganini's. We have, indeed, only to turn over any well-illustrated history of music, and look at the bull-necked, mastiff-jawed, solidly poised German musicians of the previous four hundred years, from Hans Sachs to Luther, from Luther to Bach and Handel, from these to Beethoven, to realise what a quite new tissue and facial type we have, say, in Chopin. But on the whole the most complete representative of the new spirit in music is Berlioz. He is romanticism incarnate, its new warmth of aspiration, its new truths of vision, and its failures and excesses in practice. Like the sacrificial victim of some old religion, he seems to have been chosen to atone for the sins of the whole tribe. On his own shoulders alone he bore the whole burden of romanticism in French music. The literary men and the painters fought in companies: each of them felt behind and around him the strength of the phalanx. But Berlioz had neither predecessors, contemporaries nor successors in his own sphere. And his was a double tragedy. It was not only that he found virtually no public in his lifetime; that, while he saw the Opéra opened to a score of inferior men, its doors remained closed to him nearly all his life; and that for sheer subsistence' sake he had to waste much of his genius in journalism. Worse than all this, as we see him now, was the fact that he outgrew his youthful self and could not find a maturer one of the same inner fire and self-confidence. He grew old before his time, and found himself, at the end, in a strange world that was past his understanding. No wonder, then, that his fine face moves us as perhaps no other musician's does. It reminds us of a caged and wounded eagle.

He was an impressive illustration of the truth that in music it is dangerous to be *too* original. A composer's only chance of unceasing growth throughout his career lies in his never wholly losing touch with tradition. Art, like nature, can only express itself through forms; and forms are matters of slow growth. The work of finding the final forms for wholly new ideas seems to be beyond the powers of any one artist. Sooner or later it happens with all the artists who try to cut the cable of the past—we see it clearly in the cases of Debussy, Stravinsky, and Schoenberg—that they write themselves out. They can, in their early years, throw out a wholly new shoot; but if they wilfully try to project it too far from the parent stem it dries up, sooner or later, from lack of nourishment. There was nothing in Berlioz of the peculiar self-consciousness of the later innovators. His innovations were always spontaneous, never a matter of the coldly functioning will. But all the same he was broken, as the later men are, on the wheel of his own originality. His pure Romantic period lasted only some twelve or fifteen years. In that time he put a great many new ideas into circulation. But he did not succeed in making for them a corresponding new technique (apart, needless to say, from that of the orchestra); and the result was that after the first glorious flood of Romanticism in him had lost its youthful vitality and heaven-storming audacity, when the time came, as it comes to every artist in the middle years, when the thought, if it is to function freely, must have made for itself an instrument of expression of its own that will not merely obey the imagination unquestioningly but will positively stimulate it—when that time came, Berlioz was in some respects relatively less sure of himself than he had been in the beginning.

He died fifty years ago yesterday; yet few people realise even yet his great originality, except as an orchestrator. He brought new rhythms into music, and with them, as a necessary corollary, new types of melody. It is no wonder that in his own day his melodies were regarded as ugly; for most music lovers of our own time fail to get at the secret of them. Indirectly he is a smashing disproof of the superficial theory that a "national" music can only be built upon folk-song. Berlioz was the greatest musician France had so far produced; and his music has about as much in common with folk-song as a Whistler Nocturne has with a coloured Christmas presentation plate. It was precisely because there was absolutely no common denominator between Berlioz's music and folk-music that his contemporaries missed his significance. For, whether the world realises it or not, its ideas of melody have hitherto been derived too much from folk-song and dance (especially those of Germany), which have imposed their square-cut phrases even upon instrumental music. People who had been accustomed to thinking in four-square could not adapt themselves to the seeming caprice of the conduct of Berlioz's melodies, that began and ended and ran their middle course in a way purely their own, not rhythmless but obeying a freer and subtler rhythmical impulse than classical music had ever known. His was the beginning of that free *prose style* in music that we have seen trying to establish itself in the art of the last thirty years, as against the more conventional rhythmical patterns of what may be called the verse style. But he not only left no successors; he did not even remain himself to the end of his days. He began as a Romantic; he ended as a rather tired Classic. He doubles upon his own tracks and even runs back beyond his origins: the composer of the *Symphonie fantastique*, the contemporary of Hugo and Delacroix, becomes in his later years the contemporary of Gluck.

There is, I imagine, no other case of the kind in musical history. Sometimes the style of a composer has become simplified towards the end of his career; Hugo Wolf is the cardinal example of this. But it implies no restriction of the range of the man's thinking, no cessation even of his purely musical development. It means only that he has learned the short cuts to expression, discovered how many adjectives and adverbs he can leave out and yet make the tissue of his style only the stronger for their absence. The average pressure of thought in Wolf's Italian Song-Book is not less but greater than in his settings, say, of Eichendorff; the page is now barer of notes, but the few notes that are used carry a larger burden of expression. Wolf has *trained* his style, so to speak, as an athlete trains his body; it no longer carries an ounce of superfluous fat.

This is not what happened in the case of Berlioz. What we see there is not so much the pregnant simplification of style that comes with mastery of one's maturer thinking and feeling as a narrowing of the field of thought and emotion. Berlioz had ceased to be interested in most of the moods and sensations that had meant everything to him in his youth. It looked at first as if he were going to widen the range of musical expression in the same way and to the same extent as the painters and the poets and the novelists widened the range of their own special arts. The great manifesto of Romanticism is Victor Hugo's famous preface to his *Cromwell*. The poetic Romanticists and the workers in the plastic arts were very conscious of themselves and of their ideals. Berlioz, carrying the whole burden of French musical Romanticism upon his shoulders, was intensely conscious of himself as an individual, but not as a historical or aesthetic "moment." He gave us, therefore, no manifesto; but Hugo unconsciously said for him all that he would have said for himself had he felt the need of hurling a challenge in the face of the world. The poets and painters deliberately cut themselves loose from the immediate past. It was the paradox of Berlioz that he was rooted in two great classical masters, Beethoven and Gluck, who remained the great gods of his cosmogony until the last. He was, we may almost say a Romanticist without knowing it.

But it is *his* Romanticism as well as that of the poets that Hugo voices in the *Cromwell* preface. There he insists on the need for tempering the chill of the pure sublime with the grotesque. Art was no longer to be a mere manipulation of decorous, standardised emotional patterns, but as varied as life itself. "Tout ce qui est dans la nature est dans l'art". Art should thus include the so-called ugly as well as the so-called beautiful, if only for the reason that "the beautiful has only one type, the ugly has a thousand". "The ugly", of course, must not be taken in its usual disparaging sense: Hugo means to give a concrete illustration, that in dealing with the story, say, of Beauty and the Beast, the Beast, to the genuine artist, ought to be as interesting as Beauty. Wagner was to show later that Alberich and Mime and Hagen could be as fascinating as Siegfried and Siegmund and Brynhilde. It looked at first as if Berlioz would effect this sorely-needed emancipation of music. His ideas and his technique were very crude in such things as the Witches' Sabbath, the orgy of brigands, and Faust's Ride to the Abyss; but that was inevitable. In the ordinary course of things he might have been expected to make for himself a new technique for the new pictures of which he had the first vague vision. Had he done so, he would have quickened the development of music by forty or fifty years. But the visions themselves died out in him. While poetry and prose and painting moved steadily on, never losing a foot of the new ground they won, music gave up the fight. There was only Berlioz to carry it on, and he lost faith in the ideals of his youth. Music had to wait the coming of Stravinsky before it succeeded in widening its own scope of expression as the Romantic painters and poets had widened theirs.

In his later years Berlioz turned his back on Romanticism and sought salvation in the serener classic world. Even his musical forms became what we may almost call academic. His double opera—*The Capture of Troy* and *The Trojans at Carthage*—(1856-

1858), is divided into "numbers" like any eighteenth century work. It is possible that his desire to make a stand against the rising tide of Wagnerism made him thus call pointed attention to his own adherence to classic precedents, and at the same time revert deliberately, in many places, to the style of Gluck. But this may not be the whole explanation. I have elsewhere suggested that he was mentally a tired and broken man during the last ten or more years of his life. He suffered agonies from what he calls an intestinal neuralgia, and the large quantities of opium he had to take to ease his pain must have dulled his brain somewhat. Now and then, particularly in *The Trojans at Carthage*, his new simplicity of style goes along with a new profundity of thought; but too often we feel that the simplicity, the reversion to the past, are the result of weariness of body and of soul. Berlioz's tragedy was to outlive the ideals of his youth.

THE OBSERVER 9 March 1919
16 March 1919

3

A Berlioz Revival?

THIS IS THE day of revivals and discoveries. Shall we, before long, revive Berlioz,—or, as we may perhaps put it with more truth, discover him? The tendency today is to sniff a little at the greatest masters, whose calm superiority, it must be admitted, *does* become rather irritating at times, and to take to our hearts the men a degree less great. The biggest geniuses of all are perhaps a shade too much like the impersonal forces of nature; the geniuses of the rank just below the first interest us in a peculiar way because they are more like ourselves. Your very greatest composer is a sort of summary or generalisation of humanity, the meeting-point of a hundred historical forces; the lesser men often have a more intriguing individuality.

A friend of mine used to argue with me that we ought to collect second, not first, editions. Every copy of a first edition, he used to contend, is carefully preserved by someone or other who hopes for a rise in value, whereas no one bothers about second editions. It stands to reason, then, he would say, that first editions will ultimately be a drug on the market, while the scarcity of second editions will make them so sought after that one of these days millionaires will start bidding against each other for them. There must be something in this theory, and we see to-day the application of it, in a sense, to music. All the world has collected front-rank composers so long that the value of them has depreciated a little; and now the really wise speculators are trying to corner the best specimens of the second rank. Beethoven and Brahms and Wagner are in the box labelled "Any book in this lot 6d"; it is Moussorgsky, or Stravinsky, or Honegger, or Malipiero, that the cute connoisseur now shows you and tells how he picked him up before anyone else had any idea there was going to be a boom in him.

The truth is that the average man knows very little about music, and has not room in his heart for more than one adoration at a time. For most people, music means something that began with Bach and ended about 1900. They find it hard to believe that some of the music that was written before Bach is as wonderful in its way as any of the music written since. Even within the period he knows, the plain man has so far kept only to the main roads. He gets, indeed, few opportunities of exploring the side paths, and when he does happen to be shunted on to one his chief wish is to get back to the main road as soon as he can. He knows a little, say, about Haydn and Mozart, but he knows nothing of the contemporary composers who, though they shared with Haydn and Mozart the general characteristics of their epoch, were not merely imitators of these great men but independent personalities. When he comes upon Cimarosa—as happened with *Gli Astuzie Femminili* a couple of years ago—he helplessly declares the music to be "Mozartian"; which is very much like saying that Schubert is only another Schumann, or Sullivan only another Offenbach.

But there is now springing up a refreshing curiosity on the part even of the plain man as to the music that lies off the beaten track. He is getting extremely interested in the Elizabethans. Soon his interest may be extended to Palestrina and the Continental polyphonists in general. He is learning to listen in new ways. There is a convention in listening as in everything else; and the way of listening that is right enough for a Beethoven adagio or a Wagner opera is not quite right for Dowland or Byrd. The plain man, in fact, is slowly discovering that there are fifty ways of conceiving music, and that to listen to music of one kind with ears that have been too exclusively trained on another kind is to go grievously wrong. The eighteenth century,—nay, even the nineteenth, as represented by as great a historian as Ambros —shuddered at what were thought to be the harmonic aberrations of Gesualdo, Prince of Venosa. We of today, being no longer slaves to "classical" harmony, find Gesualdo's harmonies and progressions not only not horrifying but positively pleasing. And when people have learned once more to listen in a new way, Berlioz, I fancy, will be thought more highly of than he is at present.

There are already signs of the coming reaction in his favour. He has surely been the most misunderstood composer of the last two centuries. It is hopeless to expect to see Berlioz as he really is unless you can shake off the tyranny of the German classics. His melody is not theirs, nor his harmony, nor his rhythm. Unfortunately for him, he came at the time when German music was setting out on its all-conquering career in Western Europe. German music trained people to a certain way of listening; and necessarily any music that did not accommodate itself to that way was written down as inferior. It is to the eternal credit of Schumann as a critic that he saw from the beginning that to understand Berlioz the hearer would have to place himself first of all at Berlioz's point of view, and that this was so new and purely personal a point of view that classical German music would only hinder a man from finding it.

Some day, I am sure, the public—if only it can hear Berlioz often enough—will find the right point of view. Meanwhile criticism can help a little, perhaps. France has produced lately some extremely illuminative Berlioz criticism; and one of the best specimens of it that I have met with is an article in the current number of *La Revue Musicale* by M. Paul Marie Masson, which is apparently an extract from a book by M. Masson on Berlioz that is to be published soon.* We sorely need a volume that shall state the whole case for Berlioz as the modern musician who admires him sees it, and perhaps M. Masson's book will turn out to be what we have been long looking for.

* Paris, 1923 (P.H.).

He makes it clear that, simply by judging Berlioz too exclusively by the standards of classical German art, people have double-debited him with his faults while failing to credit him with half his virtues. All the older critics fastened gleefully on his weakness in symphonic construction. It cannot be denied: here he seems only an amateur by the side of Beethoven or Brahms or Strauss. Certain kinds of technique he never mastered, and this was one of them. Where he professes to play the classical game it is only right that he should be judged by the laws of that game.

But while it is important that we shall see clearly what he cannot do, it is even more important that we shall see clearly what he can; and the things he can do best are not to be measured by the classical German standards. His melody and his rhythm do not conform to these standards. They are much freer—especially his rhythm—than the average German melody and rhythm, which have been strongly influenced by the prosody of German verse. Our rhythmical sense is expanding, largely under the influence of the polyphonic music of the seventeenth century, and when people have completely shaken off the bonds of the square German rhythms of the classical period they will be in a better position to respond to the more flexibly articulated rhythms of Berlioz.

The old view of his harmony was that it was amateurish. We cannot deny that here and there he shows in this field, as in others, the results of a lack of school discipline; but, after all, these instances are rare. What is too often regarded as technical insufficiency on his part is in reality only his thoroughly personal way of conceiving harmony. Once we get used to his peculiar tissue, with its scorn of the customary easy transitions (especially by way of the dominant seventh), his harmony has a fascinating savour of its own.

But it is in the field of colour that the ordinary ear at present lags far behind Berlioz. By this I do not mean simply that he is a wonderful colourist in the conventional sense of the term. I mean rather that the key to his seemingly strange harmony is often to be found in his colour. The piano plays a much larger part in the harmonic thinking of most composers than they are conscious of themselves. It played no part whatever in Berlioz's thinking; the logic of his harmony depends more than that of the ordinary composer does on relations of orchestral timbre.

The simplest possible illustration that I can give here is that of the harmony in the fourth bar of the accompaniment of the song "Absence". On the piano it sounds crude: on the orchestra, with each of the apparently discordant notes moving as an independent strand of colour, the effect is perfectly right. As M. Masson points out, what sometimes looks like lack of harmonic resource on Berlioz's part is really an extraordinarily fine sense of timbres indulging itself luxuriously. "We may say", as M. Masson puts it, "that he harmonises by timbres; his famous unisons become veritable harmonies." He *heard*, in fact, in a way different from that of the German classics, who mostly thought in a species of abstract harmony and then laid this out for instruments, whereas Berlioz, never having learned the piano, could not conceive abstract harmony, but only harmony in terms of concrete instrumental timbres. His day will surely come, for music everywhere is reaching out to the things he specially stood for—more particularly freedom of rhythm and the expressiveness of timbre-harmony as distinct from the abstract or black-and-white harmony of the piano.

11 March 1923

4

The Mind of Berlioz

THE PERFORMANCE OF *The Damnation of Faust* last Thursday may have set many people trying to assess once more Berlioz's real position and value in the world of music. That a number of people are conscientiously unable to see him at all as one of the great figures of the art is something which others of us can only note without being impressed by it: not all kinds of music are for all listeners, and musical criticism will not make much progress until we have recognised that the minds both of composers and of listeners fall into well-defined types, and that the mental world of one type is inaccessible to minds of an antithetical type. What is more disturbing than this frank repugnance to Berlioz on the part of many good musicians is the number of reservations that even his admirers have to make in connection with him if they are to be honest with themselves. For me he becomes a more and more interesting figure the longer I study him: I could set forth several ways in which I believe him to be unsurpassed among musicians, and, I venture to say, unsurpassable. How does it come about, then, that this extraordinarily gifted composer cannot put together a long work without grafting upon it so many things which we would have preferred to be otherwise? Why, for instance, does he spoil a work that in the main has been so consistently good as *Faust* has been up to this point by that rather absurd "Pandemonium" near the end of it?

What was it in the peculiar nature of the man's genius that

84

made it difficult for him to refrain from spoiling a fine thing at some point or other? It is frequently said that he is a poor melodist. With that I cannot agree: melody after melody of his is to me among the most moving things of the kind ever written. But I find myself again and again a little chilled by the curious lapse into commonplace in the final line of some of his best melodies: see, for example, the ending of *La Captive*, of the ballad of the King of Thule (in *Faust*), of the melody first given out by the cor anglais in the *Carnaval romain* overture, of the marvellous melody of the love scene in *Romeo and Juliet*, of the oboe solo ("Romeo alone") in the same work. Is it because the final strain left in the listener's ear is a relatively poor one that he decides that the melody as a whole is poor?

This curious inability at times to think a thing out to its impeccably logical conclusion is seen again in the haphazard structure of many of his larger works. They are manifestly an inorganic patchwork. But here a resort to aesthetic may help us to explain his failure by perceiving his difficulties.

The great German historians of art, from Wölfflin onwards, have distinguished between the "zeichnerisch" and the "malerisch" in the pictorial and plastic arts. The two terms, in the sense in which Wölfflin uses them, are not easily rendered into English. "Zeichnerisch", which relates primarily to drawing, is fairly well translatable as "linear". But "pictural", for "malerisch", is not of ordinary usage in English, while the dictionary definitions of "pictorial" or "picturesque" are apt to set up the wrong connotations. The distinction made between the two orders of art is intended to draw attention to the difference between representation that proceeds by way of clearly-edged lines in the one plane, and representation of which the essence is the mingling of planes. The linear artist draws things, as Wölfflin puts it, as they are: the "pictural" artist shows us things as they *appear* to be: working on a canvas that exists in only two dimensions, length and breadth, he succeeds in creating the illusion in the spectator that the picture exists also in a third dimension—depth.

The distinction, it should be clearly understood, has nothing whatever to do with the use of colour. It is an inner distinction of artistic vision, not an outer one of materials or treatment: the "zeichnerisch" artist who shows us a line of figures in the one plane may, if he chooses, employ colour, but he does so only in order to give more definition to his outlines. Rembrandt, on the other hand, is "pictural" in the highest degree, although he is working only in the black and white of an etching. Applying the distinction to music, a composer like Rimsky-Korsakov, in spite of the splendour of his colours, is a "zeichnerisch", not a "malerisch", artist: he thinks in contours—in extension, not in depth, in one plane, not in several. The distinction between the two "ways of seeing" in art is so fundamental that Wölfflin applies it also to architecture: a baroque building, he says, in comparison with a classical or renaissance building is "malerisch".

Now Berlioz strikes me as a truly "malerisch" musician, not because he "paints" in such rich and varied orchestral colours but because he thinks and reproduces in terms of the really "pictural". He sees everything in terms not of one plane but of several, and unconsciously tries to show us a scene as it would really appear to the eye. Compare, for instance, his handling of the Rakoczy March with that of Liszt. For the latter, with his purely linear mind, the themes just remain linear themes, to be treated with certain of the resources of art. But Berlioz's imagination works upon them in a different way: he uses them to call up before our mind's eye the coming and passing of an army: all is movement, perspective, foreground and background. Or look again at a descriptive symphonic poem like one of Smetana's and the "Chasse royale" in *The Trojans*, Smetana works in lines unfolding themselves on the flat: Berlioz's piece is a genuine *picture*, conceived in various planes, with both a physical and an aerial perspective.

I have not the space in which to elaborate this thesis, but must ask the reader to accept it, in the main, on the strength of this cursory setting forth of it. If now we take Berlioz to be a truly "malerisch" musician, we see at once where his difficulties lay. He was faced by a completely new problem of form. Each of his vignettes is incomparable in itself, but he cannot, as a rule, fuse them all into an organic large-scale work. There was nothing in previous music to help him, for the classical symphony, like classical architecture, was concerned with achieving architectonic, not "pictural", form by the symmetrical adding of self-existent unit to self-existent unit. It was a principle of structure that had its origin in a "zeichnerisch" conception of music as lines projected in the one plane. Berlioz's mind worked in quite a different way. His musical conceptions have mass and depth as well as, even more than, extension; and the forms that had been gradually beaten out to give coherence and development to an entirely different class of musical ideas were inapplicable to ideas such as his. Hence it came about that while he could make unsurpassable small pictures, he could not find the means to weave the larger vision of which these vignettes should be the components into a convincing organic whole. Works like *Faust* and *Romeo and Juliet* are just a series of independently conceived "malerisch" episodes to which a factitious air of connection has been given by a series of literary afterthoughts.

He came, in fact, before his time; his craftsmanship was not equal to his vision. A new musical content such as he had in his mind could not possibly be unified on the principles of a totally different kind of symphonic design and procedure, such as that of Mozart and Beethoven; and one man's life was too short to allow of the new type of vision working out to the full its own appropriate form. It took another two or three generations of experiment before the technical problems implicit in the new way of looking at music were triumphantly solved by Sibelius in such works as *Tapiola* and the seventh symphony.

Yet Berlioz was on the way to solving some at any rate of these problems. The "Chasse royale" is proof enough of that: here the classical apparatus to which he had clung for protection and guidance in some of his earlier orchestral works is boldly scrapped: the music evolves, and that with the most perfect naturalness, not by way of "subjects" but in virtue of the peculiar inner life of the vision as a whole. This music, like that of the later Sibelius, parts company entirely from the architectural: it is purely "malerisch". It gives us a hint of what Berlioz might have achieved had he written that symphony which, he tells us in the saddest page of all in his Memoirs, he deliberately refrained from carrying beyond the first ardent conception of it, because of the expense to which it would have put him and the chagrins it would have been sure to end in for him. He was at that time at the height of his powers, and the chances are that in this work he might have done on a larger scale what he has done so admirably on a small scale in the "Chasse royale".

That the symphony would have been abused in his own day, and perhaps, in some quarters, in ours also, we may be tolerably certain. For the academic, precepts of form that lie at the back of most people's judgment are drawn from one small genre of the great art of music, the passing product of a particular epoch intent on merely one of the many problems of musical vision and design. Any art critic who should judge, let us say, Rembrandt's "Three Trees" by criteria derived from a Raphael design would be laughed out of court. Yet a considerable section of the musical world judges music like that of Berlioz or Sibelius by standards no less inapplicable to it: and so it will be until at least the foundations of a real musical aesthetic are laid, until at least we learn to distinguish between the various types of musical imagination.

5 April 1936

5

A Man of the South

THE LAST GENERATION or two of critics and historians mis-
represented Berlioz so grossly that one can only conclude that
their acquaintance with his work as a whole was slight. They had a
predecessor in the German monarch* who remarked to him
affably, "I understand, M. Berlioz, that you never write for less
than five hundred executants." "Your Majesty has been mis-
informed," was the ironic reply: "I sometimes write for as few
as four hundred and fifty." That legend of his addiction to the
numerous and the noisy has been hard to kill.

It is true that now and then he took a fling in that direction, but
only when the occasion justified it and the milieu permitted it.
There are no absolutes in tone-mass values, only relatives.
Relatively to the orchestra of Mozart, that of Mahler is an over-
growth: but there is no reason rooted in the nature of things why
the ordinary orchestra of a century hence should not be to that of
Mahler as his to that of Mozart. There are untold glories of
orchestral volume and combination still unrealised: if they have
not been exploited already that is partly because of the economic
difficulties in the way, partly because of the lack of buildings large
enough for the purpose and acoustically favourable to it. Berlioz
was perfectly justified in writing on the scale he occasionally did
for exceptional buildings or for the open air. But to try to
give the modern public the impression that he was the victim of a

* Not a monarch, but Prince Metternich (P.H.).

megalomaniac obsession with mere volume and vehemence for their own sakes is to go a trifle too far in the way of misrepresentation. Hadow has informed us that "beside the extravagance of Berlioz, Victor Hugo is reticent." But where is the extravagance, the lack of reticence, in *Les Troyens*, in *L'Enfance du Christ*, in *Béatrice et Bénédict*, in the beautifully wrought songs, or in a dozen other works that might be mentioned? Did any composer ever engrave with so fine pointed a tool as he has done on a hundred occasions?

The critics quarrelled with him, again, over his choice of subjects, which were too "external" for them. Parry considered that the French lack the Teutonic "gift for looking inward." But why, in point of fact, should any composer, or any other artist, or we to whom their art is a joy and a refreshment, regard looking inward as more praiseworthy than looking outward? Julien Benda has some telling things to say about this fallacy in his *Belphégor*. The glories of the "mystic communion with the soul of things"—as if any of us knew what the soul of things is!—have been over-sung. As Benda says, it is only grudgingly that some people will "admit that a Gautier, for instance, who depicted Venice and Toledo *from outside*, without sharing their heartbeats or clasping them to his bosom, was still worthy the name of artist."

Berlioz had this intense perception of the interest and beauty of things as they reveal themselves to the eye that directs its vision outwards: and in censuring him for seeing the world of art like that the older critics were simply condemning him for being himself, instead of something made on the Teutonic model. Parry frowned on him for choosing such "histrionic" themes as "dances of sylphs, processions of pilgrims and orgies of brigands". But why should a composer not write about things of this kind if they appeal to him? In what way is a sylph more "histrionic" than an angel? The two fauna are equally supposititious; why then should it be counted a virtue to describe the gyrations of the one in music and a fault to describe the gyrations of the other? Putting theological considerations aside, again, are angels in themselves better material for art than witches? Have we not become so infected with what Nietzsche called moralic acid that we are inclined to over-value the moral element in art? Why should not the diabolic in nature and in man be given a fair show by the artist?

Both those among us who are interested in the latest developments of music and those who are intrigued by the problem of criticism can find much that is worthy of attention in the case of Berlioz. Musical criticism, it is evident, is every day coming a stage nearer bankruptcy in its dealings with the most characteristically "contemporary" music. So long as a composer obviously stemmed from his predecessors, no matter how individual the constitution of his own mind might be, it was possible to formulate certain criteria in virtue of which his music could be said to be very good, fairly good, or bad. But when, as is often the case today, the composer seems not to inhabit the same mental world or breathe the same atmosphere as "the classics", does not employ their vocabulary, and flouts their conjugations, declensions and syntax, criticism, in the old self-assured acceptation of the term, becomes impossible. We are left simply with naïve reactions of being interested or not.

But this problem, in a milder form, was already confronting the critics of a century ago, though they did not know it, in the work of Berlioz. For there can be no question that his was the most purely individual mind in the whole history of music. Proof of this is twofold. In the first place, he derived nothing of his artistic self from even the three or four composers preceding him and contemporary with him whom he admired, while he in turn has put in general circulation nothing whatever that the generations following him could incorporate into their own substance. He has no pride of ancestry, no hope of posterity. In the second place, while it is possible to turn out quite passable imitations of such giants as Bach, Mozart, Beethoven, Wagner and Brahms, no one can write, or will ever be able to write, two pages that could be passed off, I will not say as Berlioz, but even as a passable imitation of him. He is the one composer who defies alike the disciple, the eclectic and the parodist. I am not putting this forward, of course, as in itself a proof that he was a great composer: that issue has to be decided on various other grounds. I simply state the plain facts of a unique case.

Although no one among his German admirers in his own day was aware of it, he was unwittingly laying the axe at the root of the mighty old Germanic tree. The present day plumes itself on having shaken itself free of the Germanic influence. Berlioz enjoyed that freedom from the beginning without ever thinking about the matter—not because he was "French" but because he was himself. To call him "French", indeed, as Parry always did with a tincture of disparagement, is to misconceive him. He was a man of the south, a Dauphinois, a type not found anywhere else in France. The Dauphinois sees things without any intervening mist between himself and them, swiftly, unsentimentally, rather sceptically; he prides himself on being *jamais dupe*. Berlioz had no love for his fellow-Dauphinois Stendhal; but Stendhal, with his unsentimental directness of vision, his freedom from the conventional in his estimates and from the metaphysical fog that sometimes prevents the northern European mind from seeing the world just as it is, his style without padding, without ready-made phrases, is the nearest equivalent that even French literature offers to the music of Berlioz. Had Stendhal written a symphony, it would have been very like *Harold in Italy*, had Berlioz gone in for the novel he would have produced something like *Le Rouge et le Noir*.

As I have suggested, it was his entire remoteness from the German type of "inwardness" that made him suspect by the critics and historians who, like Parry, had come to believe that music and German music were virtually interchangeable terms. For them, German music was the predestined and final accomplishment of the musical language *per se*, the other national forms of expression that were coming into existence being merely local dialects, interesting, quaint, sometimes delightful, but to be spoken in the best circles only at the risk of your being accused of talking with a provincial or across-the-border accent. What

Berlioz essentially did, and was the first to do, was to reproduce in music the texture and colour and mental atmosphere of that "Mediterranean" which Nietzsche so longed for as an escape from the rumination of the darker, slower, thicker-blooded north.

Berlioz's biographer, Adolphe Boschot has rightly insisted on the influence on the boy of the landscape of his native Dauphiny, its dryness, its vibrating heat, its intense colour. But if we want to understand just how all these things contributed to make the mind and the temperament of the young Berlioz what they were we have to turn to a book by a brilliant Frenchwoman, Madame Bulteau (who wrote under the pseudonym of Jacque Vontade), in which she correlates the mystical and metaphysical tendencies of northern Europe and England on the one hand and the objectivity and litheness of southern art on the other, with the difference in the qualities of the light of the two milieux. As she puts it, a check to the vision has always drawn man on insensibly further and further in order to discover what may lie beyond the unclear immediate field; whereas when the light reveals everything at a glance up to the horizon limit the process is reversed— the unfrustrated eye protects the mind from the perpetual illusion that beyond the beyond is a secret it is necessary for it to know. All Berlioz's music, whether that of the painting of a scene or that of psychological probe—and he has achieved some marvels in the latter field—has the quality of controlled objectivity that is the antithesis of the northern ecstatic mystical swoon; it is the seeing of things as they appear and are, not as one would fain persuade oneself they are by calling in speculation and metaphysic to supplement the evidence of the eye.

No, to call Berlioz French and to imagine that that in any way explains him is to shoot very wide of the mark. If we turn to Stendhal we find that fellow-Dauphinois of his professing the utmost contempt for most of his compatriots of the west and north. "Civilisation", he said, "extends from Lille to Rennes, and leaves off about Orléans and Tours. To the south Grenoble is its brilliant limit." We need not take all this too seriously; but Stendhal certainly knew what he was talking about whenever he discussed the Dauphinois type of which he and Berlioz were representative. "Dauphiné", he said, "has its own way of feeling, lively, stubborn and analytical, which I have met with in no other country. . . . The character native to Dauphiné has a tenacity, a depth, an intelligence and subtlety which one would seek in vain in the civilisations of Provence or Burgundy, its neighbours." All this characterises both the human and the artistic constitution of Berlioz well enough.

But have we accounted for him fully when we have catalogued him as a Dauphinois? Can we safely speculate rather further back than that?

We have still a very imperfect understanding of the creative imagination, but at least we have learned to look for the roots of a work of art below the surface of the artist's everyday life and personality. We no longer account for a poet or a musician writing an Elegy or a Requiem by the fact that he had recently lost a second cousin of whom he was fond, or for his producing a Hymn to Joy on the Wednesday of a certain week by the fact that his wife had left him, vowing she would never return, on the preceding Monday. We have learned something of the importance of the subconscious in the artist's mental life, that immense accumulation of intellectual and emotional experience that lies sleeping in the depths of him, to awake and break through to the surface every now and then in the strangest of ways. But it is highly improbable that the cluster of experiences and habits in our subconscious is the product solely of our personal life: it may well be, though it is incapable of proof at present, that the submerged individual memories are themselves rooted in clusters of ancestral memories. And if we like to speculate to the limit on this attractive theme, what is to bar us from toying with the notion that a certain *racial* strain, after lying dormant in a family or group for many generations, may suddenly assert itself in an individual and make him something noticeably different from the mass of the beings of his time and place?

Let me plunge into the fantastic at a single leap. The young Berlioz had reddish hair; so, we discover from one of his letters, had his son. Stendhal refers to a red-haired man among his Dauphinois compatriots. Two swallows, of course, do not make a summer, and a red-headed man or two in the south of France in the early nineteenth century may seem a frail foundation on which to build a theory of why Berlioz was what he was and wrote as he did. All the same, it is clear that red hair was sufficiently uncommon in that part of France for both Berlioz and Stendhal to record their meetings with it. Now the south of France and southern Italy had from the dawn of history been populated to some extent by emigrants from Greece and Asia, coming by sea as far as Marseilles and filtering into the interior. In Vergil's time, we are told, Naples was virtually a Greek city; and well into the Middle Ages we meet with Greek personalities and Greek influences in connection with the music of the western church. And we know from various ancient sources that there was a Phrygian strain conspicuous by its red hair. Xenophanes, describing in the sixth century B.C. how men make gods in their own image, said that while those of the Ethiopians are black and snub-nosed, those of the Thracians have blue eyes and red hair. Thracian slaves at Athens, says Ridgeway, were often given the name of Pyrrhias ("Red-head").

Berlioz's son—and, I think, Berlioz himself—had "superb" blue eyes as well as reddish hair. Can the conjecture be ruled out, as too utterly fanciful, that there was a non-French strain of Thracian or some other origin in the Berlioz family? Let us note another curious fact. Stendhal surmised that he himself had Italian blood in him: "my grandfather and my Aunt Elizabeth had an obviously Italian type of face, the aquiline nose, etc." I would ask the reader now to look at a few portraits of Berlioz, noting the great aquiline nose, the finely-cut and tight-drawn mouth, the shortness of the lower part of the face, and the protuberant dimpled chin, and then run his eye over some of the Italian portraits in Burckhardt's book on the Renaissance, especially those of Lodovico, Francesco and Galeazzo Sforza (the Sforza family in general, indeed, women as well as men), Federigo da Montefeltro, Bartolommeo, Pope Colleoni,

Alexander VI, Poliziano, Pietro Bembo, Sigismondo Malatesta (amazingly like the Godebski medallion of Berlioz), and even Dante and Savonarola, where, however, the type has become in the one case super-refined and in the other thickened and coarsened. The basic resemblance between all these people and Berlioz is beyond question. Is it as fanciful, then, as it may perhaps appear at first sight to conjecture that he and they were distant waves thrown up by some racial type from the ancient world that had settled in Italy and France? May Berlioz's peculiarly individual mind be accounted for by some such freak of heredity as this?

10 November 1946

17 November 1946

24 November 1946

6

The Relations of Wagner and Berlioz

ENGLISH STUDENTS WITH a knowledge of French who want a really good book on Berlioz the man, could not do better than get the *Hector Berlioz et la Société de son Temps* of M. Julien Tiersot, published in the early part of the present year. The work is done with German thoroughness combined with French ease and grace of style, and altogether it is the most complete and reliable study of the personal Berlioz that has yet appeared. From so sane a study as this, Berlioz comes out a bigger man than ever. He has generally served as a mark for the wit or the abuse of people who knew next to nothing about him; to see the man as a whole is to realise that the undeniable follies of his early years can be made too much of, and that so far from being merely the romantic *poseur* of the popular imagination, he was really a man of culture and intelligence, quite as well balanced as the average great musician, and with a much better all-round brain than the majority of them. We have heard a little too much of the mad, effusive Berlioz; it is time that overworked legend was put to sleep, and the complete Berlioz allowed to be seen.

Perhaps the false opinion of him that has so long been current, both as man and as musician, has been partly due to the ill-considered zeal of the Wagnerians for their great idol. Both Berlioz and Liszt, having had so much of the root of Wagnerism in them before Wagner, were *a priori* subjects for Wagnerian dislike; but Liszt, of course, was graciously tolerated, not because he was Liszt, but because he was an unselfish supporter of Wagner —a distinction to which Berlioz could not lay claim. M. Tiersot has done us all a service in making a connected story of the relations of Wagner and Berlioz from first to last. He presents the facts impartially, and sums up upon them judiciously; and most people will agree that on the whole Berlioz comes the better out of the examination. Neither man understood the other properly —that goes without saying; each forgot himself at times and behaved foolishly towards the other; but on the whole Berlioz's errors were less gross than those of Wagner. He did not make Wagner's mistake of impertinently patronising his opponent; nor did he, like Wagner—as I shall try to show—condemn some of the works of his opponent without knowing anything about them.

Most people, when they think of Wagner and Berlioz, have in mind that dramatic episode between them in 1861, when Wagner was in Paris. Berlioz declared against him—partly out of real dislike and misunderstanding of *Tristan*, partly goaded to a momentary loss of all self-restraint by the long neglect of him at the Opera, followed by this sudden lavishing of favour upon his foreign rival. His article, read calmly, really contains much sound æsthetic; but he made the cardinal mistake of attributing to Wagner opinions which the latter never held. Wagner had an easy case in replying; and he replied with commendable dignity and good taste. It was the hour of his triumph; he could afford to be magnanimous to his unsuccessful rival.

But Wagner had previously spoken of Berlioz with irritating, patronising ignorance. In *Opera and Drama* there is that famous passage of pseudo-criticism, which with many good souls no doubt passed for a genuine analysis of Berlioz. Wagner, with sad lack of humour, speaks of Berlioz's dependence on mechanism, of his being buried hopelessly beneath his machines, and so on— Wagner, who is dependent as no musician ever has been upon machinery, who relies for a thousand effects upon the stage carpenter and the limelight man, and who often revolts our dramatic sense by being so much beholden to stage trickery! No one can take him seriously here; but there is another reference of his to Berlioz that is worth looking at for a moment, if only to ask the official English Wagnerians if they are quite sure they have clean consciences in the matter.

In 1852 Liszt meant to give *Lohengrin* at Weimar; Wagner thought it all right. Then Liszt took up Berlioz's old opera *Benvenuto Cellini*, and Wagner thought it all wrong. He wrote Liszt a letter that apparently throbs with love and pity for Berlioz, but in which the parade of patronising goodwill cannot hide from us the annoyance that underlies it. In his letter to Liszt of September 8, 1852, he says, "If there is one composer I expect something of, it is Berlioz; but not if he follows the path that has led him to the platitudes of his Faust Symphony, for if he goes any further in this way, he can only become quite ridiculous. If any musician needs a poet, it is Berlioz. . . . He has need of the poet to penetrate him," and so on, in the well-known Wagnerian æsthetic. He offers Berlioz his own libretto of *Wieland*, which Berlioz wisely declines.

Now, two or three points in the letter need elucidating:

(1) Wagner speaks unsympathetically of *Cellini*. Did he know anything of it? What are the facts? The opera was produced in Paris on September 3, 1838, and withdrawn after only three performances. Wagner, being at this time in Riga, could not have heard the opera. Could he have acquired his knowledge of it from the score? After the Paris fiasco only the overture and eight vocal pieces were published. The opera underwent many changes. It was given in Weimar in 1852, altered again, and given in 1856, and *then* published. Apparently Wagner, in 1852, could have known absolutely nothing of the work.

(2) Every schoolboy knows that Berlioz's *Faust* is not a symphony, but a dramatic cantata or opera. The original *Eight Scenes from Faust* had been published in 1829. Wagner seems to have known nothing of these. The complete work was produced in 1846, failed, and was not published until 1854. Wagner's use of the term "Faust Symphony" clearly points to complete ignorance

of the work which he has the impertinence to describe as consisting of platitudes. (About 1830 Berlioz really thought of doing a
Faust *Symphony*, and it is quite possible he may have mentioned
the idea to Wagner at some time.)

(3) It is not surprising to find Wagner thus depreciating other
men's works of which he knew nothing or next to nothing; there
is testimony that he did the same thing in the case of Schumann.
But why is it that the phrase "Faust Symphony"—which, in the
language of the vulgar, at once gives Wagner away—has been
carefully withheld from the English public? Turn to Hueffer's
translation of the Wagner-Liszt letters, revised by Mr. Ashton
Ellis, and you will find that the word "symphony" has been
deliberately omitted. The sentence runs, "the absurdities of his
Faust". Turn next to the big Glasenapp biography which Mr.
Ellis is translating and expanding, and on page 337 of Volume
III you will find that Mr. Ellis, though he is so prodigal of space
that 1,300 pages are devoted to getting Wagner up to 1853,
cannot find space to quote the incriminating lines of this letter.
He omits all reference to *Faust*. He gives the sentence, "If there
is one composer I expect something of, it is Berlioz"; then he
omits the rest of the sentence, making it appear that Wagner was
simply bursting with generous artistic sympathy, and hiding that
tell-tale passage from the innocent reader. Discreet dots do the
work of concealment, and the letter is resumed with the sentence,
"But he needs a poet who shall fill him through and through."
Mr. Finck, again, in his biography, prints the words "Faust
Symphony", but without comment, and without any attempt
to discover whether Wagner could have known Berlioz's work
at all.

With a knowledge of these facts the English reader has a
rather better chance of appreciating the letter of September 8,
1852, at its true value. Berlioz did at least "read and re-read"
the prelude to *Tristan* before he said he could make nothing of it;
Wagner disparaged *Cellini* and *Faust* upon the basis of an ignorance about as complete as one could imagine. Yet there is talk of
the "ingratitude" of Berlioz, while Wagner, thanks to the care

with which his admirers revise his correspondence for the English public, is made to appear scarcely one degree lower than the angels. Thus—as I had occasion to remark once before—thus does Wagner-worship make for the "truly human".

THE SPEAKER 8 October 1904

7

Miscellaneous Comments

PARIS, IT MUST be remembered, was not a very large place in Berlioz's early days, and a young man of his pronounced characteristics and gift for making himself prominent must have been an almost too familiar figure. Who can doubt now that to the Parisians of that time Berlioz must have been a figure of the sort that it is difficult to take seriously? He advertised himself extensively, and not always with good taste. All the world knew of his absurd passions and his equally absurd marital relations. His very appearance must have gone against him. Somebody described him as having the face of an owl in his younger days: and what with this, and his meagre little body, and the great shock of red hair, he could hardly have been a figure to command the respect of the irreverent Parisians.

And they must have known all sorts of things about him that, for us, have been made clear only by M. Boschot's painstaking biography. He was evidently very pushful and a great intriguer. Not a post fell vacant, or looked like falling vacant, but he applied for it; not an occasion for ceremonial public music occurred but he began to pull innumerable strings to secure the commission for himself. For the greater part of his career he had to earn his living by musical journalism. His essential honesty cannot be doubted, but there was inevitably occasions when it would have been impolitic of him to express his real opinions—as when a feeble opera by the daughter of his employer was produced—and every such lapse from his usual outspokenness was remembered against him. And though there is no evidence that he himself ever used his position in the press to damage those who were not so friendly to him as he thought they might have been, there is little doubt that Jules Janin, and others of his journalistic friends, did so for him. M. Boschot gives ample evidence of his habit of supplying these friends with bulletins for public use. In a word, he must have been exceedingly pushing, and all Paris must have known it.

As regards his music, it has to be remembered that his output, on the whole, was rather small, and that the public must have grown tired of the constant repetition of the same works. M. Boschot shows that in some fifteen years he had given more than forty concerts of his own works—necessarily the same things time after time. Can it be wondered at that, apart from the faithful few, the public showed no great inclination to go again and again to hear works that it had already heard and not particularly liked.

I am not contending that its attitude towards him was justifiable: but it is understandable. He was a great man, but he had not the art of impressing the Parisian public with his greatness, and he had a most unfortunate way of parading all his littlenesses before them. Like many another young composer, he was his own worst enemy. Only music of the most enchanting kind could have enabled its composer to live down a legend so plentifully touched with absurdity as that which Berlioz made for himself as a young man; and, unfortunately, Berlioz's music, in the mass, has no enchantment for the ordinary concert goer.

22 May 1921

*　　　*　　　*

If Berlioz is to a great extent better understood today than he was in his lifetime, that is because the general musical consciousness has now caught up with the elements in his make-up with which his own generation and the next found it hardest to keep step. The fusion or parallelism of the musical and the visual in him, which puzzled the armchair aestheticians who wrung their hands over the impurity of any kind of music but "pure" music, causes us no difficulty today. We realise, for one thing, that if the classical composers never got beyond a nursery innocence in the "descriptive" genre it was not because the genre itself is alien to the "true" nature of music, but simply because they had neither the orchestral apparatus nor the craftsmanship for a job with which, as their fumbling attempts at it show, they would gladly have grappled if they could.

Thanks largely to the symphonic poem, the opera and the song, the ordinary listener of today has developed a new technique of musical apprehension. Even the more intelligent of Berlioz's contemporaries, such as Wagner, while recognising his genius, regretted that in such episodes as the "scène d'amour" in *Romeo and Juliet* or the "scène aux champs" in the *Fantastique* he should have tried to do by means of the listener's inner eye alone what ought really to have been done by a visible stage setting. The musical mind of today, however, has no difficulty in *seeing* what it is hearing; in Strauss's great work, for instance, we not only feel with Don Quixote in his reactions to each of his adventures but visualise with the greatest ease the milieu and the attendant circumstances of each adventure.

13 November 1949

*　　　*　　　*

From the Opera he was mostly barred by intrigue and misunderstanding. The result of it all was that he was driven again and again, by sheer necessity, into the mistake of trying to do in concert form something the proper place for which would have been the theatre, and vice versa. Works like *The Damnation of Faust* and *Romeo and Juliet* fall between two stools; they are too dramatic for the concert room and too "symphonic" for the theatre, and so a great deal of unique music never gets a fair chance. Even *The Childhood of Christ*, which Berlioz regards as an oratorio, sets us dreaming of a stage setting when we hear it under concert conditions; yet the only result of an attempt to link up the episodes continuously in the theatre would be to drive the work back to the concert room.

28 February 1943

*   *   *

There is a further problem—that of performing his bigger works to-day under the same conditions as those implicit in his conception of them. He designed such things as the *Te Deum* for a great church, in which the organ at one end and the orchestra at the other could set each other off with a sort of aerial perspective between them. (The effect of the antiphonal opening chords of the *Te Deum*, for example, depends entirely upon this. For his "third choir", again, he wanted six hundred children in unison, whose tone would afford a contrast to that of his two main choirs of mixed voices that is unobtainable in a makeshift present-day performance.) The instrumental perspective of which I have spoken is cancelled out when the work is given to-day in a concert room with organ and orchestra cheek by jowl on the platform. The only possible way, I imagine, to overcome this difficulty would be to give the work in a large church, with an orchestra placed at the furthest remove from the organ. But that raises a further problem: the acoustics of a vast and lofty cathedral are not those of the concert room. And out of this practical consideration arises yet another. If, as I suppose we must, we give the *Te Deum* in the concert room, ought not the conductor to adopt in some places a rather faster tempo than that indicated by Berlioz? Being a consummate practician, he no doubt took into account the relative lethargy of a sound-mass in a church such as that of St. Eustache and allowed for it in his metronome marks. But should not these compensatory slow tempi be modified to some extent in the quicker-speaking concert room of today?

1 August 1943

III

Berlioz and the Academics

1

The Case for the Prosecution

I F, A S H A S been said, the correct definition of a classic be simply
a work that has a continuing vogue, then undoubtedly the
Symphonie fantastique is a classic. It was produced 105 years ago,
and it is still in the repertory. Moreover, it is the only symphony produced in any country in the years immediately following the deaths of Beethoven (1827) and Schubert (1828) that *is*
in the repertory today. It has been cursed and derided and
patronised by the partisans of one school of musical thought for
more than three generations: yet it is not only still in the repertory but it and its composer are more generally respected today
than they ever were. The only possible inference is that, whatever faults it may have, in its way it is a vital and a remarkable
work.

The Berlioz question is of peculiar interest to the students of
musical criticism, if only because it shows, even better than the
Wagner question, how little influence the critics have upon public
opinion in the long run. But it shows more than that: it reveals
how infirm the basis even of reasoned musical criticism always has
been and still is. Anyone who will take the trouble to read what is
said against Berlioz today by people who do not like him, and
then what was being said against him 80 years or so ago, will make
the rather painful discovery that in criticism, as in other things,
there is nothing new under the sun: anti-Berlioz criticism has not
progressed an inch since the days of Scudo, Castil-Blaze and Otto

Jahn. From this fact we are driven to the awkward inference that criticism can sometimes be at its most fallible when it appears to be at its most rational. For the ancient Berlioz critics were anything but fools. They did not regard themselves as merely sensitised plates, but as having an armour-proofed philosophy and aesthetic at the back of their judgements: they reasoned logically about the nature of music, or what they held to be the nature of music, and, as they thought, they *proved* Berlioz to be a bad composer in terms of what were to them the eternal verities. Scudo in particular went about his business of trying and sentencing Berlioz with the utmost care and conscientiousness, examining first of all his relation to his predecessors, then the special constitution of his mind, and condemning him finally on what he took to be principles rooted in the very nature of music.

The faults, or supposed faults, of Berlioz have been set forth by no modern critic more systematically, more comprehensively, or more searchingly than they were by Scudo about 1855. He pointed out that Berlioz, in common with the other romanticists, went to an extreme in his passion for local colour, sacrificing "truth of sentiment" for "exactitude of costumes and decor"; that he "transported into the symphony a compound of bizarre naiveté and philosophical pretension, of common reality and lyrical enthusiasm"; that there was a fundamental disunion between his ambitions and his powers—"we see him laying out an immense area and then not knowing how to fill it, stretching out eagle wings yet not being able to raise himself from the earth: this disproportion between his desires and his faculties, between the audacity of his will and the mediocrity of his work, is the most salient feature of M. Berlioz's physiognomy"; that his swelling phrases ring hollow, image being heaped upon image, pell-mell; that he is poor in melodic ideas; that even when he has a good idea he does not know how to develop it; that he resorts to violence because he cannot persuade; that there is a wide gulf between his mind and his hand, between the capacity to conceive and the capacity to realise; that he is excessively bent upon reproducing the actual or the picturesque in music; and so on almost *ad infinitum*.

This is the utmost that the anti-Berliozians have to say today; and much of it is true, if not of the whole Berlioz as ardent students now know him, at any rate of the youthful Berlioz. Yet in spite of it all, Berlioz not only still lives but, so far as public performances are concerned, is more alive than he ever was. What can the inference be but just this—that criticism can sometimes be just as rotten at the core when it reasons as when it merely reacts, because critical tests derived from historical aesthetic data, valid as they may be up to a point, are apt to break down when it is a question not of what the new composer is in relation to other and older composers but what he is in himself. It is *this* factor which declares itself in time; and everything depends upon it. If there is something in the man's music that appeals for its own sake to a fair number of people he will become a classic in spite of all that criticism can urge against him. His defects will not be hidden from them—indeed, they will be less in dispute than they formerly were; but listeners will take these in their stride, frankly recognising the alloy in the metal but still feeling that there is more than enough gold in it to compensate them.

This, I take it, is the general attitude towards Berlioz today of all but the people whose temperament is constitutionally alien to his, and who therefore do not come into the reckoning. We others admit that he was a flawed genius; but we claim that all the same he was a rare genius. He never quite achieved the inner harmony of being of the other great composers, and in his earlier work in particular he is visibly pulled in different directions by contradictory elements in his nature. But all the same he cuts, at his best, as deeply into us as any composer has ever done: he is as supreme in his own sphere of imagination as any of the others is in his; he has given to certain emotions an expression which, we feel, will never be surpassed.

Some of his most obvious faults are the product of his personal and local circumstances: he was driven, for instance, to attempt too much story-telling, too much description of externalities in his earlier works, in large part because he was barred from the theatre: he had to try to do by means of music alone what ought to be done by a stage action and setting. But his judgment and his taste were often at fault less because of outward constraint than because of inner dis-harmony. For two-thirds of his life he was a bundle of warring impulses. His mind was fundamentally classical, but he had the misfortune to be thrown as a young man into a world of romanticism: his real lifelong love was Vergil, but he had slowly to cut his way to the clarity of Vergil through an absurd romantic murk. What beat him in the end was not his own nature, which, I believe, was in itself strong enough to solve, in time, all its own peculiar problems, but the infirmities of his body and his ill-luck in being a citizen of a country that had no use for music such as his. There can be little doubt that in his later years he could have produced orchestral works that would have been as far above the *Fantastique* as *Les Troyens* is above *Benvenuto Cellini*. But his body failed him, and mortification at the indifference of his countrymen helped to break the spring in him. There are few things in autobiography so pathetic as the passage in his *Memoirs* in which he tells us of the symphony he dreamed one night but, on cool reflection, deliberately refrained from writing, because of the long and painful labour it would have cost him and the expense to which the production of it would have put him in the Paris of that epoch.

As it is, the modern public can estimate him as a symphonist only from the *Fantastique*, which is a youthful work patched up from all kinds of scraps of pre-existing material, held together only by virtue of the programme he chose to foist upon them. But even in the *Fantastique* he reveals himself as one of the most original minds that has ever worked in music. Without models of any kind he produced, within a year or two of Beethoven's death, a work which, as I said at the beginning of this article, is the sole survivor of all the extensive symphonic output of that period. It was not merely that he created in the *Fantastique* orchestral colours of which none of his predecessors or contemporaries had ever dreamed, but that he gave, at a stroke, its final expression to a whole new world of inner feeling and outward movement. In spite of its youthful faults, the *Fantastique* remains a masterwork in its special genre.

3 November 1935

2

The Real Berlioz

Let us run a quick eye over some of the grievances of the musically virtuous against Berlioz.

They say he could not construct. The truth is that works like the "Royal Hunt" or the "Hungarian March" are more firmly, more connectedly wrought than some of the most admired classical works in the repertory. They hold together without a bar of padding: the trouble is that our schooldozed pedagogues do not see the standardised padding—they call it "working-out"—for the bogus thing it too often is. They say, again, that he is not a melodist. The truth is that he is free of the obsession of the simple four-square symmetries that constitute the essence of "melody" for people who know no better. Berlioz's melodies have a more flexible articulation and soar on a freer wing. Nor does he repeat himself, as the "classical" melodists do, with only slight changes in one tune after another in one work after another that has a different psychological genesis and a different ambitus. He draws from the life, not from a studio plaster cast.

They say, once more, that he was no harmonist because he had not done enough "technical exercises" in his youth. The answer to that is that Berlioz's often unexpected harmonies are the natural expression of his thought. To say that he wrote as he did because he had not sufficiently studied the grammar of music is like saying that a Browning or a Bacon or a Sir Thomas Browne did not understand English grammar because the pungent individuality of his thinking sought and found other modes of expression than those expected of a student by a school examiner in school-examination "English".

Two other points remain to be considered. Berlioz's music was amazingly colouristic; and the old-style academics frowned on colour as being a manifestation of original sin. The proper thing to do was to make your music, conceived in terms of the piano and then "orchestrated", sound as if it had been dipped in a mixture of beer and brown sugar. That proved you to be a profound thinker, a "master of pure line" and all that sort of thing, a virtuous Odysseus who wasn't going to succumb to the blandishments of "mere sensuous beauty" and its siren gauds.

Finally there was Berlioz's extension of the range of musical expression to bring the diabolical within its circle. The celestial was permissible, the diabolic not; though I doubt whether our oratorio writers and other musical moralists really had any more first-hand acquaintance with the Gates of Heaven than they had with the gates of hell, though they knew, of course, that the former always called for the musical equivalent of the reverent use of capital letters and the latter for small. Berlioz was as interested in the sinner as in the saint, perhaps more so. A good stringy devil-dammed witch, complete with goat and broomstick, meant far more to him than the whole white company of St. Ursula and her eleven thousand virgins. And since all these picturesque but hypothetical fauna are alike the creation of man's romantic imagination, it is not quite clear why this artist should be commended for specialising in the one and that excluded from the best circles for showing a partiality for the other. When a Goethe gives us a real live Witches' Sabbath in words the poetical world delights in the unholy spectacle; when a Berlioz does the same thing the musically pious behave like the Sacristan when he sees Cavaradossi painting not a Madonna but the portrait of the worldly Floria Tosca—they cross themselves and go off muttering "He turns his back on the saints and consorts with the ungodly!" You may say that among really nice people such things are not done in music. Then it is high time they were. Our aesthetic criteria are in sore need of a good overhauling.

14 March 1943

3

An Answer to Ravel

RAVEL, WHEN HE was interviewed in London the other day, made one or two remarks that suggested that if, as a composer, he has no longer anything to say that is likely to astonish us, he might add considerably to the gaiety of nations if he were to turn critic. "Berlioz?" he said in reply to a question by the interviewer; "he was the worst musician of all the great musical geniuses. He had astounding genius, and he could not harmonise a simple waltz correctly."

On the face of it, it looks like a contradiction in terms: one does not quite see how a man can be one of the great musical geniuses and yet be a bad musician. The alleged grounds for this curious statement are apparently that Berlioz's harmony was not "correct". I could understand this being the view of a pedagogue of the old academic type; but I thought the species was now extinct. It is curious and humorous to see it coming to life again in Ravel.

It seems that poor Berlioz, astounding genius as he was, could not even harmonise a simple waltz correctly. The only waltz Berlioz ever wrote was that in the *Symphonie fantastique*; and it would be interesting if Ravel would analyse the harmony of that for us, showing us where it is not "correct," and what harmonies he would propose to substitute for those of Berlioz. Wagner used to amuse his friends by playing the first page of the *Tannhäuser* overture as some well-known German academic of the day, who objected to its harmonisation, would have written it.

I fancy we should have a gay quarter-of-an-hour listening to the waltz in the *Symphonie fantastique* as "corrected" by Ravel.

The charge that Berlioz's harmony is not correct is an old one. It was intelligible enough in the nineteenth century, when harmony was supposed to be something that could be taught, and when professors and the compilers of text-books used to concoct "bad" harmonic sequences and show how they could be converted into "good" ones—the only trouble being that, to a non-academic ear, the "bad" harmonies were often more appetising than the "good". (I believe someone amused himself once by taking a number of the condemned harmonies, stringing them together, and making quite a jolly piece of music out of them. They were unconscious humorists, the professors of those days. Dear old Ebenezer Prout, for example, when illustrating a certain melodic "rule", wrote a phrase which he qualified as "very bad"—in blissful ignorance that it is with this very sequence of notes that Brahms begins one of his loveliest songs, "Wie Melodien zieht es.")

But in these days, surely, it is recognised that a composer's harmony is part of himself. It is an element in his style, which in turn is the expression of his mental idiosyncrasy. You may like the idiosyncrasy or you may not; that is a matter of personal predilection. But you have no right to say, offhand, that the reason for a composer having chosen to harmonise his music in his own way rather than in yours is that he was not a musician and could not harmonise correctly; any more than you have a right to say that Browning was no poet and could not speak correct English because he wrote

> For I am ware it is the seed of act
> God holds appraising in his hollow palm;
> Not act grown great thence on the world below,
> Leafage and branchage, vulgar eyes admire.

It may be that you would have expressed the idea differently; but that would only be because you are you, while Browning was

Browning. We must let our great men express themselves in the language that seems to them, not to us, the most fitting medium for their thoughts.

Undoubtedly Berlioz often harmonises a passage in a way that seems odd to the rest of us, who, do what we will, find it difficult to rid our minds of the academic preconceptions of our early training. But it would be easy to quote from, let us say, Sir Thomas Browne a hundred passages that the ordinary writer would have expressed differently, more "correctly", as Ravel would say. But the peculiar angles of Browne's style comes from the fact that there are peculiar angles in his way of thinking; and to round off the former according to standardised notions of English prose would be to take all the character out of the latter. I submit that what the academic mind regards as "incorrectness" of harmony in Berlioz is not technical in competence but part and parcel of his thinking.

For observe, to begin with, what the "incorrectness" theory implies. Suppose, if you like, that Berlioz, as a young man, had not learned correct methods of harmonic progression. But are you going to suppose also that, after thirty years' exercise of his craft, after having heard and studied scores innumerable, he was still unable to make one harmony lead into another with conventional "correctness"? For really it does not take a vast amount of intelligence to write "correct" harmonies; a moderately intelligent horse could learn it all in three weeks. Are you going to suppose that this "astounding genius" of a Berlioz was yet such a *crétin* that he could not see that a Niedermeyer or a Clapisson would have harmonised such and such a passage differently? The supposition is nonsensical on the face of it; the more reasonable view is that Berlioz knew perfectly well what he was doing when he wrote non-academic harmony and preferred his own way because it corresponded to the way of his thought. For in his latest and greatest work we find him harmonising in the style that had been characteristic of him from the beginning; a thousand examples in proof of this could be quoted from *Les Troyens*.

I would not dream of denying that many of his harmonic

sequences strike us as odd; I only protest that we have no right to call them, "incorrect," the truth being that they represent the matter as Berlioz saw it, and as we learn to see it when we become thoroughly accustomed to his style. I remember how, years ago, I used to be pulled up by such passages as this from the superb "Marche Troyenne" in *Les Troyens*.

My ear kept expecting the A flat again in the first chord of the last bar but one; while in the light of what has gone before, I did not expect the final progression to the tonic to be conducted in the way that Berlioz has chosen to conduct it. But now, having assimilated his idiosyncrasies by long experience of them, I think I can see this and hundreds of similar passages as he saw them.

Two other considerations may be briefly indicated. Berlioz's harmony is always astonishingly simple and unadventurous; compared with Wagner's, it was quite "unmodern" even in his own day. The truth is that no genius whatever can innovate consistently well over the whole field of music. (Much of the sterility of present-day composers comes from ignorance of this simple fact.) Wagner himself saw that his extraordinary expansion of the resources of harmony was made possible to him only by his keeping to a few simple rhythmical formulæ; there is a passage in one of his letters in which he points out the absurdity of expecting music like his to show much variety of rhythm. Now it was precisely in the field of rhythm that Berlioz was far ahead of the music of his time: and Wagner would have been as incapable of such a piece of rhythmical articulation as the "Cortège des ouvriers constructeurs" in *Les Troyens* as Berlioz would have been of the harmonic subtleties of the second act of *Tristan*.

Secondly, we must never judge Berlioz's harmony from a piano score. He was fortunate enough to have escaped, through his ignorance of the piano, the malign influence of that instrument upon orchestral composition. He thought naturally in terms of the orchestra; and the passages that seem harmonically illogical on the piano have a logic peculiarly their own when they are heard in their orchestral colours. I would cite, as one of the simplest illustrations of this, the effect of the fourth and fifth bars of the song "Absence" in the piano version and in the orchestral version. And because Berlioz did not understand the piano he had no idea how to arrange his scores for it in such a way as to suggest the orchestral original. The piano version of *Les Troyens* is particularly bald; if we only had a piano score of this with something in it of the genius that fills Liszt's marvellous piano transcription of the *Symphonie fantastique* I fancy we should hear less about the "incorrectness" of Berlioz's harmony.

8 October 1928

* * *

It is really astonishing how long and how persistently criticism has taken for defects in Berlioz what were actually the sign manual of his individuality. Some twenty years ago I had a little public controversy with Ravel on the subject of Berlioz's harmony, of which Ravel took the conventional view that it betrays technical incompetence, whereas in point of fact its peculiarities are simply part and parcel of his general conception of musical "meaning", and to censure him for not having swum in the general academic stream of harmony is like censuring original prose writers like Doughty or Proust for not constructing their sentences on the same lines as Pater or Burke.

The strange thing with Ravel was that while he refused to try to see Berlioz's harmony as Berlioz himself conceived it he fell foul of Rimsky-Korsakov for occasionally substituting his own more "correct" harmonies for those of Moussorgsky. Apparently this sort of thing was "vandalism" on Rimsky-Korsakov's part where Moussorgsky was concerned, while it would have been legitimate "correction" on Ravel's part where Berlioz was concerned! Berlioz's mind was all of a piece; his imagination, his general conception of music, were his own, and until that fact is clearly recognised, with all its practical implications, rational "criticism" of him is impossible and ideal performance difficult.

25 March 1956

4

Berlioz's "Irregularities"

THE COVENT GARDEN prospectus for the coming season is unadventurous; and the indications are that it will be some time yet before we are allowed to see any one of three works that are long overdue in London, *Wozzeck*, *Mathis der Maler* and *Les Troyens*. The BBC's two broadcasts of the Berlioz work have created a general desire to see it in all the fullness of its life on the stage, in its entirety if possible, but if not, then in some such condensed form as that of the Paris revival of 1921. It would have to be, of course, an all-French affair so far as the singers and the staging were concerned.

While I was musing wistfully on this matter my gaze happened to light on the little book of M. Maurice Cauchie, *La pratique de la musique*, about which I had something to say a few weeks ago; and I read again the timely short essay in it on "L'harmonisation de Berlioz".

As M. Cauchie points out, while the new musical public is taking more and more to Berlioz, he is still in the bad books of certain "professeurs d'harmonie" who cling to the thesis of their predecessors of eighty years ago that Berlioz is not a good harmonist. Even a master like Ravel, who ought to have known better, confidently assured the world that Berlioz was "incapable of harmonising a simple waltz tune properly,"—an *obiter dictum* which M. Cauchie rightly declares to be "complètement dépourvu de sens." It came, as he says, from a one-time conception of harmony that is now entirely discredited.

There are no "rules" in virtue of the observance or non-observance of which harmonisation can be declared to be right or wrong. These fictitious "rules," M. Cauchie continues, were arbitrarily framed by our great-grandfathers from the music of the German classics of the eighteenth century and given the status of a "catechism." Today it is taken as axiomatic by every modernist that a composer is at liberty to employ any combination of tones whatsoever which he feels are the necessary and inevitable expression of his idea. "Why should Berlioz alone be denied the right to harmonise in his own way? Why is he charged with ignorance of harmony by people who adore the crack-brained harmonies of a whole host of composers of today and yesterday—pseudo-harmonies which for any sound ear are a tissue of wrong notes?"

Harmonies of themselves, of course, can be neither good nor bad; it is only in the manner of their enchainment that they can come before the tribunal of aesthetic judgment. It is the musical *idea* that matters, not the degree of physical consonance or dissonance—purely arbitrary terms, by the way—between this note and that. If the idea is intelligible to us and appeals to us, we accept the structure and the concatenation of the chords as a matter of course. That, surely, is a self-evident proposition.

What apparently is not so self-evident is that a certain conventional manner of chord enchainment can become second nature to a man to such an extent that it bars him from apprehending the *idea* of a piece of music in which the chord-linking flouts this convention. This is the real trouble with the type of anti-Berliozian which M. Cauchie and I have in mind. These people jib at Berlioz's harmonisation because they are out of sympathy with his way of thought.

To hear some of these "professeurs d'harmonie" talk, one would think that the kind of harmonisation they would like to substitute for Berlioz's is something that only initiates like themselves can achieve. The simple truth, however, is that the youngest and slowest-witted boy in any conservatoire can pick it all up in a few weeks. Basically it is nothing more than a series of variations and expansions of what Miss Œnone Somerville used to call ironically the three chord trick. Some day, I am convinced, a more than usually gifted dog or monkey will be taught to perform that trick.

M. Cauchie is right to express surprise that the very people who rejoice in the present-day emancipation of music from the tyranny of certain classical German procedures should fail to give Berlioz credit for the pioneer part he unconsciously played in that emancipation. Today we regard it as a point in any composer's favour that he inhabits, more or less, a mental world of his own and expresses himself, more or less, in an idiom of his own; yet critics can still be found who sniff at Berlioz for having done both these things. For their ostensibly technical disapproval of him is, at bottom, simply due to the fact that he was wholly and truly himself and not a derived personality.

I would like to put some of these good people to a public practical test—the harmonisation of a few typical Berlioz passages in a way which they would regard as "correct". For this purpose I would choose first of all the second movement of *Harold in Italy*, where the Pilgrims' Evening Hymn is presented in a variety of forms. They would soon discover, I fancy, that Berlioz's handling of the melody is first and final; alter the harmonisation anywhere and the thing ceases to be Berlioz at all, for the reason, among others, that here, as always with him, the whole texture—melody, harmony, rhythm, colour—is one and indivisible.

To rewrite his harmony on textbook lines would result in as great absurdity as would the rewriting of *The Ring and the Book* in the manner of *Idylls of the King*; for Berlioz, like Browning, has a sound-sense, a syntax, a construction of his own, the natural expression of his own way of thinking, capable neither of being applied to, nor "corrected" in terms of, any other way.

The tune played by Berlioz criticism, ancient and modern, has always been the same, a lament, angry or pitying according to the temperament of the critic, over the composer's "irregularities", his "caprice" and so on in the matters of melody, harmony and rhythm. Today it is precisely those "irregularities" that delight the true Berliozian and the general musical public, who find

Berlioz's unusual phrase-articulation refreshingly vital after an overdose of the easy, over-obvious, almost mechanical symmetries into which "classical" melody and rhythm in particular have always tended to petrify.

Reaction against these facile symmetries raised its head much earlier in poetry than in music. Arthur Hugh Clough, defending, in a preface to his *Dipsychus*, against an imaginary Uncle, the metrical freedom of that poem, pointed out that "there is an instructed ear and an uninstructed. A rude taste for identical recurrences would exact sing-song from 'Paradise Lost', and grumble because 'Il Penseroso' doesn't run like a nursery rhyme."

The music critics and textbook writers were reluctant to abandon the norms which they imagined to have been established for all time by the mighty German masters, and particularly the drift to "identical recurrences" in melodic structure. The criticism of Berlioz in his own day was one long whimper over the "irregularities", the "lack of symmetry" of his melodies and rhythms. Adolphe Adam felt he had almost a personal grievance against him in this matter.

A former critic of *The Times* seems to have suffered the tortures of the damned: "the rhythm is often broken and irregular", he wailed, "so as to torment and puzzle the ear; and several of the melodies which begin happily are spoiled by being tortured into strange and unexpected cadences"—the implication being that no composer had the right to employ any but an "expected" cadence. Yet, oddly enough, there is a grain of truth in what *The Times*' critic had to say about Berlioz's cadences; for it cannot be denied that his cadences are to a great extent peculiar, so that occasionally the whole effect of a melody comes near being dissipated in the last phrase of all.

This is a problem of Berliozian style on which I have reflected for years without being able to feel that I really understand it. Had I a whole page of the *Sunday Times* at my disposal it would be easy to show, by means of a large number of musical quotations from his work of all periods, that while he is infinitely inventive in the main body of his melodies his cadences are to a large extent simply variant after variant upon a single basic procedure—a mannerism, if we like to call it that. As things are, I must ask the reader to accept this statement without present proof.

But why, as each melody neared its close, Berlioz's mind should have taken, as it were automatically, a course apparently pre-destined for it by some kink in him is a question to which I can supply no convincing answer. I only know, after a long and detailed analysis of his cadences, that that is what happened; and it is this disappointing feeling we so often get that the melody is ending strangely or weakly that makes some people declare that melody is not his strongest point.

14 May 1950
21 May 1950
28 May 1950

5

Berlioz and his Critics

Of ALL THE great composers, Berlioz has been the one least understandingly dealt with by criticism. None of the older writers came within measurable distance of a true understanding of either the man or his music. There were many things in the latter which they admired, and in some cases admired enormously: Hueffer, for example, thought the "scène d'amour" in *Romeo and Juliet* "perhaps the divinest song of love ever conceived by human heart", the "divinest of elegies", a judgment from which few who know that profoundly moving scene will dissent; but not one of Berlioz's critics had any real insight into the peculiar, the unique constitution of his musical being.

Critical understanding of him, intellectual oneness with him, as distinguished from simple instinctive ardour of emotional response to some of his music, involves the consideration of a number of problems—of ethnology, of national or local predispositions and cultures, of aesthetic in general and of musical aesthetic in particular, of the ever-expanding resources of musical expression, of the different types of musical mentality, in both composers and listeners, of which we are now beginning to be aware, etc. About none of these fundamental problems had any of the older critics of Berlioz (or indeed of composers in general) ever done any serious thinking.

We have only to read Hubert Parry on Berlioz—and Parry's is a name not to be mentioned without respect—to realise how utterly without any sort of a rationale of judgment was the "musical criticism" of a generation or a half-century ago. For Parry, with his Teutonic bias in music ("his head has a twist Allemagne," as Lamb said of Crabb Robinson), it was *a priori* impossible for Berlioz's music to be anything more than good in parts.

"The French have never shown any talent for self-dependent instrumental music," said Parry, and then blandly took it for granted that because they had hardly done so in the Bach to Beethoven period they were constitutionally barred from doing so in either the present or the future. "The kernel of the Gallic view of things", he went on to say, "is moreover, persistently theatrical", Berlioz being in this respect "typically French". But there is no such thing as "the" Gallic view of things, for "Gallic", like every other facile generalisation of the kind, is seen to mean precisely nothing when we demand a definition of it. It is a lazy, slovenly, question-begging abstraction, arbitrary and worthless.

Jules Lemaître, who can be presumed to have known something about "Gaul", has told us that no other nation contains so many types as the French; what, indeed, is there "persistently theatrical" about the "view of things" of a score of great French writers one could easily name from Ronsard to Proust, and why should there be a "Gallic view of things", "persistently theatrical", common to French musicians any more than to French poets, prosaists or painters?

The current view was that the only possible way of writing great music was the German way. The magnificent German achievement of the preceding century-and-a-half had generated the illusion that the "legitimate" aims and methods of instrumental music had been decided once for all. The pedagogues, like all myth-makers from the beginning of time, had created out of their inner consciousness a god in their own image, to which they gave the name of "sonata form"; then they managed to persuade themselves that this "form" was form *per se*, Very-form of Very-form, an emanation from the being of music itself, which instrumental music could turn its back upon only at its peril.

We had a singular instance of this aberration in the case of Hadow's book on Sonata Form. Having deduced the rationale of this "form" from the practice of the great German classics Hadow went on to consider what he quaintly called "extraneous influences"—dilutions of the pure wine of "sonata form" by liquors alien to it. Instead of regarding form as the external realisation of the inner nature of the ideas, and therefore under the obligation to vary with the varying nature of these, he saw it as something to which the ideas should conform *a priori*; and impulses that dictated at this point or that a departure from the mode of thought to which sonata form really applied were stigmatised as "extraneous". The cart was put before the horse.

Berlioz, of course, was the head and front of this offending on the part of instrumental music in the mid-19th century. He rarely troubled about "pure" instrumental music; when he did, the occasion calling for it, as in the overture to the second part of *L'Enfance du Christ*, he made no bad job of it. The biographers have attached absurd importance to his boyish quarrels with Cherubini at the Conservatoire over fugue; they have drawn from them the conclusion that he had shirked discipline in the ordinary technique of composition. That is a mistaken idea; he had worked hard enough under first Lesueur and then Reicha. He recognised the utility, in certain junctures, of fugal procedure; what he jibbed at was grinding out fugues for fugue's sake.

A vast amount of nonsense has been written about the rudimentary quality of the fugue sung by the roisterers in Auerbach's cellar in *The Damnation of Faust*. Its innocence has been taken as damning proof that Berlioz could not write a fugue—a feat performed daily, by the way, after a fashion, by a million students of composition every day in the year! What Berlioz is doing is to poke fun at the quaint notion that the writing of fugue is the supreme test of musicianship; this he does by showing a handful of half-drunk German students improvising a primitive fugue on the "subject" of Brander's song. The key to the situation is given us in Mephistopheles's call to the company—"for the Amen (after the "Requiescat in pace" for the deceased rat) let's have a fugue, a choral fugue"—followed by his aside to Faust, "Now listen to this, Doctor, you'll see bestiality at its topmost."

Berlioz saw nothing sacrosanct in any technical device: these things were not ends with him but simply means to an end of his own, which was to say what he had to say in the manner most natural to it. And what he had to say was something quite new in music. The old notion of a composer as existing in a sort of insulation from the material world around him, creating disembodied fantasies in "pure sound", has at last gone by the board. We see now that the types of musical imagination are many. Some composers and listeners are by nature wholly or relatively insensitive to poetic or pictorial suggestion: others are extremely responsive to these "extra-musical" influences, as they are falsely called. Of this latter type Berlioz was the first great representative. He flung open the door to a treasure house the riches of which it has been the business and the profit of music since his day to exploit.

His historical significance is that he was the first to put his shoulder to that door with any energy or persistence or purpose. He was fortunate enough to escape "musical education" of the conventional kind in his childhood; until he went as a young man to Paris, though his mind was volcanically charged with musical impulses, he had heard virtually nothing of the music of the past or present, so that he began on his own account without the substance of his musical ideas being unconsciously pre-determined for him, and their routes canalised for him, by the daily absorption of other men's music—which has been the unfortunate case with all other composers. He is the one real "independent" in musical history—a position, of course, not without its dangers.

23 October 1949
30 October 1949

6

Cherubini and the Fugue

Berlioz is sometimes weak because the very originality of
his mind alienated him from the school devices that often make it
possible for a stumped composer to go on talking fluently until he
can think of something to say. In a word, he could not pad—
could not "botch", as Wagner said of himself when telling King
Ludwig of the fascinating difficulties he was coming upon in his
work at the *Götterdämmerung*.

Berlioz never learned, and never troubled to learn, the tricks
of faking that often serve even a first-rate composer in such good
stead. When he was in the right vein he wrote very good music;
but if the real ore ran out for a few moments he could not complacently make do with one of the baser metals or one of the
convenient school alloys: he just went on in the way native to him
and wrote less good music, but still *his* music. It is for the individual listener to decide for himself, according to his taste and
his knowledge of the time-honoured tricks of the composing
trade, whether little failures of the Berlioz kind are less or more
dreadful than the sham successes won by padding and botching.
For myself I have no difficulty in deciding.

It was not that Berlioz could not have acquired the ordinary
school procedure had he wanted to: after all, what any pedagogue
can teach and any duffer can learn would not have been beyond
the capacity of a Berlioz. It was simply that his instinct—a
perfectly sound instinct—revolted against forcing his muse to

wear clothes that did not suit her. He was never more right than in his obstinate refusal as a student at the Paris Conservatoire to take fugue and all the rest of it as seriously as Cherubini would have had him do. Cherubini spoke more wisely than he knew when he growled that Berlioz "did not like fugue because fugue did not like him". When we find learned pedagogues of the Cherubini type solemnly telling the student that not a single one of Bach's fugues is "correctly" written, we can only hold up our hands in pious amazement at the cast of mind that can so complacently mistake shadow for substance, dead molecules for living vitamins, where the musical faculty is concerned.

Perhaps we ought not to censure the good Cherubini too severely for not seeing that music is, or should be, a matter not of forcing the imagination of the composer to take the route of standardised forms and textures but of leaving it free to create its own forms and textures afresh each time out of its own inner necessities. That point of view does not seem even yet to have established itself in academic circles, where the most distracted and ludicrous attempts are still made to elucidate the works of Beethoven's last phase in terms of "modified sonata form"— the truth being that by that time Beethoven's perpetually evolving mind had moved on into a domain in which the ancient writ of "sonata form" no longer ran. Musical exegesis will never achieve anything vital until it reverses its whole procedure and replaces the mechanical by the psychological, trying to understand the inner nerve and circulation of a great composer's mind instead of complacently regarding him as primarily a dealer in keys and subjects and all that sort of thing.

Any dolt can write a fugue a day; some do; but if, musically speaking, he is of feeble mind his best-made fugue will never be anything but a piece of doltish music. Only the completest ignorance on Cherubini's part of the varieties of musical psychology could have blinded him to the absurdity of trying to force the genius of so rare a bird as Berlioz into channels that had no validity whatever for his special type of imagination, and made him doubt whether a composer who so frankly "did not like fugue" would ever come to anything. Cherubini himself was a fine composer in his own way; but if ever I come across him in the Elysian Fields I will watch his face as I tell him that the Berlioz he so despised gets a thousand performances today to his one, while of the young rebel's fellow-students at the Conservatoire who did so well in the examinations not so much as the name of one of them is known to the ordinary music lover today.

7 March 1943

IV

Berlioz as Melodist

1

The Eye and the Ear

SOME TIME AGO I had an article in the *Sunday Times* in which I spoke of the delights of score-reading, which, under certain circumstances, can bring the intelligent reader into closer touch with the mind of the composer than the average concert performance can do. This innocent thesis of mine evoked a good deal of disapproving comment from some of my honourable confrères. It left me unmoved, because obviously none of them had more than an elementary idea of what I was really driving at. One criticism I particularly remember, however, for its pathetic naïveté. I was gravely told that a musical work does not really exist until it is realised in performance; the inference clearly being that whenever we hear a performance we have the work as the composer conceived it! In face of innocence so complete as that I could only hold up my hands in pious astonishment.

I will say nothing on the subject of colour, as it must be fairly evident that the same orchestral score can sound in a hundred subtly different ways according to the size of the orchestra, the quality of the orchestra, the ear and taste and knowledge of the conductor, the construction of the hall, where we happen to be sitting in the hall, and so on. Today I wish to ask another question: Do we always hear even so simple a thing as a melody as the composer intended it to be heard? I make bold to say that frequently what the listener hears is something quite different from that. Ask anyone to play or sing you the opening unison phrase of Schubert's Unfinished Symphony.

I

and it is a practical certainty that you will get it in the form indicated by the short upper ties, the first limb of the phrase ending with the fourth note. The correct phrasing, however, as indicated by the composer, is as shown by the lower ties, the first limb consisting of three notes. That this articulation was a vital element in Schubert's conception of his work is shown by the fact that whenever, later on, the theme is used with a harmony, the proper grouping of the notes is not merely indicated by the ties but implied in the chords themselves. An example will be found just after the double bar; while at the end of the movement we get the two forms marked respectively A and B in the following quotation:

2

Anyone, therefore, who, at the commencement of the symphony, hears the theme phrased, or conceives it as phrased, with the first limb terminating at the fourth note instead of at the third, is simply not hearing what Schubert had in his own mind. Yet this is undoubtedly how most listeners hear it. It is, indeed, as most orchestras play it. I once spoke to an orchestral 'cellist about the matter the day after he had taken part in a performance of the symphony. He was incredulous as to the correctness of my view, and would not believe me until I showed him the score: he then admitted that all his orchestral life he had been phrasing the theme wrongly. It is not to be wondered at that players and listeners should go wrong over the theme as often as they do, for some of the Schubert editors evidently have not the least perception of its true shape; I have before me, as I write, an edition in which no attempt even is made to group the notes as either 3 + 4 or as 4 + 3, but a single tie is drawn over the whole body of the theme, as shown at the top of Example No. 1 above!

This Schubert illustration is elementary but instructive. It shows, in the first place that though the actual *notes* of a melody may be correctly played, an incorrect notion of the structural essence of it may be given by a wrong phrasing. But the trouble does not end there. A more serious feature of it is that even if the correct ties were observed at the commencement of the work, the chances are a thousand to one that the ordinary listener would still hear the phrase as 4 + 3—partly from old habit, partly from the fact that there is something in the melody itself that almost irresistibly forces the 4 + 3 phrasing upon our consciousness. An orchestra would probably have to insist on the 3 + 4 with exaggerated emphasis before the casual listener noticed it—and then as likely as not, he would feel there was something wrong! It is only when we know, from the evidence of the eye, what is the right phrasing, that the mind can correct the tendency of the ear to mislead it.

Here is a slightly more subtle example of the same phenomenon. The second section of the cor anglais melody that occurs soon after the opening of the *Carnaval romain* overture is invariably heard thus:

3

and is invariably rendered in that form by a player who has not been taken severely in hand by a conductor who really understands his Berlioz. The correct phrasing, however, is this (the ties, of course, are Berlioz's own):

4

The distinction is vital, and no conductor who is not acutely sensitive to it can have the slightest understanding of the peculiar build of Berlioz's musical mind, or the slightest right to be conducting any of his works. This brings us back to an old thesis of mine—that you cannot properly play or sing any one work of a composer unless you know inside out the whole of the works of his that matter. For every composer has a mentality of his own that writes itself not only upon a work as a whole but upon the smallest details of it; and unless a performer has studied the peculiar personal functionings of the man's mind both as a whole and in detail, he cannot possibly see a single work as the composer composer saw it. The results of this failure are evident almost every evening in our concert rooms; it means that instead of a composer being interpreted in terms of himself he is often interpreted in terms of a kind of broad generalisation derived from the music of all schools and all periods.

No composer suffers in this respect so atrociously as Berlioz. He articulated the limbs of his melodies on a system so completely his own—answering, of course, to a vision of his own—that to phrase him in the ordinary way is to misrepresent him grossly. When superficial people speak of Berlioz being a poor melodist they do not realise that, as likely as not, they have been listening to a Berlioz melody in quite the wrong way. They group the limbs of it according to a standardised category derived from melodies in general, especially those of the classical German schools; and because the Berlioz melody does not make sense of the finest kind when sung or played in this way, they deny Berlioz the title of melodist. It is quite a different matter when you train yourself to hear his melodies as he himself conceived them, with an articulation that cuts sharply across the ordinary four-square, of, say, German melody. This latter, roughly speaking, corresponds to the four-line verse in poetry, with clinching end-rhymes and with the accentual footfalls occurring in virtually the same place in each line.

A Berlioz melody is a different thing altogether. It is often a series of non-rhyming lines in which the caesurae fall irregularly and come in the most unexpected places; and as Schumann pointed out a century ago, in his analysis of the *Symphonie fantastique*, it is seldom that in a Berlioz melody the second limb corresponds to the first, or the fourth to the third, or indeed any one of them to the others, in the way that is customary in melody of the ordinary type. Play or sing—or listen to—a Berlioz melody as if it were by Wagner or Mozart, and you ruin it utterly.

I will ask the reader to glance again at the theme from the *Carnaval romain* overture in the two forms in which it is quoted above. No. 3 shows what the listener always hears; No. 4 shows what he ought to hear. The trouble is that even if the conductor insists on the correct tieing of the melodic notes, and the cor anglais player does his conscientious best to reproduce it as in No. 4, the listener who does not know the score is still virtually certain to *hear* the passage tied as in No. 3. The reason for this is that he hears not only with his ear but with the whole background of his mind; and his mind has a natural bias towards imagining that the melodic line is shaped to the same pattern as the harmonic shift.

It will be seen that each bar is constructed upon a separate and distinct chord. These pull the listener's mind along with them, so that he thinks in chord-bar units; and this "pull" now transfers itself to the melody, so that he can hardly help conceiving that this also is shaped strictly according to the bar, as in No. 3. It is as in No. 3, accordingly, not as in No. 4, that he hears the melody, let the player phrase it as accurately as he will. In actual performance it takes both a knowledge of the score and an act of the will to sense the correct irregular tieing of the notes in spite of the pull of the regular bar-formation of the supporting chords. The eye, in fact, must help out the ear.

Berlioz's music is full of these little problems for the un-suspecting listener. He is pretty certain to hear the first main theme of *Harold in Italy*, for instance—

with the limbs shaped as shown by the lower ties, whereas the correct articulation is as indicated by the upper ties. (The current carelessness in these matters is shown by the incorrect placing of some of the ties in the quotation of the opening theme of *Harold in Italy* in a recent concert programme. The listener was thus misled from the commencement.) In the Prelude to "The Flight into Egypt" (the second part of *L'Enfance du Christ*)—

the listener is certain to hear the opening theme as shown by the lower ties instead of the upper ones. If he thus goes wrong at the commencement he is not likely to perceive the true meaning of the tieing in the later portions of the movement: this, for instance—

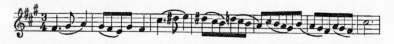

The reader must beware of thinking that in all these examples (which might be multiplied indefinitely) Berlioz is merely "tieing across the bar" as other composers do. (Examples of this latter will be found by the handful in the Schumann symphony we heard the other evening). There is a radical distinction between the two procedures; and the conductor or the player who is not conscious of it would be well advised to leave Berlioz alone, for it is evident he has not the most elementary understanding of the mind of Berlioz.

It has long been recognised that Berlioz thinks harmonically in a way of his own that is not the textbook way, or the way of the Germans and Italians. As Saint-Saëns pointed out long ago in an admirable essay (not on Berlioz, by the way, but on Liszt), Berlioz had the unique advantages of not having been brought up on the piano, so that he escaped the "devastating influence" of the enharmonic. The academic railed, and still rail, at Berlioz's harmony—even going so far as to say that he did not understand harmony!—merely because his harmonic sense was different from, and subtler than, their own. His rhythms, we all know, are peculiarly his own. It has not yet been sufficiently recognised that he had also a melodic articulation of his own, and to play or hear a Berlioz melody articulated as Wagner or Mozart would have articulated much the same sequence of notes is to misconceive it utterly; the result is neither true Berlioz nor good anything else. Yet the ear of the average concert-goer is quite incompetent, of itself, to perceive the true articulation; the pull of the other type of melody is too strong for that. It is only when we have studied Berlioz with the eye that we can train the ear to take the right road.

Much of the misunderstanding, of course, is due to sheer carelessness or sheer ignorance on the part of conductors and players; they also are the victims of the conventional "pull", and are insensitive to either Berlioz's peculiar caesurae or his peculiar nuancing. But it must be admitted that in performance it is sometimes absolutely impossible to reproduce the fine shades he intended, if only because of the rapid pace of the music. Here, for instance, is a passage from the "Feast at the Capulets" (in *Romeo and Juliet*) that has never yet been heard, and never will be heard, as Berlioz imagined it—

What we always hear is—

the fine and vital distinction of the tie and the dots in the first (complete) bar being lost in the commonplace dead level of five absolutely uniform notes. The reader may think it does not make much real difference. If, however, he will train himself to hear the passage mentally—and indeed the whole of this movement—correctly nuanced according to Berlioz's markings, he will in time realise that what he has heard in the concert room or on a gramophone record was the clumsiest travesty of what the composer had in his mind.

The truth is that musical instruments, even the most delicate among them, are much too crude a medium to allow of the passage of the composer's thought through them without a certain amount of distortion. Unless we hear with the eye, so to speak, as well as with the ear, we often miss the very essence of the musical idea, especially in the case of music so subtly organised as that of Berlioz.

21 January 1934
28 January 1934

2

Closing Phrases

IT IS OFTEN said that Berlioz is no melodist. The importance of "melody" in music can easily be over-estimated; one symphony, for instance, can be packed with good melodies and yet be, as a symphony, quite second-rate, while another can have hardly anything to show that will bear detached consideration as a melody and yet be first-rate. Or again, to reduce the matter to a smaller scale, a miniature like Grieg's "Erotikon" can be built up out of two charming melodies and yet not be comparable, as an effort of the musical imagination, with this or that fugue of Bach's that is evolved out of half a dozen notes at which one would scarcely give a second glance if they stood alone. There is a whole field of music in which the vital thing is not the germ-notes but the organism that somehow or other develops out of the germ; could anything, for instance, be less notable in itself than the absurd little phrase to which Mariandel, in the *Rosenkavalier* sings "Nein, nein, nein, nein, I trink kein Wein," and anything more notable than the great trio that is afterwards evolved out of this melodic snippet?

Nevertheless, when a composer says, in effect, "Here is a melody which I confidently invite you to consider purely and simply as a melody and to judge it as such", we are bound to apply to it the tests of its own nature. Subject a long melody of Grieg or Rimsky-Korsakov to these tests and it emerges triumphant; apply them to a Berlioz melody and it too often fails somehow or other. It is not that one agrees with his detractors that he is "no melodist"; on the contrary, we who are endlessly fascinated by his peculiar though undeniably flawed genius feel again and again, when listening to certain of his melodies, that they move us as few things in this line do. They inhabit a world of their own, which is one of the reasons why they appeal so little to some people and so much to others. The former cannot reconcile themselves to the absence from a Berlioz melody of the conventional movements and balances of the typical German or Italian melody: while for the other people it is precisely the unexpectedness, the pure incalculability of a Berlioz melody that gives it its interest and value. Yet the fact has to be faced that comparatively few melodies of his will bear critical examination throughout. Their great defect, very often, is their way of concluding; and it is perhaps the sense of something emotionally flat or technically helpless in the closing phrase of an otherwise fine melody that makes the anti-Berliozians decide that he is a poor melodist.

It is hardly an exaggeration to say that in a work of art there are only two really difficult moments for a creator of genius—the beginning and the end. More particularly the end, and still more particularly in the case of music, which is hampered in the first place by the fact that its essential material is limited to a mere twelve notes, and in the second place by the fact that a final cadence is restricted to the merest handful of possible harmonies. The eighteenth century had no difficulty with its endings; it was a formal age, and there were certain recognised ways of leaving a musical work, as of leaving one's company, with proper ceremonial: a Bach or a Handel could elaborate the same cadence a thousand times without anyone blaming him for repeating himself. A more difficult problem confronted composers when music became a more personal matter; as soon as pattern was abandoned, as soon as a piece of music aimed at being the expression of something peculiar to the individual and to the moment or the situation, it necessarily had to have an ending in keeping with its general character, not constructed according to a standard recipe. This new problem was often too much for Berlioz: in the body of his melody he could paint, and paint most convincingly, with his eye on the object, as it were, but he could not always maintain the individuality of his idea to the end, for there he came up against the natural limitations of cadence-material. And so it is in the final phrase of a melody that he frequently fails us.

Let us look at a few of his best-known melodies. Marguerite's song of the King of Thule (in *The Damnation of Faust*) is a creation of genius until we come to the feeble closing bars:

Can anyone really feel, again, that the ending of Marguerite's romance ("D'amour l'ardente flamme"):

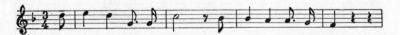

is the best ending conceivable for that moving song?

The oboe melody depicting "Romeo alone," in the introduction to the second part of *Romeo and Juliet*, is one of Berlioz's best efforts; especially fine is the way in which he delays the expected cadence for bar after bar. But how lame and impotent is the actual conclusions:

Few things in romantic music are as moving as the orchestral adagio of the garden scene in the same work: but how sadly the final phrase of the passionate melody disappoints us:

So again with the ending of an admirable song, *La Captive*:

and with that of Chorebe's aria. "Mais le ciel et la terre," in the first part of *Les Troyens*:

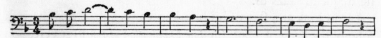

Berlioz was strangely liable to lapses from good taste, or even from musical commonsense, and they generally occur at or near the end of a train of thought; apparently he saw nothing absurd in foisting the following absurd melodic line upon the tenor part in the third line of the opening stanza of the great duet between Dido and Aeneas in *Les Troyens*:

It is as true of his faults as of his virtues that one never knows what Berlioz will do next; he is as capable, at a critical moment, of an absurdity or a commonplace as of a stroke of genius. And nowhere does he so frequently fail to keep his ideas on their highest level as in the cadences to his melodies; and I suspect it is because of a fine idea of his so often ends in deflation that many listeners feel that he is a poor melodist. The rather ignominious exit of the melody cancels all the effect of its fine bearing up to that point.   20 December 1936

3

Phrasing in Berlioz

Berlioz seems at last to be getting in this country something like the attention he deserves, and I propose to talk about his mind and art in general in a following article or two. But first of all it is necessary to say a word about our manner of performing him. If that be largely wrong, the impression the ordinary listener will get of him will be wrong; and no one familiar with the mind and the style of Berlioz can doubt that in most performances of him there is a good deal that not merely fails to represent him accurately but positively misrepresents him.

This comes about, for the most part, through players and singers indulging, from force of habit, in a system of phrasing and accentuation that does not apply to him, and against which he has done his best to protect himself by his markings—a system in which the bar line reigns supreme, with the conventional "strong" and "weak" beats as its henchmen. Unfortunately the disastrous effect of this kind of metrical tyranny is less easily perceivable in the case of the performance of music than in the reading of poetry, because even if a succession of musical sounds is bound together in the wrong way it may still make a pleasing pattern. The least literate person would laugh if he heard Shakespeare's or Milton's blank verse read aloud as a cast-iron sequence of iambics, without any flexibility in the distribution of accents and time-values within the theoretical scheme of scansion; but a piece of music played with the accents corresponding mechanically with the bar lines may still make some sort of musical sense, even if it is not the sense the composer had in his mind.

Even a ridiculous re-phrasing of a classic by some modern editor or other may not reveal its absurdity to a listener who does not know the original. Take, as an example, Riemann's nonsensical phrasing, made to suit his own pet theory of musical rhythm, of the andante grazioso of Mozart's piano sonata in A major (K.331):

As Schenker has pointed out, the build of the piece, the course of the thought, show that Mozart conceived the rhythmical articulation along the lines indicated by the slurs here placed below the notes. Riemann's slurs (shown here above the notes) are the aberration of a mind that could not listen to a piece of music without wanting to impose its own theories upon it. Yet I have heard the andante played in public in Riemann's way without either the pianist or the bulk of the audience realising that they were taking part in a farce.

Our orchestral players all too frequently misrepresent Berlioz's melodic line in the reverse way to this, by ignoring or inadequately reproducing, the delicacies of his irregular accentual footfalls and forcing the melody into the conventional four-bar groups. Listen, for example, to some of the phrasings in the Pilgrims' Hymn in the recent excellent records of *Harold in Italy* made by William Primrose and the Boston Symphony Orchestra under Koussevitzki. Take the following fragment:

What the uninformed listener perceives here in the third, fourth and fifth bars is three groups of two notes with an implied stress on the first of each group, whereas what Berlioz wanted was a first phrase running as far as the first note of bar 3, followed by two groups of two notes with accents *across* the bar lines. Ask anyone who does not know the score to write out this passage for you after hearing it on the records, and you will find that he has heard the melody wrongly as made up of two limbs of four bars each: the fact that the first note of the fifth bar is the highest and most forceful of them all makes it inevitable, if the players are not aware of the danger and do not guard against it, that the listener will conceive it as marking the beginning of a second four-bar phrase balancing the first one, which itself has been wrongly conceived by him as a four-bar limb because it has not been slurred and accented as Berlioz marked it.

I willingly concede that to get all Berlioz's phrase-markings faithfully reproduced in a long orchestral work would need a vast amount of rehearsal. But that does nothing to reconcile us to the plain fact that the phrasing we hear is often sadly wrong, that, to go back to the analogy with poetry, his music is being read to us not in his own flexible way but according to a mechanical scheme of scansion. I am sure that in many cases we are given the wrong rhythmical articulation not because the players have made no effort to play the passage as Berlioz has marked it but because of the difficulty of realising these good intentions in an orchestral mass without more rehearsal than is possible under ordinary conditions. A good orchestra might perhaps get this passage from *Béatrice and Bénédict* right:

But how much rehearsal would it take to get this from the same work right in an ensemble of flutes, oboes, clarinets and horns, at a speed of minim 108?

I have given only one or two of the simplest illustrations of a problem of performance that confronts us on almost every page of Berlioz. I am afraid conductors and players are apt to imagine that because they hear the correct phrasing and accentuation mentally it is equally evident to the listener. A thousand experiences in the concert room and by wireless, with the score in front of me, have proved the contrary.

27 October 1946

V

Individual Works

1

The "*Symphonie fantastique*"

Sir Henry Wood's fine performance of the *Symphonie fantastique* a week ago may have made a few new friends for Berlioz. As I have often said in this column, Berlioz is not everyone's composer: one is born either a Berliozian or an anti-Berliozian, and there's an end of it. It is useless for one who is sympathetic with him to argue with one who is antipathetic: the two will never understand each other. There is always hope, however, that by more frequent hearings of his music new admirers of it may be made.

The trouble with him has always been that while some of his most characteristic qualities cannot be appreciated all at once, the public does not hear enough performances of him to carry them, as it were over the first hurdle. In spite of everything that the historians and critics say against him, he remains one of the most extraordinary figures in the history of music. With all his faults, there is something in him that perpetually intrigues us. Even the general public, that knows next to nothing of him apart from the *Faust*, feels vaguely the uncommon quality of his music.

One proof of this feeling is the revival every now and then of the *Symphonie fantastique*. We may greet a good deal of it, if we like, with an indulgent smile: but the fact remains that, with the exception of the Beethoven symphonies and a couple of Schubert's, no other symphonic works of the first thirty years of the nineteenth century have any life today in our concert rooms, and no other non-German symphony whatever has survived from that time. A work of which this can be said is not negligible.

Perhaps people would see the *Symphonie fantastique* more truly for what it is if some of the legends that have settled round it could be dissipated. The ordinary music-lover regards it as the first of the programme symphonies,—which, in a sense, it is; and, following the lead of the historians and the æstheticians he imagines Berlioz to have created deliberately a new genre out of his inner consciousness, much as Liszt did with the symphonic poem. But there are grave reasons for doubting whether Berlioz meant to do anything of the kind. The probability is that the new form came to him more or less by accident. Certainly the *Symphonie fantastique* did not, as is popularly supposed, come into being as a piece of music worked out systematically to illustrate a preconceived programme.

It would hardly be too much to say that had Berlioz been able to force the doors of the Opera he would never have written programme symphonies; there would have been no *Symphonie fantastique*, and the world would have been spared a great deal of acrimonious æsthetic argument. Berlioz's object from the very beginning of his consciousness of himself as a musician was to write operas: the one idea possessed him to the end of his days, and it was the failure of *Benvenuto Cellini* and his vain struggle to get *The Trojans* performed that sent him to his grave a disappointed, embittered man. Debussy has said that Berlioz was never really "un musicien de théâtre". That is only a half-truth; and Debussy's amazingly superficial estimate of *The Trojans* is enough to make us distrust his judgment in everything concerning Berlioz. But whether Berlioz was a theatrical composer or not in the popular sense of the term, the theatre was always his land of heart's desire. And it was really out of the theatre that the *Symphonie fantastique* came.

The Symphony is generally dated 1830. But parts of it are older than that. At the Ambign-Comique Theatre there had been given in 1823 a play entitled *Les Francs-Juges*. Berlioz conceived the idea of writing an opera on this subject, and got his friend Humbert Ferrand to put together a "book" for him. He seems to have worked intermittently at the opera from about 1825 to 1829. We have the overture (which is occasionally given at concerts): a few scenes only of the opera itself were actually composed.* The careful researches of M. Adolphe Boschot have revealed the fact that, as usual with him, Berlioz utilised some of the abandoned fragments in his later work.

The second act of the opera is laid in "a wild valley", between "high mountains crowned by thick forests. In the distance are some chalets . . . gypsies, shepherds, shepherdesses. . . . The cornemuses are heard answering each other from one mountain to another." "Music written", Berlioz has noted on Ferrand's manuscript. "One remembers", says M. Boschot, "the 'Scène aux Champs' (the andante of the Symphony) where the two shepherds answer each other as here. Further, the second act ends with a storm: between the thunder-peals the cornemuses of the shepherds are again heard in dialogue. There is the same effect in the 'Scène aux Champs'." Now these pages are *missing* from the manuscript of the *Francs Juges* score at the Bibliothèque Nationale: the clear inference is that Berlioz had used them for the andante of the Symphony.†

"Music written" is noted, again, on the libretto in a scene in the third act, in which the Francs Juges enter a cavern to the strains of a "marche lugubre". This "marche lugubre" became, in 1830, the "March to the Scaffold" of the *Symphonie fantastique*. The programme would account quite satisfactorily for its introduction here: all he would have to do would be to give it a sort of organic connection with the rest of the symphony by means of the "idée fixe" (the theme representing the Beloved). Nothing was easier, as M. Boschot shows, on the evidence of the manuscript itself. Berlioz simply holds up the orchestra for a moment on

* The entire opera was composed (P.H.).

† These pages survive and are unrelated to the "Scène aux champs" (P.H.).

the dominant of the last fortissimo, inserts four bars of the "idée fixe" in the clarinet, and the thing is done. There can be no doubt of it: the interpolation is written on a slip: when this slip is lifted from the manuscript, the original music of the *Francs Juges* march at this point is seen underneath.

It is probable, too, that the last movement of the Symphony, the Witches' Sabbath, had an origin earlier than the Symphony itself. Berlioz has told us that part of the Symphony was written under the influence of Goethe's *Faust*. We know that in 1828 he was planning a *Faust* ballet: it is very likely that he had the Walpurgis Night scene in his mind, and that his sketches for this were worked up into the Sabbath scene of the *Fantastique*.

The melody of the "idée fixe" had already been used by him in the cantata *Herminie*, in the *Prix de Rome* competition of 1828; and the opening theme of the Symphony was taken from a work of his boyhood. He did, in fact, what he always did; if a good idea had no chance of being heard in the work for which it was originally written, he put it in another work. The motive for the *Symphonie fantastique* was not, as is generally supposed, the desire to create a new musical genre. The Symphony came into being in a more or less haphazard way. Perhaps the root of it all was the desire to make public his feelings with regard to Harriet Smithson; he had a certain amount of music already written that he thought it a pity should never be heard, so he worked out a programme that would permit him both to use these fragments and to tell the story of *l'affaire* Smithson, and any new music he wanted to fill up the picture he wrote.

When we realise the happy-go-lucky way in which the Symphony was put together we are less critical of its defects of structure: it would obviously be unreasonable to expect from a work of this kind the organic unity of an orchestral work conceived and executed with a single musical purpose in view. We must be chary, too, of arguing too solemnly from the obvious defects of the Symphony to the essential flaws of programme music in general. But when everything has been said against the *Fantastique* that can be said, it remains a marvel for a young man of twenty-five or twenty-six in the most unmusical period of a not particularly musical country. The novelty and the sureness of the orchestral colouring are not the least of the marvels.

19 February 1922

2

The Origins of the "Symphonie fantastique"

As is usual with him, Berlioz, in his autobiography, succeeds, without the slightest intention of misleading his readers, in giving them quite a wrong notion of the nature and genesis of the *Symphonie Fantastique*. One would suppose, from his account, that the work sprang complete from his brain as an organic conception. The facts, which are fully and lucidly set forth by Mr. Wotton in his analysis of this work in the excellent "Musical Pilgrim" series, tell a very different story. As with many another piece of programme music, the music came before the programme and independently of it. The youthful genius had on his hands a quantity of music that he rightly thought too good to be lost to the world for ever merely because the world showed no great desire to hear it in its original form. His experience of Beethoven's fifth symphony in 1828 seems to have fired him, at the age of twenty-five, with the ambition to write a symphony of his own, the older form, of course, to be vivified by the new poetic and romantic spirit.

In July of that year he began work on a "Faust" ballet for the Paris Opera; as Mr. Wotton says, it is probable that not only the "Witches' Sabbath" movement of the symphony but the Waltz formed parts of this ballet. During the next year he worked at an opera *Les Francs Juges*, that was not accepted by the authorities. This contained a March, which now figures in the *Fantastique* as the "March to the Scaffold". The transfer was not so reckless as it may seem at first sight: in the opera the "March of the Guards" accompanied the conducting of a condemned man to execution in a setting of romantic horror. Finally there were two themes in Berlioz's head for which he had a great liking. One was a melody written by him when, as a little boy, he was in love with that Estelle, who was destined to play so strange a part in his strange life: this melody reappears in the Introduction to the *Fantastique*. The other was the "idée fixe" of the symphony, the principal theme of the first movement. Berlioz had already used this in his Conservatoire cantata of 1828, *Herminie*.

His problem now was to find a scheme that would permit of the use of all this material and give it a plausible unity. After much racking of his brain he hit upon the idea of a story that would not only suit the material but give him the opportunity to tell the public all about himself and Harriet Smithson. The story was that of a young artist who, in the first movement, romanticises over his beloved, in the second meets her at a ball, in the third finds her presence a disturbance of the peace brought to his ravaged soul by the beauty and quiet of the country, in the fourth dreams that he has killed her and is being led to execution and in the fifth sees her as not the least horrible part of the grotesque horror of a Witches' Sabbath.

The programme was obviously intended, in large part, to make the Parisians sit up and take notice—for Berlioz knew as well as any modern sub-editor the value of "the human interest" in attracting the great bourgeois public—and there are evidences that, its purpose once fulfilled, he would not have been sorry to have had its wealth of detail forgotten, and his work accepted or rejected on its purely musical merits alone. Unfortunately it has proved impossible to delete the programme from the public mind; and one of the results of the association has been that many people have been too busy smiling at the early-romantic absurdities of the programme to see how much of the *Fantastique* can stand on its own feet without the assistance of the story-teller.

The task of organising the old material on new lines was not quite so simple as it appears on the face of it. It is to Berlioz's credit that he succeeds best where he confines himself to purely musical problems, as in the first three movements, and particularly the first. The further he plunges into his programme, the more difficulties it creates for him. As happens not infrequently in this world, a work of art has turned out less well than it might have done because the artist was foolish enough to mix up art and woman. If only Berlioz had had the sense to go on dreaming about his Estelle—who, being merely an artist's dream, would have done his art the maximum of good and the minimum of harm—instead of fretting about the much too real Harriet, who was never anything but a nuisance to him as a man and a drag on him as an artist, the *Fantastique* might have been even better than it is.

But he made the mistake, common to lovers, and especially to frustrated lovers, of imagining that his personal feelings about a rather commonplace bit of femininity were stuff out of which to make enduring art. As soon as he allows his rage against poor insignificant Harriet to get the upper hand of the artist in him, his symphony begins to weaken in its texture. He managed tolerably well in the fourth movement; having in his portfolio a "March to the Scaffold" that fitted in well enough with his programme, all he had to do was to cut out the original ending, paste in the "idée fixe", and add a few finishing bars. We are conscious of the mechanics of the procedure; we can see that the "idée fixe" has been dragged in by the hair of its head; but we can pass it all off with a smile. In the finale, however, in spite of the technical cleverness of much of it, we can see too clearly that the tissue is a patchwork. It is in the three earlier movements, where the programme is less obtrusive, that Berlioz comes out best as a musician. I am inclined to believe that the lovely scene "In the country" was originally complete without the present programme. Mr. Wotton, following the lead of

Berlioz in his programme note, sees "Her" appearing in the threatening passage for basses, 'cellos, and bassoons—as Berlioz puts it, "*She* appears anew, and a spasm contracts his heart, black presentiments assail him: should she prove false. . . ." But this passage could quite well have represented, in the original picture, the distant muttering of a storm. It was easy enough to impose a suggestion of the "idée fixe" upon it; but both here and in the later passage in which the "idée" occurs (at No. 47 in the full score), the music really seems complete without it, though Berlioz achieves a subtle touch, which we should have been sorry to lose, in the magical reintroduction of that drop of a seventh that is one of the most characteristic features of the development of the "idée fixe" in the first movement. (Mr. Wotton points out the similarity of the figure to the "Reflection" motive in *Siegfried*, but apparently has not correlated it with the earlier falling seventh.)

A touch like this shows what Berlioz could do when he let the musician in him come uppermost. It is as a symphonist, indeed, a musician evolving new shapes out of old material and endowing them with new meanings, that he shines in the opening movement and the third. The prelude to the first movement is a truly extraordinary piece of writing for its period; and if we wish to see how far Berlioz had travelled as a musician pure and simple in the course of a year or so, we have only to compare the fumbling treatment of the "idée fixe" theme in *Herminie* with the richness and freedom of its handling in the opening movement of the symphony. There is genius, for example, in the alteration of the octave fall in the *Herminie* melody at one point to that drop of a seventh that is one of the most expressive moments of the melody as we have it in the *Fantastique*.

All in all, it seems to be true that Berlioz is best when he is developing his work along purely musical lines, and only becomes more or less awkward when he thinks too much of Harriet and his programme. I have a subconscious feeling, though I cannot produce any valid evidence for it, that the changes of key in the "Ball" movement when the "idée fixe" is introduced, and the rather clumsy method of its first introduction in particular, point to a none too skilful plastering of the programme motive upon a piece of music that was originally complete and self-sufficing without it.

3 November 1929

3

Schumann on the "Symphonie fantastique"

I WANT TO TALK today about Schumann and Berlioz, *à propos*
of the two performances we have had broadcast this week of the
Symphonie fantastique at the BBC concert on Wednesday under
Weingartner, and from Birmingham on Thursday, under Sir
Hamilton Harty.

I have been reading again Schumann's famous essay on the
Symphonie fantastique, written in 1835. Schumann could be an
extremely bad critic at times. Peter Raabe, in his recent book on
Liszt, has pointed out his grievous misunderstanding, and
occasional complete misrepresentation, of one of Liszt's early
epoch-making Etudes. But at times he was extraordinarily acute;
and his article on the *Symphonie fantastique* is perhaps the best
thing he ever wrote. It is interesting today not only because of the
insight it here and there shows into the real quality of Berlioz's
mind—to appreciate this feature of Schumann's article it is only
necessary to read the imbecilities of Fétis about the Symphony
—but because it incidentally illustrates once more the saddest of
all facts in connection with musical criticism, that nine-tenths of
contemporary criticism of composers is hardly worth, for future
generations, the paper it is written on.

That Schumann had done his work with the utmost care is
everywhere evident, and he says some admirable things about
Berlioz. He was the first to point out that we simply cannot
judge a Berlioz melody by the standards that apply to German

melody, for it is a different thing altogether, not only in feeling but in structure—a point that our German-music-sodden criticism of today has still not fully grasped. But Schumann wastes a good deal of his time and ours on matters that have no importance today outside the textbooks—the sequence of keys in the Symphony, and so on; and, for all his latitudinarianism of mind, which was often quite remarkable for a German composer and critic of that epoch, he is sometimes quite unable to see the point of certain harmonies of Berlioz that present no difficulties at all for us. Schumann did not possess the full score of the Symphony: he wrote his article on the basis of Liszt's amazing piano arrangement of the work; and unfortunately the reader who does not possess the original edition of that arrangement, or a later French one printed from the same plates, cannot check Schumann's numerous references to this page and bar or that. But for those who have Liszt's score in its first form it is extremely interesting to follow Schumann point by point through his objections to Berlioz's harmonies.

No real understanding of the Symphony, of course, can be had from the piano score. Schumann goes sadly wrong more than once. Without the full score to turn to, he often does not realise that the difficulties of transcription for the piano have baffled even the genius of Liszt, and that the music is something quite different on the orchestra, as regards not only colour but line. Melodies have sometimes had to be taken out of their proper octave; at other times a melody is broken up into cascades that do, in a sense, trace a certain connected line on the piano, but a very different line from the continous sweep of Berlioz's strings or wind. Sometimes the whole meaning of the music is altered because the harmonic texture is necessarily deprived, by reason of the limitation of the human hands, of a significant thickening an octave or two lower. Schumann, again, thought that "the chromatic heavily ascending and descending chord of the sixth" (in the first movement), was "nothing in itself, though it may be uncommonly imposing in its place here". He could not possibly, however, have heard or imagined this passage as it actually sounds on the orchestra. Liszt could do no more than transcribe the long ascents and descents of sixths; he could not work in the hoarse cries in the woodwind and horns with which the passage is punctuated, and that give it its real character and force. (He might possibly have conveyed something of this had he confined the sequences of string sixths, where necessary, to the left hand, instead of giving them to both hands; this would have left the right hand free for the harsh ejaculations in the other orchestral instruments.) But in spite of everything, Schumann's article is often astonishingly percipient for its time.

One thing, however, he could not do. Perhaps no critic of that epoch could have done it, for it is possible to us of today only in virtue of the evolution of the symphony during the last fifty years or so; and even today most people miss the point—I refer to the new symphonic style of structure of the first movement—because they are too much accustomed to thinking of symphonic structure in terms of German practice. The *Fantastique*, as we know, is a composite work. The "March to the Scaffold" is taken from a March already written for an opera on the subject of *Les Francs Juges*; the Witches' Sabbath movement is probably a re-casting of a *Faust* ballet that Berlioz had planned some time before; while the marvellously eloquent Introduction to the Symphony is an expansion of some music Berlioz had written, as a boy, to a poem, commencing "Je vais donc quitter pour jamais mon doux pays, ma douce amie", from Florian's "Estelle". (Julien Tiersot has shown that the words of the poem can be fitted perfectly to the music of the opening melody of the Symphony, except at the finish, "where the end of the musical phrase is lost in the symphonic development".) What holds the *Fantastique* together throughout its five movements is the programme, which was an afterthought, hit upon by Berlioz as a peg upon which to hang a good deal of already existing music which he was reluctant to sacrifice. But the first movement is a genuinely symphonic piece of writing, which hangs together, purely and simply as music, even if we put the poetic idea out of our minds.

This first movement is not only splendid stuff in itself but is of exceptional interest to us of today who have seen composers like Sibelius trying to sweat all the old superfluous tissue out of the symphony and make it compact and meaningful throughout. Berlioz was at least half a century before his time in his contempt for the bogus sort of writing, the note-spinning, the mere talking when you have nothing to say, that is the weak point of much of the music that passes for symphonic and "classical" in Germany, and in countries, like ours, that have followed too blindly in the German wake. Berlioz did not put together his music in the conventional German way, not because he had not the craftsman-ship for it, but because it simply did not appeal to him. He saw no sense in plodding away at a "form" that had no real relation to what he had to say. He could handle fugal imitation in masterly style when it was vital to his thought, as is shown by the first number of his *Faust*, by the scene of Faust alone in his study, and by the orchestral introduction to the second part of *L'Enfance du Christ*; but he saw no reason to persist doggedly with a fugue for mere fugue's sake, in the plodding academic way. The pedants have solemnly assured us that the "Amen" chorus in *Faust* is a poor fugue; they have not perceived that Berlioz (as is shown by a correlation of the words he puts into the mouth of Mephisto-pheles with his own remarks on bad academic fugues here and there in his prose works) meant it to be an ironic commentary on the flatulent school-work of the academics.

He could construct logically enough in his own new way, which was the way first of all of having something to say, then saying it as lucidly and expressively as possible, avoiding the bogus sort of manipulation that passes for "working-out" in the schools, and finishing the moment the topic was exhausted, without troubling himself in the least whether he had complied with "form" as the academics conceive it. In a word, he was in this respect, as in so many others, a man of our day. If any teacher of "form" in the conservatoires thinks he could improve on the form of the first movement of the *Fantastique*, he would oblige us, and perhaps add to our gaiety, by favouring us with a sight of his attempt.   19 November 1933

4

The "Symphonie fantastique" . . . as ballet

WE NEED NOT anticipate any such dead set being made against Massine for having decoyed the *Symphonie fantastique* into his lair as has been made against him for his "outrage" on the Brahms No. 4: for Berlioz has never been, among "sensitive musicians", the Sacred Person, the sort of Grand Lama of Music, that Brahms has always been to certain communities in this country. The *Fantastique*, indeed, so obviously calls out for balletic treatment that many people must have wondered why it was not taken in hand by some choreographer or other long ago.

If ballet is an outrage on symphony, here at least is a symphony which, so far from fleeing in horror from the vile seducer, has always stretched out appealing hands to him—very much like the neglected elderly ladies in Byron's "Don Juan" who, some hours after their town had been captured by a brutal and licentious soldiery, were heard asking anxiously "wherefore the ravishing did not begin?" And if any purist should still object that even if the *Fantastique* is a programme symphony it is still a symphony, and should therefore be immune from stage treatment, we have only to point out to him that we know for certain that Berlioz himself saw a considerable part of his work in terms of the theatre, while it is probable that the idea of a stage setting of some kind or other was at the back of his mind when he wrote the other portions also. Berlioz could never reconcile himself to letting a piece of music of his be wasted merely because he could not float it in its original form; again and again he patched up a new work with fragments from old ones.

Nor was he too particular as to the new application he would sometimes give to an old idea. We can understand his later use of the theme of the "Et iterum venturus est", from his early "Resurrexit", for the "Tuba mirum" of the *Requiem*, for after all there is some consanguinity between the two religious conceptions. At first sight, however, it is less easy to understand how he could use the second portion of this theme in his opera *Benvenuto Cellini*, where the chorus sings it to the words "Assassiner un capucin, un camaldule, ah, c'est infame!": but a little reflection on our part serves to dispel the mystery. Berlioz's commonsense told him that a musical theme intended to express terror and horror was equally suscepible of a sacred and of a secular application where terror and horror were concerned: the words are a matter of minor importance. In the same spirit he had no hesitation in using the melody of "Cujus regni non erit finis" (in the "Resurrexit") for the words "Ah, cher canon du fort Saint Ange" and "Ah, quelle nuit noire et profonde" in *Benvenuto Cellini*. And the *Fantastique* came into being primarily, not because he wanted to tell symbolically, in symphonic form, the story of himself and Harriet Smithson, but because he had some good music on his hands from previous works which he thought it a pity to consign to oblivion. The March to the Scaffold is merely a march from his youthful opera *Les Francs Juges* to which he has added a few bars introducing the *idée fixe* motive of the Beloved.

We may take it as certain that the Witches' Sabbath movement was derived from the *Faust* ballet of an earlier date; and even the Ball Room scene and the Scene in the Country may have come from that. What makes a unity of the five movements of the symphony is merely the story imposed on them later, and the employment of the *idée fixe* motive in each of them.

There can be no possible ground of complaint against Massine, therefore, in this instance, for having put a symphony on the stage: one feels, indeed, that had Berlioz had a choreographer like Massine ready to his hand it would have been in some such form as this that he would have planned to have his work presented. But in that case he would probably have modified the musical part of it at one or two points. Having to tell the whole story to a concert audience in music pure and simple, he naturally turned his incomparable gift for orchestral description on to the business of suggesting the atmosphere of the scene to the eye through the ear; and now and then he has done his own part of the job so thoroughly that nothing that the choreographer can put before the eye can be anything but the faintest shadow of what Berlioz makes us visualise, so to speak, through the ear.

Take, for instance, the seventh and following bars of the Witches' Sabbath scene. No one knew better than Berlioz the uncanny effect to be obtained from certain woodwind lines and colours suspended high over the bass. The oboe melody in the Ride to the Abyss, in *Faust*, is one of the most notable illustrations he has given us of this. In the preamble to the Witches' Sabbath he sets flute, piccolo and oboe piping in octaves miles above a grisly chord of the diminished seventh in the bassoons and deep brass, with a baleful, bodeful distant answer in a muted horn. This passage has beaten even Massine, for all his capacity for making sound quasi-visible on the stage: the little gnome-figures of the ballet that creep on here have nothing, can have nothing, of the suggestion of horror that is in the music itself. It may be that Massine has been faced here with an utterly insoluble problem, or it may simply be that he has not found, at this first attempt, the best way of dealing with the music in terms of his own special material. Anyhow, I venture to suggest that he should run his mind over this passage in the choreography again, and see what can be done with it in other terms.

Perhaps, after all, the best thing would be to leave Berlioz in undisputed possession here—till, indeed, the 29th bar of the score, a matter of only a minute or two after the curtain has gone up— and begin the choreography with the furious outburst in the whole orchestra at the allegro, the preceding parodistic theme of the *idée fixe*, hinting at the coming of the Beloved, thus being heard "off", as it were. The stage thus being left empty for a minute or so our imagination would get the fullest possible horror-value out of Berlioz's grisly scoring. One does not, without considerable diffidence, make suggestions to a Massine; but the point I have put forward may be worth considering by one so extraordinarily sensitive to music as he is. It is true that the procedure I have suggested would mean the sacrifice of some quaintly sinister-grotesque gestures on the part of the chief Demon (and others) just before the *idée fixe* motive is heard; and these we should be sorry to lose. But if the music *must* be accompanied by choreography from the very first bar of the finale, then I would ask Massine to revise the opening entry with a view to giving it more of the grisly horror of the music.

For the rest, one is lost in admiration of the skill with which he has reproduced in his choreography the suggestions of movement and gesture in which Berlioz's music is always so rich—for if ever there was a "visuel" in music it was Berlioz—and the art with which all these points of detail have been blended into an organic choreographic whole. One's great difficulty in writing about ballet is that one cannot quote from it; if one could do this it would be instructive to take any three minutes of what we may call Massine's score and set forth the curious unexpected felicities of it. As regards the general treatment of the story his course has been easy: he has only had to follow Berlioz's programme in its broad outlines, creating the illustrative detail for himself. Nothing so pungently realistic has yet been seen in ballet as the March to the Scaffold and the Witches' Sabbath.

Perhaps Massine's greatest triumph, however, is in the Scene in the Country. This scene has perhaps been the reason why the *Fantastique* as a whole has not been treated in ballet form before now. Its difficulties frankly seemed insuperable to all of us who had given any thought to the matter. Without it, of course, the result would not have been the *Fantastique* as musicians know it; yet how was this slow, contemplative music to be translated into terms of choreography? Better than to have lost the symphony altogether to the ballet on account of the adagio would have been to have cut this movement to about four minutes in place of the normal twelve; and indeed a cut and join could have been made that would have preserved fairly well the essence of the character of the movement, and thus have afforded an opportunity for the insertion of this so necessary slow reflective section between the vertiginous waltz and the harshly realistic March to the Scaffold and the Witches' Sabbath. Without this adagio wedge in the very centre of the piece, indeed, any ballet on the *Fantastique* would lack balance and relief. But a shortened version of the movement would not only have left the musicians in the audience with a sense of loss to which they would have found difficulty in resigning themselves, but would have provided the ballet with too little time for adequate mediation between the first half of the symphony and the second.

It evidently had to be all or nothing, and as the nothing would have meant no ballet at all on the *Fantastique*, Massine wisely decided to tackle what seemed, on the face of it, a sheer impossibility. The result has been as convincing a demonstration of his genius as he has ever given us, an idyll of the first order, with a new miming and a new translation of music into terms of dance. So skilfully and imaginatively has it all been done that there is soon an end of our first fears of a too intrusive realism when we catch sight of the deer in the background: even this animal is woven harmoniously into the general texture of the idyll.

There are one or two things in the ballet as a whole, and the manner of presentation of it, that raise a little doubt in my mind, at any rate at first. I am not quite sure that I like the floating figure (on wires in the air) of the Beloved in the Scene in the Country, though I must confess that I cannot see how the affair could have been managed in any other way. We may argue that here the Beloved comes into the drama not as a reality but only as a vision in the mind of the Artist; but unfortunately an abstraction of this kind cannot be made actual to the audience. There is nothing for it, then, but for the Beloved to be shown as a physical reality, though her (for the moment) fictive, not real, existence may be suggested by her hovering over the head of the Artist, visible only to him, in the upper air. At the fifth performance of the ballet I was more reconciled to this device than I thought I should have been at first; but I still think that the device itself could be better managed in practice. Perhaps some trick of lighting could be called in to do what is necessary to throw the floating figure back into a deeper and more mysterious perspective. To some of Berard's costumes, I am afraid, I shall never become reconciled, especially those of certain of the male figures; in some mysterious way or other they cut too violently across my Berliozian sensations. The orchestra has the amazing score well in hand, and Mr. Efrem Kurtz, who conducts the work, is thoroughly alive to all its possibilities.

The ballet as a whole is the most varied in the company's repertory: each of the five movements is an independent creation of the sharpest individual definition, yet, thanks in part to the cement of the story, is only a detail co-operating to the creation of a singularly unified whole. Almost the entire company appears in the ballet, and while the natural character of each dancer's art has been studied, Massine has succeeded in evoking new or further expressions from them all. Massine himself plays the Artist, Toumanova the Beloved. Worthy of particular mention is the lovely part for Verchinina in the adagio movement.

2 August 1936

5

"Lélio"

I<small>T</small> <small>WAS</small> <small>AN</small> excellent idea of the BBC the other evening to follow up the *Symphonie fantastique* with its sequel *Lélio*; not that the two constitute anything like an organic whole, but it was pleasant to be able to see, for once, the crazy, delightful scheme as its proud creator saw it. We may smile at *Lélio* today, but Berlioz never ceased to believe in it. Twenty-four years later, in 1855, he conducted a performance of it in Weimar, with no less a personage than Liszt taking the piano part.

The early Berlioz was a paradoxical mixture of qualities and defects: he was doing things in music which till then had not been regarded as within either the province or the scope of the art, and doing them with a technical certainty that is to this day amazing, yet going about the business of co-ordinating them in larger units with a naïveté almost beyond belief.

The best he could do to achieve some semblance of over-all design was to tack one picture on to another by means of a literary scheme which (even when the tacking is most plausible, as in the *Fantastique* or *L'Enfance du Christ*) leaves us unconvinced, though of course never uninterested. There is no over-riding design even in *The Damnation of Faust*, where he had a ground-plan provided for him by Goethe's poem; all he did in 1846 was to take up again the amazing *Eight Scenes from Goethe's Faust* of 1829 and tack others on to them.

He wrote completely absorbed in some visual or auditory

image that appealed to him at the moment for its own pure sake; then, finding himself with a number of vignettes in his portfolio, all of them too good to be left to slumber there unknown, he set to work to fabricate a make-believe armature for them. He himself never tried to put a better face on this constructional botchery than it really has. His whole attitude towards the tiresome problem of large-scale structure is seen in his gay *fait justificatif* for taking Faust into Hungary; "I have been asked", he says in a preface to the full score of the *Damnation*, "why I have made Faust go to Hungary. The answer is, because I wanted to get a hearing for an orchestral piece the theme of which is Hungarian [the famous Hungarian March], I admit it frankly; and I would have taken Faust to any other place on earth had I had the smallest musical reason for doing so." With a mentality like this, is it any wonder that he rarely gets beyond fairly plausible bluff in his attempts at a rationale of structure? He did better when he had some sort of design provided for him by the very nature of his subject, as in the great *Requiem Mass* and the *Te Deum*.

After completing the *Fantastique* he found himself with a number of musical sketches for which a public hearing would have to be devised by hook or by crook. So he hit upon what seemed to him the bright idea of not merely fathering them on his hero of the *Fantastique* but showing him actually composing them. The young artist who, in the Symphony, had had so strange a series of adventures in an opium dream is now supposed to recover from the effects of the drug, try to take his bearings in an uncomprehending world, and at one point after another embody his emotions or his philosophy in a piece of music composed *ad hoc*. The motivation is naïve, but at all events it serves to introduce us to some remarkable speciments of Berliozian painting. Is there anything else of the kind in all music, for example, that can bear comparison with the "Harpe éolienne"?

If the BBC should contemplate broadcasting the work again I would suggest condensing Lélio's long speeches into a few explanatory words by a commentator: the plan adopted the other evening rather over-estimates the linguistic accomplishment of the average listener.

Perhaps, however, the whole thing could be realised integrally some day by means of television, in a setting of the kind of scene Berlioz describes—a theatre stage with Lélio perambulating and declaiming (in English) in front of the curtain, and the orchestra, soloists and chorus concealed behind it, doing their stuff as and when called upon by the text, the curtain being raised at the finish to allow Berlioz-Lélio to give them (and the audience) his little lecture on how music should be performed. Lélio should be dressed and barbered in the fashion of the *Jeune-France* of 1830; he might be made to look like the striking Signol painting of him in 1831, with luxuriant side-whiskers, that tremendous mop of red hair, and a nose like the beak of an eagle of the Alps. The actor should speak the long tirades with perfect seriousness; the ineffable solemnity of Lélio's rantings would be their own most exquisite burlesque. Given in this way, *Lélio* could be immense fun.

5 June 1949

6

"Harold in Italy"

HAROLD IN ITALY is perhaps the best orchestral work through which to approach the study of Berlioz, for it reveals everywhere the individual nature of his musical mind. Even in his attitude towards the music of other men he was peculiarly himself: he knew comparatively little of the music of the two centuries that had preceded him and as, the *Tristan* episode proved, had hardly any understanding of the significance of the contemporary Wagner.

Even his attitude towards some of the objects of his adoration we occasionally find difficult to understand; from Beethoven, for instance, he assimilated nothing that was truly Beethovenian. The great German's way was to work from the core of a symphonic idea to the periphery; Berlioz's way was generally to cover a surface and then find, by hook or by crook, a unifying "programmatic" idea for all the detail. He took from others only what he needed at the moment to feed himself.

In *Harold in Italy* he had no use for Beethoven except to take over for his own ends the opening procedure of the finale of the Ninth Symphony: in *his* finale Berlioz introduces five tentative "reminiscences", as he calls them, type-themes from the three earlier movements, embedding them, à la Beethoven, in the quasi-recitative tissue of the imprecatory ejaculations of his brigands. And the astonishing thing about it all is that the device comes off.

It would be interesting and instructive to know precisely all the details of the processes by which *Harold in Italy* came to assume its ultimate form, how much of it had been planned as an "Italian symphony" before Paganini and his viola made their way into the scheme, and just when and how the idea of a perambulant Byronic hero imposed itself on it. To read overmuch Harold into the present symphony, and more particularly to identify him only with the solo viola part, is to misunderstand the work. For "Harold" himself is not a character undergoing psychological or circumstantial mutations, like the Don Quixote of Strauss or the Faust, Gretchen and Mephistopheles of Liszt and Wagner, but simply a mood, a melancholy mood and nothing more. He is not like Strauss's dynamic Don Juan, for example, for a setting of whose activities a number of scenes and episodes have to be devised, but a static element in Nature scenes that are constantly changing; and he does not so much make his stage entry into these scenes as emanate from them, materialise from them, as it were, either by oneness with the essence of the scene of the moment or in momentary dissent from this.

It is not Harold but the scenes that constitute the basis of the work, as is shown by Berlioz's general description of it—"a symphony in four movements with a solo viola"—and his titles for the four movements: (1) "Harold in the mountains; scenes of melancholy, happiness and joy"; (2) "Procession of Pilgrims singing the evening prayer"; (3) "Serenade of a mountaineer in the Abruzzi to his Beloved"; (4) "Orgy of Brigands, with reminiscences of the preceding scenes". The "scenes" are the vital things.

And what wonderful scenes they are, especially those of Nature! Berlioz, as always, is a *visuel*, a translator into tone of things that have impassioned in the first place his eye and ear. He is the greatest of all Nature painters in music; no other composer has written anything to compare with the Invocation to Nature in *The Damnation of Faust* or the Royal Hunt and Storm in *Les Troyens*. And the remarkable thing is that all this vivid suggestion of the scenic is achieved by Berlioz practically without resort to realism.

Contrary to the general notion, he is the least realistic of the "pictorial" musicians. He scorns the customary cheap "effects" of tonal imitation of material things: what he gives us, particularly in *Harold in Italy*, is the spirit of a scene, its settled or changing moods, its space, its light, its vibration. One movement of all would suffice to establish his claim to priority in these matters—the Pilgrims' Procession and Hymn. And this may be profitably studied as an illustration of what we mean by the individuality of his genius; for no one else could have written a page of it.

Ravel, who could be surprisingly stupid at times, was once indiscreet enough to join in the old foolish chatter still current in some quarters about Berlioz's imperfections as melodist and harmonist, especially the latter. The simple truth is that both his melody and his harmony are the natural and only valid expression of what he had it in his mind to say; they are what we would call in a poet or prose-writer his style, his manner, his accent, and to suggest that it could be improved or even altered without damage to the thing being said is to imply that this theorist or that could have made a better job of the creation of Hector Berlioz.

There is really not a misplaced or a fumbled note in either the melody or the harmony of the many transformations of the Pilgrims' theme; to accept and enjoy them we have simply to listen to them with ears unspoiled by old-fashioned text-book theory. If any professor of composition thinks he could improve upon the texture of this movement in any way I suggest that he favour us with a demonstration of how Berlioz ought to have gone about the job.

27 December 1953

7

"Romeo and Juliet"

DURING THE COUPLE of weeks before the newspaper strike the BBC gave us broadcasts of the customary excerpts from the earlier part of Berlioz's *Romeo and Juliet*, which are always welcome for their own remarkable sake. It would be as pleasant as instructive, however, to hear oftener than we do the whole of the "dramatic symphony," as the composer styled it. He felt justified in giving it that ambitious title, for in purpose and design the work is indeed "symphonic" according to Berlioz's notions: to the Queen Mab episode, for instance, he has affixed the label of "Scherzo".

Contrary to the accepted dogma Berlioz was always strong, at any rate in intention, on the point of "form": the trouble too often in his larger works is that his ideas of form are not always ours. Sometimes we have to make a conscious effort to see the "form" of one of his works as he presumably saw it: and the effort is not always successful.

While always having his eye on the Paris stage—for it was there alone, not in the concert room, that he could look for anything like an income from his music—he never, until the days of his full maturity, seems to have thought out the problem of an opera from its foundations upwards: in *Les Troyens* he had the good fortune to find a single self-contained heroic subject practically made for him by his adored Vergil, the whole superb action developing naturally from a single germ.

His taste in subjects was as a rule far from impeccable; how, for instance, could he ever have seriously thought of making an opera out of Scribe's absurd *La Nonne Sanglante*? (The subject, by the way, was later taken up by Gounod.) The only reason we can think of was that one or two macabre situations in the play had appealed to his pictorial imagination at a first reading, and as usual he proposed to start from these points and build up round them some sort of plausible operatic structure. As a rule, though of course the statement calls for frequent modification, he began not with a predetermined whole but with a succession of details which he was sanguine he could weld into some sort of a dramatic unity. Sometimes this rather haphazard method succeeded astonishingly, as in the case of *L'Enfance du Christ*. But not always.

Fundamentally he was what the Germans call an "eye-man," a "visuel," his imagination seizing instantly and surely on some character or occurrence in a moment of objective realisation. It had been thus, for example, with his youthful *Eight Scenes from Goethe's Faust*, that ultimately expanded into the quasi-opera *La Damnation de Faust*.

It was so again with the masterly *L'Enfance du Christ*, with which, as one critic after another has sagely pointed out, Christ has hardly any connection at all. Berlioz saw the subject primarily as a series of episodes each of which could serve as a "cue" for a monologue, an essay in pictorialism, an instrumental divertimento, and so on. There is no real "action" in the work, but only a succession of charming or impressive vignettes: things indeed happen, the characters keep moving, the *milieu* keeps changing, but invariably only as motivating pretexts for some musical "piece" or other that does indeed, in a sense, arise out of the situation of the moment, but actually has itself predetermined the introduction of the situation.

The plan of *L'Enfance du Christ*, strictly speaking, is not good drama, nor good narrative, nor good oratorio, nor good cantata, but it is undoubtedly, in the totality of its realisation, good Berlioz. Why is not the basic plan of the *Romeo and Juliet* a comparable success? The verdict of the musical world has been given against the work as a whole, and it has never established itself firmly in the concert repertory, despite the fact that it contains a great deal of the finest music ever written by Berlioz.

The answer seems to be that although he must have put more and harder constructive thinking into *Romeo and Juliet* than he did into *L'Enfance du Christ*, and there are some felicitous features in the layout of the "symphony", Berlioz has on the whole failed to accommodate his symphonic intentions to his dramatic, or *vice versa*. His lovers do not sing, never appear, as it were, in person—a stroke of true genius this, as I shall point out in more detail. But this means that after their death the whole dramatic interest, such as it is, rests on the shoulders of Friar Laurence and the quarrelling Capulet and Montague factions, in neither of whom can we take the interest we do in their Shakesperian prototypes. The good Friar's long concluding harangue to the rival houses to reflect upon the error of their ways, bury the sword, and live henceforth in amity, leaves us cold; what should have been all along only the background to the tragic pair of lovers has now become the foreground of the drama; and we are left with a sense of anti-climax.

We have, in fact, here as elsewhere, to take Berlioz frankly as he is, recognising that his faults and his limitations are not, as generally in the case of other artists, merely lapses from his best self but an organic part and parcel of his veriest self; and now that he is on a rising wave of public appreciation it is incumbent on criticism to admit his faults without reserve, and to suggest an explanation of them.

There are occasions, indeed—happily rare in his work as a whole —when we simply cannot understand how an artist of his calibre could bungle matters so grossly, in a way that is obvious to the most casual observer. Someone (I think it was Heine) remarked acutely that the trouble with Berlioz was that he hadn't enough talent for his genius. That is not a mere epigram: it goes to the heart of the matter. Every genius requires a certain dexterity of talent to see him safely through a temporary difficulty; signal examples of this are Shakespeare, Beethoven, Wagner and Brahms, in whom the useful talent has sometimes to carry on as best it can until the genius can take full charge again.

A notable example of the disaster that comes upon a genius when talent fails to do its work properly is seen in Berlioz's taste-less—and, not to mince our words—stupid handling of the "pre-lude" he found it necessary to write for the second part of his great Trojan opera. (The reader will recall that he succeeded only in getting this second part, *The Trojans at Carthage*, produced, and he felt under the necessity of spatchcocking into his score a "prelude" that would enlighten the spectator as to what had happened in the suppressed first section of the opera, *The Fall of Troy*.) The poor best he could do was to insert a "prelude" that monstrously perverts the duet of Cassandra and Coroebus in the *Fall*. Bad taste could hardly go further than Berlioz has done here.

Another instance, which the concert-goer can more easily check for himself, occurs in the garden scene of *Romeo and Juliet*. While the feasting and dancing are going on in the Capulet palace Romeo pours out all the sadness of his young heart in one of the most moving melodies ever entrusted to a solo oboe. At its conclusion the roisterers break in on the scene with a vigorous, jubilant dance. Ultimately there comes a moment when Berlioz realises that we must be reminded that Romeo is still in the back-ground, still musing on Juliet, still pouring out his adolescent grief on the night air. Now a reminiscence of his melody in an oboe—the colour and the tang of which are bone of the bone and blood of the blood of the emotional expression—could never assert itself through the massive orchestral texture of the music of the riotous young Capulets. So, in a lapse into the worst taste imaginable, Berlioz thunders out the Romeo melody in the brass, thereby completely destroying its true character; it is as if the poor boy were trying to bear the others down by sheer lung power.

Nor is this all; worse is still to come. When finally the crowd departs and the orchestral turmoil dies away, Berlioz has at last a chance to let us hear the Romeo melody in its proper oboe medium. But now it sounds, by sheer contrast, absurdly anaemic: this is not the apotheosis of Romeo but an abject deflation of him. How, we ask ourselves in despair, could Berlioz ever have committed so great a sin against not merely good taste but simple common sense?

And then, the talent having done its sorry best, the genius takes charge once more, and there comes a world's wonder—a love scene that is without a superior in music. Here the taste is impeccable. With consummate tact Berlioz entrusts the whole expression to the orchestra; the intrusion of the voices of Romeo and Juliet in person would have imported too mature, too fleshly an element into it all, would have de-spiritualised the young lovers. The orchestral scoring, too, is a miracle of colour, the utmost intensity of emotion being conveyed in a texture that is consistently subdued. Truly Berlioz in his totality is one of the enigmas of music.

24 April 1955
1 May 1955

8

"La Damnation de Faust"

NOT THE LEAST curious thing about Berlioz's *Damnation de Faust* is its title. Why, we may ask, insist so pointedly on Faust's mere damnation? As a piece of tone-painting that episode occupies a very small part of the score, while there is nothing whatever in the previous portraiture of Faust in the work to suggest that what Berlioz has been leading up to from the first is the rightful punishment of him: considering, indeed, that after the short Ride to the Abyss and the Chorus of the Damned, Berlioz takes leave of us with the Apostheosis of Margaret, surely a more appropriate title for it all would have been this last. But the title is only one of the oddities *La Damnation de Faust* presents.

There need be no hesitation in adapting the work for the stage, as has been done at Covent Garden this week, for it was never, as Berlioz made it and left it, a steadily planned organic unity in itself. It began in the winter of 1828–29, as *Eight Scenes from Faust*: the pieces set by Berlioz were (1) the Easter Hymn, (2) the song and dance of the peasants, (3) the chorus of sylphs, (4) Brander's song of the Rat, (5) Mephistopheles' song of the Flea, (6) The Ballad of the King of Thule, (7) Margaret's song, "My Peace Has Fled," to which Berlioz arbitrarily attaches the march and chorus of the soldiers, whom, for his own purposes, he sends past Margaret's window at this juncture, (8) Mephistopheles' Serenade. Faust, it will be seen, does not enter into the work at all as yet. Berlioz at once had the full score engraved at his own expense, and in April 1829 he sent a couple of copies to Goethe. The 80-year-old poet could make nothing of such music; so he sent a copy to his friend and musical mentor Zelter in Berlin, who pronounced it to be about the worst nonsense he had ever come across.

Although Berlioz, of course, had already tried his hand at several things, he issued the *Eight Scenes* as his Opus 1. The work is certainly the most astounding Opus 1 that the world of music had ever known, or, in all probability, will ever know. It contained, in addition to numbers such as the song of the Rat and the song of the Flea, which can still hold their own among their competitors, such immortal masterpieces of expression as the two songs of Margaret and the serenade, and, in the chorus of sylphs, a piece of tone-painting that is as remarkable today as it was a hundred years ago. And all this was the work of a young man of 25 who had had so little formal musical "education" that the academics who write about him today still feel it safe to speak of him with the mixture of pity and impertinence that has been characteristic of the academic mind, in all epochs, towards whatever is different from, and better than, anything it is able to produce itself.

When this splendid and extraordinarily original music was written, Beethoven had been in his grave less than two years; Schubert did not die until November, 1828. Both imaginatively and technically this work of Berlioz's was, for its time, a world's wonder, had the world but known it. Poor Zelter, of course, could make nothing of it; the mere sight of the orchestral lay-out of the sylph music must have given him vertigo, while the clue to the two incomparable songs of Margaret necessarily escaped him. He would no doubt subconsciously think of these songs in the simple poetic rhythms of Goethe's lines and the correspondingly simple musical metres of the German Lied of the period; the rhythmical novelty and subtlety of Berlioz's settings, and the complete originality of emotional experience that spoke through them, were utterly beyond him. And, as final scene in this historic comedy, there came the failure, in the summer of 1829, of the composer of these masterpieces to win the *Prix de Rome*!

The idea of expanding these fragments came to Berlioz in the eighteen-forties, and *La Damnation de Faust* was completed in 1846. Even in 1828 he had had a vague notion of an opera, or an elaborate mimo-drama, on the Faust subject; and as he pondered over it, it naturally came to take a more and more dramatic form in his mind. It is significant that on the title page of the manuscript of the *Damnation* he styles the work an "Opéra de concert"; afterwards, feeling perhaps that this was something of a contradiction in terms, he struck it out and substituted for it "Légende." As was so often the case with him in his earlier years, he plunged into the subject without having thought it all out organically, fascinated by certain outstanding episodes in it, and then, as was the case with the *Symphonie fantastique*, had to cut and rearrange and add to the first material in order to give a semblance of unity to the larger plan.

He had to scheme entrances and exits for Faust and the others, and, as we have seen, to write the whole of the music for Faust's part. He re-grouped and expanded or curtailed this movement or that in order both to keep the action going and to modulate from one scene into another. He transposed the ballad of the King of Thule from G major to F major, leaving, however, both versions in his manuscript, the former for a soprano, the latter for a mezzo-soprano. (It would be interesting, by the way, to have it restored, in our modern concert or operatic productions, to its original G major, in which key the exquisite phrases for the solo viola would be even more poignant.) In the *Eight Scenes*, Mephistopheles' serenade is written for a tenor (in the key of E major), with a guitar accompaniment. But as Faust, by convention, would have to be a tenor, Mephistopheles had to become, in the larger scheme, a bass; so Berlioz transposed the song down to B major (with an alternate version, in C major, for a baritone), and expanded the guitar strumming into the marvellous orchestral accompaniment that we now know so well.

Faust's own music called out all that was best in him in the period of his maturity. The opening solo (Faust alone in the fields),

Faust's Invocation to Nature, his song in Margaret's chamber, his meditation alone in his study, and the duet are all in his finest vein: as was more than once the case with him, he gave the lie to the academic Beckmessers who said that fugue was beyond him by using the fugal method admirably, at times, to give substance to his ideas and extension to the development of them. He was blamed, from the first, for having made such drastic alterations in Goethe's text. He replied to his critics, with considerable force, in the preface to his score, in which he points out that Goethe had no monopoly in the Faust subject, and that Shakespeare and the Greek dramatists have been made possible in opera only by a very free handling of the originals. When reproached for having taken Faust, contrary to the legend, into Hungary, his reply was that he had already written a Hungarian March which he wanted to use, and that if he had had a piece of music relating to any other country he would just as cheerfully have taken his Faust into that country in order to introduce it. His audacity has been justified. For the rest he pieces his scenes together, and writes connective verbal and musical tissue for them with considerable skill; and all in all the work goes very well on the stage.

A modern version exists in which the arranger for the stage has added words and music of his own at various points. Sir Thomas Beecham has shown that these can be dispensed with. His own modifications and additions have been very slight: they were forced upon him by stage exigencies. For example, the monologue of Faust in Margaret's chamber is followed, in the original score, by an orchestral postlude. This is very short, lasting, in all, only about a minute and a quarter; but even that, apparently, is too long for the average tenor to fill up with convincing action. Sir Thomas has therefore shortened the postlude slightly; and though we are sorry to lose the full sweep of the lovely wandering line that Berlioz has written at this point, the curtailment is a practical necessity. On the other hand, something had to be added to the score in order to keep the audience from chattering during the longish interval occupied by the change of scene from the Hungarian plains to the study of Faust. It was a happy idea on

Sir Thomas's part to give us here the lovely fugal introduction to "The Flight into Egypt" (the second part of *L'Enfance du Christ*.) This, which is in F sharp minor, proceeds quite naturally from the A major of the Hungarian March, and leads as naturally, when the curtain rises, into the F sharp minor of Faust's monologue: the mood of this blends well with that of the movement from "The Flight into Egypt", while the crime has been avoided of adding to the score of *Faust* any music that is not Berlioz's own.

28 May 1933

9

"L'Enfance du Christ"

To suppose *L'Enfance du Christ* to be a work peculiarly appropriate to the Christmas season is to misunderstand it and its composer sadly. Berlioz was a pagan of the ancient Mediterranean tradition, and the Christian story meant no more to him than any other story from any other religion or mythology would do: his mind never warmed to these figures as it did to those of his beloved Vergil—for in one sense Berlioz was the most "classical" of all composers. He had no religious feeling whatever of the conventional kind, and was incapable of trying to persuade himself, for the purposes of art of the moment, that he had. The whole case of his curiously objective mind made conventional accommodations of that or any other sort a sheer impossibility to him. It was not that he deliberately rejected them; it was simply that they never occurred to him. His oratorio has virtually no connection with the Christian story as such; this serves him only as a pretext for a sequence of dramatic or pictorial or idyllic musical miniatures.

He begins with the Narrator telling us of the birth of Christ. But he betrays no emotion over it. It has no religious connotations for him. His concern with it is of quite another order: he needs it only as a spring-board from which to plunge into a description of the hag-ridden sleep of Herod and the picturesque mumbo-jumbo of the Hebrew soothsayers. About Jerusalem, as he sees it, there is no mystical aura; he sees it only as a street at night that may serve as setting for a colloquy between a centurion of the guard and a soldier, lately drafted from Rome, who is bored and exasperated by his exile from civilisation. For Berlioz, again, the manger at Bethlehem is not the focal point of a world-embracing religious emotion but merely the excuse for a tender eclogue in the Theocritean or Vergilian manner.

At Sais he is interested first of all only in the very human weariness of the much-travelled Joseph and Mary and the brutality of the inhabitants towards them, then in the charming idyll for two flutes and a harp, the introduction of which is the sole reason for the whole episode of the Ishmaelite family. From first to last he is innocent of all religious prepossessions; he is simply the poet, the painter, using the Christian legend to provide him with opportunities for human drama or pastoral. The point needs insisting on because the listener who goes to *L'Enfance du Christ* expecting to find the regulation religious feelings in it is approaching it from the wrong direction and in the wrong mood, and, in his disappointment at not finding what he had hoped for, is in danger of missing the true nature of the exquisite work.

17 January 1943

10

"La Marseillaise"

———————————

IT IS STRANGE that no attempt has been made to introduce "La Marseillaise" into our ordinary concert life during the past year. It does not seem to be generally known that there is an arrangement of it by Berlioz for orchestra and chorus. (This arrangement is to be had, I think, only in the Malherbe-Weingartner edition of Berlioz's complete works, which may account for the ordinary conductor's ignorance of its existence.) There is an interesting description, in the first volume of Berlioz's *Mémoires*, of the singing of the melody by a Parisian crowd during the July revolution of 1830. Berlioz had been shut up for some days at the *Institut*, undergoing examination for the *Prix de Rome*. He was released on the 29th July, plunged among the crowd in the Palais-Royal courtyard, and found a handful of young men, to his delight, singing a warlike hymn of his own from the Irish Melodies. Later they burst into "La Marseillaise", in which the crowd of four or five thousand was gradually induced to join, the effect, according to Berlioz, being overwhelming. He remembered that he had just made an arrangement of his own of the song, to the choral part of which he had prefixed, in place of the usual "Sopranos, altos," &c., the direction, "Everything that has a voice, a heart, and blood in its veins." In December of the same year, on the eve of his departure for Rome, the ebullient young musician wrote to Rouget de l'Isle—then an old man of seventy—desiring permission to dedicate the arrangement to him.

Rouget sent him in reply the charming letter that is to be seen in Berlioz's *Mémoires*. The composer of "La Marseillaise" invited his young admirer to visit him at Choisy; but Berlioz had to set out at once for Italy to comply with the conditions of the prize. When, later, the visit became possible, Rouget de l'Isle was dead. Berlioz afterwards heard that the old man had meant to offer him an opera libretto of his own on the subject of Othello.

Berlioz's setting of "La Marseillaise" is for an orchestra composed of strings, two clarinets, four horns, two bassoons, six trumpets, three trombones, two tubas, three kettledrums, and bass drum. There is no attempt at embellishment or transformation of the melody, the orchestral mass being simply employed to obtain a colossal sonority and an insistent martial rhythm. The opening lines of the fifth stanza, urging magnanimity towards those "tristes victimes" who have unwillingly taken up arms against the French, are accompanied softly by the string quartet alone; but there is a formidable crescendo of passion in the orchestra as the chorus goes on to vow vengeance on the "despote sanguinaire" and his accomplices who have brought about the war. The total effect of the work must be most stirring. It is interesting to observe, by the way, that at the words "Marchez, marchez," in the refrain to each verse, Berlioz retains Rouget de l'Isle's version of the melody, the first syllable of the second "marchez" being sung to the same note as the last syllable of its predecessor. In modern versions the melody is made to ascend a tone at this point. One hardly knows which form to prefer; each of them has a peculiar effectiveness of its own.

BIRMINGHAM POST, 26 July 1915

VI

"Les Troyens"

1

"Les Troyens" in Paris

BEING COMPELLED TO spend three or four days in Paris last week on my way home from Switzerland, and having heard no music for a month except that of cow-bells and goat-bells (an enchanting symphony in the Swiss meadows), I naturally thought of the opera. August is not the best time for music in Paris, and the performance of Massenet's *Werther*, that I heard at the Opéra Comique would have been thought a pretty poor one for the "B" company of one of our English touring organisations. I should have been even more sorry than I was already at having to waste some days of precious time in a dull, dirty, and dingy city, had I not the good fortune to strike Berlioz's *Trojans* at the Grand Opéra. I cannot be too grateful to Providence for making the revival of this opera last so long: I have been longing to hear it for about twenty years, and no doubt it will be another twenty before it is given again. Why it should be so I do not know. It seems to get good houses, and apparently it pleases the audiences; but Berlioz has always had the worst of luck in the theatre, and probably always will.

I have long known *The Trojans* from the score, and admired it exceedingly; but not until now, after having heard it on the orchestra, have I realised how remarkable a work it is. Even a performance that was mostly mediocre could not kill it. Dido (Mme. Gozategui) and Cassandra (Mme. Courso) were very capable, and Aeneas (M. Sullivan) fairly good; but the rest of the cast was merely so-so, with the exception of the lady (Mlle. Daunt), who mimed the part of Andromache.

Still, if there was little on the stage to rouse one to wild enthusiasm, there was little to annoy us, and I should have been quite happy had the orchestral part of the performance been reasonably good. But the orchestral playing was of the sort that offends the trained listener most deeply; everything was correct and technically competent, but there was no beauty, no sensitiveness. It was typical of that last stage of the degeneration of a good orchestra, when the players cease to be artists and become only artisans. The oboe tone was an especial infliction on me; in colour, in substance, and in sentiment it was first cousin to an ox-horn, and there is such lovely music for the oboe in *The Trojans*! Nor is the Paris Grand Opéra, with its shattering vulgarity—the building suggests a publican's dream of a grand hotel—the place for a drama so finely wrought as this. But in spite of everything the greatness of the opera was unmistakable.

I came away with a deepening of the conviction that has been with me for years—that Berlioz has never yet had justice done to him as a composer. Criticism has not known where or how to "place" him because he did not fit any of the accepted categories, and was obviously a misfit in some of the most cherished of them. In an article in the *Sunday Times* a few weeks ago, I pointed out the peculiar loneliness of Berlioz, both as man and as artist. For all the noise and commotion he made in the Paris of the first half of the nineteenth century, he had a very small circle of real friends, and for the main music-loving public was little more than a somewhat grotesque myth.

He died a hopelessly disappointed, disillusioned man, worn out physically by the opium he had had to take for years to still the atrocious pangs of his intestinal neuralgia, and broken spiritually by the indifference not only of the public but of his colleagues. There is no more pitiful story in musical history than that of his long, partly vain struggle to get *The Trojans*, which he knew to be his greatest work, put on at the Opéra. Not more than one or two of his intimates really understood him as a man; hardly more than a dozen musicians in Europe really understood him as a composer. Many people, especially in Germany and Russia, liked a good deal of such music of his as they were able to hear; but hardly anyone comprehended him as a whole and saw his true greatness.

His last years were embittered by that combat between Wagner and himself for the Grand Opéra and for the French public that ended in the complete victory of the German composer. It looked then like a purely personal affair; we can see it now as the conflict between two different musical civilisations, as it were. For serious-minded musicians of that day the only music that really mattered was German music, or music written in the German tradition. Unfortunately for Berlioz, the best criticism, even down to our own day, also took its rules from that tradition. People knew what it was in the music of Bach, Beethoven, Brahms, Mozart, Schumann, Schubert, and Wagner that made it good music: and as this was in the main the best sort of music then existing they naturally assumed that music could be good music only in that particular way.

Berlioz's music was not good in that way. It was good in its own way, but this was a way to which the ordinary critic's classical training gave him no clue; and so he dismissed Berlioz as an eccentric, or regarded him as, at the best, no more than half a musician. Here and there in his orchestral works he made a clumsy attempt to employ the typically German instrument of "development". The critics could see the clumsiness of these portions of the music, but could not see the originality of the rest.

He reminds me in some ways of Sir Thomas Browne. We can no more classify the one than we can the other. Each is himself and himself alone, owing practically nothing to any artistic operator, and leaving no artistic posterity. If English literature were "taught" as music is, if academics had grown up with a vested interest in certain rules and a certain etiquette of writing, we should have Browne despised as an eccentric and disparaged as a semi-illiterate. His construction, his rhythm, his cadence having nothing in common with the sort of generalised notion of English construction, rhythm, and cadence that one gets from the classics of our literature, the academies, that always play for safety, would have pecked him to death as birds peck to death one of themselves that is not of the general colour of the flock. Berlioz has been pecked almost to death by critics who knew no other instinct than that of the German flock. It is now time, and our duty, to restore him to life.

The developments of the last twenty years have made us better able to understand these rare individualists of music. Moussorgsky, Debussy, and Stravinsky have given us the new technique of appreciation that enables us to see Berlioz as he really is. But no one really knows Berlioz who does not know *The Trojans*. Spiritually the work moves me deeply; but if other people are unmoved by it I shall not quarrel with them, for, as I have remarked before, some men are born Berliozians and some anti-Berliozians, and neither party can see into the mind of the other. But all parties, I think, must recognise the originality of the idiom of *The Trojans* and the certainty of its technique.

Those who long for redemption from the traditional German methods of "developing" music and who are inclined, perhaps, to over-rate some of the attempts of Stravinsky and others to create a new and swifter method, will surely recognise that the composer of *The Trojans*, was a pioneer in this field. With the exception of a page or two in Cassandra's music that reminds us faintly of Gluck, there is nothing in the whole opera that suggests any other composer than its own. That is a most exceptional thing in music, where even the very greatest cannot help showing their spiritual ancestry at every turn. About the time when Wagner, in *Tristan* and the *Meistersingers*, was carrying the traditional symphonic method to its further possibilities, Berlioz, in *The Trojans*, was showing how music could be put together without any of these stereotyped formal aids.

That was his offence in the eyes of a generation that had no standard but that of German symphonic music. In our eyes it is one of his greatest virtues. We can admire now the originality of this mind that found a way of its own of striking at once into the heart of its subject, of talking about it lucidly and concisely and without repetition of formulae, and not only of making a personal idiom and a personal texture, but of using the instruments of the orchestra in a personal way. Not until we hear *The Trojans* can we realise how Berlioz's colour schemes grow out of the psychology of his music, and how different from Wagner's is his whole conception of the orchestra.

4 September 1921

2

"The Trojans" in Glasgow

THE GLASGOW GRAND OPERA SOCIETY, which already
had several bold deeds to its credit, has distinguished itself during
the past week by producing Berlioz's *Trojans* for the first time in
this country. I remember a concert performance of a portion of it
by the Liverpool Philharmonic Society some 40 years ago, and I
believe the Hallé people have given it in a condensed form at
Manchester during the last four years; but to Glasgow has fallen
the honour of first producing the great work on the stage, and
that in virtually complete form, only a few pages of no surpassing
importance having been omitted.

A performance of the whole work in a single evening is, and
always has been, a frank impossibility.* Berlioz calculated that
the five acts, with four intervals of a quarter of an hour each, would
take four hours and 26 minutes—that is to say, from 7.30 till
midnight. The feat of either performing it or listening to it under
such conditions would be beyond average human endurance.
Even with the cuts specified by the composer it would take
practically four hours to play the opera continuously. Only two
courses are possible then: either there must be liberal cuts to make
a working version for a single evening, or the opera must be given
in two parts, *The Capture of Troy* on one evening and *The Trojans
at Carthage* on the next. This latter procedure was adopted at

* Scottish Opera performed the entire work successfully in a single evening
in 1969 (P.H.).

Glasgow. It is the ideal one, of course, for enthusiasts, but it is not practicable except under festival conditions; and so, for ordinary opera house purposes, we are driven back to the Paris method of condensation. Personally I would much rather have the work established in the Covent Garden repertoty in that form than never have the opportunity to hear it at all.

The Trojans will never be as popular as *Tosca* or *Faust*, but I am sure that if it were once given in something like a representative form in London it would draw the more musical section of the public several times in the course of each season. It is a work that has to be seen and heard to be really known. To approach it in the first place from the piano score is to remain insensitive to a good deal of it; and it was only through the piano score that we *could* approach it until quite recently. Berlioz's music in general does not lend itself to transcription for the piano; and the case for *The Trojans* was particularly prejudiced by the fact that the first piano score, made by Berlioz himself, has all the faults to be expected under the circumstances, for Berlioz had not the slightest feeling for the piano, or the faintest knowledge of how to make the approximate best of the bad job of arranging one of his own orchestral scores for that medium. In the later editions of the piano score—i.e. those now on sale—the work of transcription has been much better done, by someone with more technical knowledge of how to reproduce something of the essence of an orchestral texture on the piano; but even here there are innumerable instances in which the piano does not merely conceal the real character of the music but actually distorts it. No one who has not heard *The Trojans* on the orchestra can have much more than a rudimentary idea of what a great deal of the music is like. I speak feelingly on this subject, for I myself, in days gone by, underestimated the work through having only Berlioz's own wretched piano transcription by which to judge it: it was not until I saw the opera in Paris in 1921 that I fully realised its greatness.

Masterpiece as the work is, taking a broad view of it, it has faults or peculiarities that go against it now as much as they did seventy years ago. So individual a genius as Berlioz was bound to be a bundle of contradictions and paradoxes in almost everything he did. It is equally true of him, at various times, that he had the most consummate sense of the stage and an imperfect sense of it. He does things that no one but a musical dramatist of the first order could have thought of: he is equally capable of falling down at the first fence where dramatic construction is concerned. There are not many operas that contain so much fine music as his early *Benvenuto Cellini*; yet all attempts to maintain that work on the stage have failed. Bülow analysed it most sympathetically and at the same time most searchingly in an article of 1852; and his summing-up is as valid today as it was then—"*Benvenuto Cellini* is not a dramatic art-work in the higher sense, but the dramatic study of a musical genius." No amount of re-casting of the work, either by the composer or others, has ever sufficed to assure it life in the theatre. Berlioz never thought out the new problems of nineteenth century opera from the foundations upward as Wagner did: too much of the old convention clung to his thinking for him ever to achieve perfect dramatic connection and consistency. In the first act of *Cellini*, for instance, he writes a trio that is not only of the utmost musical piquancy but scores a direct dramatic hit. He is so much in love with it for its own sake, however, that he cannot resist the temptation to repeat it, to achieve which end he resorts to the innocent device of making one of the characters say in effect, "To make sure that you have fixed in your mind all the details of the time and place of our next meeting, let us go over the arrangements again"; and, not satisfied even with that, he makes the characters break out into the same strains a third time.

There are one or two instances in *The Trojans* also of this inability to distinguish between the demands of pure music and the exigencies of dramatic action: one or two instances also of that curious failure of taste that every now and then puzzles us in Berlioz. In the scene of Romeo in the garden (in his *Romeo and Juliet*), for example, he paints the longing and the youthful romantic heartbreak of his hero in an exquisite long-drawn oboe melody that has hardly a rival in its own sphere in all music;

afterwards he needs must bellow this same melody at us in the cornets and trombones for no logical reason that can be discovered: one wonders that Berlioz, of all people, with his rare ear for colour in conjunction with psychology, should not have seen that the melody is no longer the same thing when transferred from its first medium to its second. The procedure hardly makes dramatic sense at all, while it comes perilously near making musical nonsense. And again in *The Trojans* he commits precisely the same kind of error, the same kind of sin not only against taste but against sense; for his orchestral "Lament for the House of Priam" in *The Trojans at Carthage* he can think of nothing better than to take the theme of the duet between Cassandra and Chorebus (in *The Capture of Troy*) and drag it out at a tempo and in an orchestral colour that merely cheapen it.

Nor is the music of the opera as a whole consistent with itself. In the *Troy* he goes back at times to the idiom of the "classical" opera of the eighteenth and early nineteenth centuries—to Gluck, Spontini, and the Mozart of *Idomeneo*; he even makes liberal use of that venerable stand-by of the dramatic music of that period, the diminished seventh as an expression of tension or horror, to an extent that no one could have anticipated from the works of his first and second periods. There was something "old-fashioned" about *Troy* from the first, something to which we of today have found the key again, but which was alien to the temper of the 1860's. We can quite understand now the reluctance of the Paris theatre authorities to give anything but the *Carthage* in 1863: both the music and the dramatic action of the *Troy* must have seemed to them, in large part, a reversion to a period and a style that was as remote from them as the crinoline is from us, and as outmoded.

It is another of the paradoxes continually facing us where Berlioz is concerned that this daring innovator was always, in one sense, a little behind his own time. He missed the boat with the marvellous *Damnation of Faust*, because in 1846 the Parisian tide had already definitely turned against the romanticism of the 'thirties; and in 1863 he was more or less tolerantly regarded as a back number because his spirit, always more classical at the core than romantic, went back to Vergil, Gluck, and Spontini. That epoch preferred the antique as seen through the derisive eyes of comedy; Offenbach's *Orphée aux Enfers* (1858) and *La Belle Hélène* (1865) were typical of this tendency to tolerate the ancient gods and heroes on the stage only in so far as they could be subjected to what in these days would be called debunking. Berlioz himself, in his Memoirs, tells us of the cruel irony the Parisians brought to bear upon his subject and his treatment of it; they laughed at his rhapsodist with a lyre, at his use of a poetic diction that seemed to them affectedly antique, at Mercury with wings on head and heels, and most of all at Aeneas appearing on the stage in a helmet—for one of the "characters" of the Paris streets was a certain old Mangin who sold pencils in the streets and also wore a helmet. We have passed beyond all this now, into a phase when every period but the one or two immediately preceding our own has ceased to "date". The antique idiom of Berlioz's *Troy* is for us old-fashioned only in the sense that the idiom of Gluck or Mozart is.

In *Carthage* Berlioz parts company from his classical models, but not to take up again the romantic idiom of his early and middle period. He now develops a third style, marked by a peculiar intimacy and delicacy of characterisation. His Cassandra is cast in an antique mould: his Dido, for all her distinction of manner, her sculpturesque quality, has the modelling of a portrait bust. She is life-size, not of heroic proportions as Cassandra is. She is wholly human, and every fine shade of her woman's nature is reproduced in music that never orates at us, as Cassandra's does, but simply talks to us. Anna, again, is purely human and feminine. We can best study this new type of Berlioz music in the charming duet between Dido and Anna in the first act of *Carthage* and in the quintet ("Tout conspire a vaincre mes remords") in the second act, with its curiously fine-spun psychological characterisation.

Though *The Trojans* as a whole has nothing of either the fundamental dramatic compression or the consistency of musical style of such a work as *Tristan*, it is still anything but a mere patchwork. It achieves the paradox of sacrificing to all the gods of operatic convention and yet being intensely original and personal. Berlioz was too much the Parisian of his epoch to be able to think operatically in terms of anything but opening chorus, aria, duet, ensemble, ballet, and so on; but all the same a real dramatic imagination has been at work in him upon the great story given him by Vergil, and each episode is so vital in itself, and follows so logically, without haste and without delay, upon its pre-decessor, that in the end we have little feeling of a convention that dates, but rather of a dramatic evolution that could not have been otherwise. The music is no less remarkable. The really weak pages in the score are few, and are confined to the moments in which Berlioz is hopelessly hampered by some contemporary stage formula or other. The test of a dramatic composer is not in his ability to write fine music for outstanding lyrical episodes but in his capacity for filling the veins of the action as a whole with living blood; and judged by this test Berlioz, in *The Trojans*, stands out as a genuine musical dramatist. (Once more, however, I would warn the student against being misled to a contrary conclusion, as I myself was at one time, by a study of the piano score alone: *The Trojans* must be seen on the stage if it is to be grasped as a whole). Marvellous as is the music to this episode or that—the quintet, the septet, the love duet between Dido and Aeneas, the "Chasse royale," and so on—no less marvellous is the treatment of some of the choruses, the handling of certain vital dialogues, and the characterisation in certain fugitive scenes. There is little in the best dramatic music of the last 300 years that can compare in impressiveness with that of the scene in which the ghost of Hector appears to Aeneas.

The Glasgow people, with their limited financial resources, could not reasonably be expected to do justice to all the stage pageantry of the work, nor can amateurs anywhere sing some of this music as it needs to be sung. But in spite of some lapses the performances I saw were highly creditable. The opera was sung to a good working English version by Professor Dent, but the words were not always as audible as one could have wished. The orchestral playing was fair: no doubt it would improve as the week went on. Dr. Erik Chisholm, who conducted, had orchestra and stage well in hand: there were some ticklish moments, but his resource never failed him.

24 March 1935

3

Before the Beecham Broadcast

On Tuesday and Friday next we are to have a BBC broadcast of Berlioz's *The Fall of Troy*, and two performances of its sequel *The Trojans at Carthage*, are to follow in a few weeks' time. No one should miss the opportunity of hearing this remarkable work, which is kept out of the ordinary theatre repertory by its length, its difficulty and the expense it entails. It was originally planned for performance as an opera (*Les Troyens*) in five acts. Later it was spread over two evenings, acts 1 and 2 being now called *La Prise de Troie*, acts 3–5 *Les Troyens à Carthage*. Later still it was produced in a condensed form occupying a single evening; this is better than nothing though it fails to do full justice to the work.

It was in this form that I heard it in Paris about 1921. It was a revelation to me, for previously I had known the opera only in Berlioz's own arrangement for piano, which conveys hardly the smallest notion of the quality of most of it.

He began work on the opera in the spring of 1856 and finished the music in April, 1858. Into no other work of his had he thrown himself with such ardour, in connection with no other work had he done so much planning of design and structure. He had been a Vergil worshipper since his boyhood, and the great figures of the Aeneid were more real to him than most of the people he brushed shoulders with from day to day. But this Mediterranean classicist at heart was also a romantic and an admirer of Shakespeare; and so, when he left Troy and the Aeneas of Troy and came to Dido and to Aeneas as the lover of Dido, he could without any sense or any effect of incongruity draw upon the scene between Jessica and Lorenzo in *The Merchant of Venice* ("The moon shines bright; in such a night as this", etc.) for the text of his duet between Vergil's Carthaginian queen and Trojan hero. (This episode was the first he set to music.)

Not the least curious and interesting feature of the opera, indeed, is the change in atmosphere and idiom from the Gluckian classicism of the earlier acts, in which Cassandra had been the dominant figure, and the romanticism of feeling and of milieu in the Carthage scenes.

I will go into a few details later with regard to the music of *Les Troyens*. Before doing that I want to suggest to the reader how and how not to approach the work. It must on no account be listened to with any Wagnerian, or indeed German, pre-possessions regarding opera. It is pure Berlioz, that is to say, the expression of the most independent artistic personality in nine-teenth-century music; and we must listen to him, here as else-where, in terms purely of himself. The first thing to be clear about is that his strength was always in the moment-to-moment definition of character or scene rather than in architectonics. This is not to say that *Les Troyens* was not con-ceived as a whole. Far from it. Some of his other large-scale works we know to have been pieced together primarily for the dear sake of their component parts—some of which had previously come into being in quite other connections—Berlioz giving them what coherence he could by means of a programme. But during the making of *Les Troyens*, as we can see from his letters, he thought long and hard in the one direc-tion.

His mind worked in the opposite way to that of the great Germans, who had a gift for seeing a whole work, in a sense, before they were quite clear as to some of the constituent parts. Over each of the works of Wagner's maturity, over the Eroica and the Ninth Symphony and the last quartets, a certain spirit can be seen brooding from the first bar to the last, something that animates every cell and shapes every limb of the particular work.

Berlioz evidently strove for a unifying principle in *Les Troyens*: it took the form of the concept, derived from Vergil, of the mission imposed on Aeneas to find Italy and found there another and greater Troy. Berlioz was conscious all along that this motive of the foundation of a Roman empire by Aeneas ought to be the energic core of his opera. But with the native bent of his mind towards seeing a work as a series of incidents composing into a whole by juxtaposition rather than by coalescence or interfusion, he realised this central conception in the end only imperfectly, and had many a stumble before it became even as effective as it is in the opera.

"I had forgotten", he wrote in one of his reports of progress to the Princess Sayn-Wittgenstein in September, 1856, apropros the second act, "to bring out properly the future grandeur of Rome"; and to remedy the omission, he said he had now added a couple of lines to the monologue of Hector: "Go, find Italy", he makes the shade of Hector say to Aeneas, "and there, after many wanderings over the sea, found a mighty empire that shall one day rule the world."

But how lacking in central energising power this dominant motive—as it should have been—was for him is shown by the fact that in the first draft of his poem he had somehow—one strives in vain to imagine how—managed to make Dido, in her dying monologue, speak of "the French domination in Africa"! This, he saw later, as he told the Princess in December, 1856, was "a mere chauvinistic puerility; it will be grander and more dignified to keep to the line indicated by Vergil himself"; therefore now, he says, Dido will refer prophetically to the coming of a Hannibal who shall be a thorn in the side of conquering Rome.

His handling of the "Italy" motive, indeed, is never as convincing as we could have wished. But, as with most other works of his, we must judge *Les Troyens* by its splendid parts rather than its totality.

What we have to bear in mind when listening to Berlioz is that he was primarily *un visuel*; his gift was always to see his subject as a particular individual in a localised milieu. He generally began with a series of sharply etched dramatic or pictorial situations to which he tried to give unity by means of an action, a programme or a narration. Always his lively, penetrating musical imagination worked in terms of individuals and situations that defined themselves sharply before his eye. If a link had to be made between two pictures he generally effected it by inserting another picture. His letters to Princess Wittgenstein, which are invaluable for an understanding of his peculiar mentality in general, throw a good deal of light on this aspect of his genius. When his poem was already well under way, he tells her, he became conscious of an awkward gap between act 4, which had ended with the love scene between Dido and Aeneas and the summons to the latter by Mercury to remember his Italian mission, and the opening of act 5, in which the Trojan chiefs are seen making preparations for the departure of the fleet.

Any modern German composer—Wagner for certain—would have effected this transition by means of an orchestral interlude during the changing of the scene, that would weave past and present and future of the drama into one in terms of the "Italy" motive. But Berlioz's starkly objective imagination never worked along "symphonic" lines of that kind. The problem and the solution of it presented themselves simultaneously to him in terms of the actual and the pictorial. He had been faced with a somewhat similar problem just after the commencement of *L'Enfance du Christ*, where he motivated the tortured dream of Herod by prefacing it with a street scene between a Roman centurion on night duty and one Polydorus, lately arrived in Jerusalem from Rome; the pair discuss the general situation, and the centurion tells his friend of the terror to which the King is now a prey.

For the transition he saw to be necessary at the commencement of the fifth act of *Les Troyens*, Berlioz, obeying his irresistible bent towards the visual concrete, repeated, in effect, the device to which he had resorted in the trilogy. He had now decided, he told the Princess, to introduce here a scene of "two Trojan soldiers on night guard before the tents, one of them marching from left to right, the other from right to left, and grumbling, when they meet in the centre of the stage, about the obstinate intention of their chiefs to go off to the conquest of this plaguey Italy, when life's so agreeable here in Carthage, where there's plenty to eat, good lodging, and the rest.

"Then one of them informs the other—in common language, of course—that the court of Dido has been much upset for the past week, that Aeneas had told this worthy Queen that he must leave her soon, etc." Not only will this device, says Berlioz, "fill up the gap there was between the fourth act and the fifth and give the audience an idea of the time that has elapsed during the entr'acte", but "the contrast between the low instincts of these common soldiers and the heroic aspirations of the royal personages will be effective."

Someone—was it Heine?—said that Berlioz was hampered by not having enough talent for his genius. The remark shows insight into not only Berlioz but the artist in general, whose genius has often reason to be grateful to his talent for helping it over a stile. By talent I mean, in this connection, the routine facility, partly the artist's own acquisition, partly a lien upon a common fund, that gives him such complete unconscious ease in the handling of his material that he can mark time competently at a lower level of "inspiration" until the genius in him can take up the running. Bach, Mozart and Brahms are supreme examples of the importance of what we may call the machine in the artist's equipment; in each of them it functioned so efficiently that, to the uncritical eye, his second-best is often barely distinguishable from his best.

This machine had been withheld by the gods from Berlioz: he had neither the long artistic heredity nor the contemporary

affiliations that provide genius with the backing of talent which it
sometimes finds so useful. The result is that he cannot, like Bach,
Mozart and many others, shake good ordinary music out of his
sleeve whenever he likes, giving us a sort of second-drawer
thinking that looks as like that of the top-drawer as makes no
matter. If his genius is not functioning in top gear he simply fails
altogether.

But on the broad view this lack of a talent proportionate to
his genius is in his case a characteristic of his physiognomy rather
than a fatal blemish on it. It would decidedly have shown itself
as a defect, and a grave one, had he been prone to getting into
situations in which he would have had to rely on the communal
fund of talent to keep the thing in hand going until his individual
genius could get into its stride and take command. But he was
saved from that by the very nature of his peculiar gift. As a rule
he had little need of what I have called the machine because the
whole bent of his artistic nature was away from what, without dis-
respect, may be called, in the case of certain other and greater
composers, the factory product. Never thinking along conventional lines, he had no need of the generalised procedures
and constructions that were sometimes such a support to
them.

As I have already pointed out, with him everything is *pris sur le
vif*; he plunges straight into his main business of characterisation
very much like the medieval sculptors who did not make pre-
liminary casts but began right away with hammer and chisel on
the block of stone in front of them, digging out of it what they
saw within themselves. Everything vital that Berlioz creates in
music relates specifically to this character or scene or that and to
no other; all he is concerned with is to reproduce what he sees.
When Schumann has to write music for the Gretchen of his
Faust he writes essentially the same kind of music as he does for
this or that woman of his songs or for the Genoveva or the
Margaret of his opera. Essentially the thinking and the method
of characterisation are the same everywhere; the only difference is
in the name of the character. But Berlioz's Gretchen belongs not

merely to Berlioz alone but to Berlioz's *Faust* and no other work of his. He writes for her at one point what he describes, in a contemporary letter and in his score, as a "chanson gothique"; being the *visuel* he is he sees her as a medieval maiden in a "Gothic" setting, and in some strange way or other—partly by the curious points and angles of a melody that is quite unlike any other of his—he really does project a sort of "Gothic" figure upon our imagination. Wagner's pilgrims, again, are pilgrims of any place, any period, any opera: the pilgrims' hymn in *Harold in Italy* is unthinkable in any other milieu than the one in which Berlioz has set it.

Or take the superb Trojan March. Other composers' marches, like Schumann's women, are fundamentally the same thing with different titles or opus numbers. But the Trojan March came straight out of Troy as Berlioz's vivid imagination saw it, and could have come from nowhere else. Not only is it a march that no other composer past or present could possibly have written, but it is a march which Berlioz himself would not, because he simply could not, have conceived in connection with any other work but *Les Troyens*. (Let the reader put on the recently issued brilliant record of the March made by Sir Thomas Beecham and the Royal Philharmonic Orchestra and judge for himself.)

So with Berlioz's nature painting. The Germans have produced some lovely music of field and stream and forest, with here and there a horn call or a bird song piercing the brooding stillness; but on the whole it is music of a restricted imaginative range and with a number of family traits in common. Berlioz's great nature scenes—the Invocation to Nature in *Faust*, the landscapes of *Harold*, the "Scène aux champs" in the *Fantastique*, the Royal Hunt and Storm in *Les Troyens à Carthage*, etc.—are in a different category altogether; not only is each of them totally unlike any other music ever written but each of them is unthinkable in connection with any other work of his than the one for which it was composed.

The listener by wireless to *Les Troyens* who has not seen

the opera on the stage and does not know it in the score is bound to miss some of the force of Berlioz's characterisation by being unable to visualise this or that scene. This is particularly the case with the remarkable episode of the appearance of Hector's shade to Aeneas, and even more, perhaps, with that of Andromache and her little son, robed in white—the mourning colour of the ancients—bringing their offerings of flowers to the altar. This episode is in dumb show, and one has to see it on the stage to realise the noble and penetrating pathos of it.

With the incomparable Royal Hunt and Storm the case is different. Here it is impossible for any combination of producer and choreographer to realise for us Berlioz's inner vision of the naiads, fauns, satyrs, wood nymphs, hunters and so on who are supposed to take part in the scene in the forest. On the whole it is best, even in the theatre, to play the great music, which is now fairly well known in the concert room, simply as a symphonic interlude; the way to listen to it is to read Vergil's description of the scene, then Berlioz's stage directions in his score, and then close one's eyes and let one's imagination call up the details.

There are few episodes in *Les Troyens à Carthage*, however, in which the wireless listener will be at any serious disadvantage. He will find the work more accessible in every way at a first hearing than its predecessor. For one thing, the characters, the milieux, the psychological motives, being more "romantic," are nearer to us of today than their classic counterparts in *La Prise de Troie*; for another, the musical idiom does not demand of the listener, as the other work sometimes does, a certain sympathetic familiarity with the Gluckian style that was so dear to Berlioz from his boyhood.

Les Troyens à Carthage is a succession of scenes vibrating with romantic life and aglow with romantic colour. The figures and the movement are no longer like those of a Greek frieze. The action is faithful to Vergil, but the people draw much of their life from the second of Berlioz's great admirations, Shakespeare.

As I have already pointed out, we are not conscious of the smallest incongruity when he draws upon *The Merchant of Venice* for some of his lines in the duet in the moonlight between Dido and Aeneas.

Listeners who know him only by the standard pieces of the concert room will find in *Les Troyens à Carthage* another Berlioz whose existence they have never suspected. There has been a vast amount of mistaken criticism of his harmony by people who in the first place lacked the right imaginative approach to him, and in the second place could conceive harmony only in text book and examination room terms, failing to realise that it should be the instrument of a composer's thought, not the determinant and, as it too often has been, the constrainer of it. Berlioz's unorthodox but personal harmony was the natural product of a very personal way of thinking.

In *Les Troyens à Carthage* we see him indulging in what is for him a new type of chordal flow, which makes possible a lissomness and graciousness of melodic line such as he had rarely achieved in his earlier days. The change came not as a matter of conscious reflection but from absorption in a new type of character and episode.

We see the new style at its finest in the duet between Dido and Aeneas, the sad colloquy between Dido and her sister near the end of the opera, and above all in the quintet in which he paints the slow undermining of the resolution of Dido, seduced by the example of Andromache, not to re-marry. This exquisite vignette has no parallel in music; nowhere else has Berlioz spun psychological threads of such fineness and woven them into so delicate yet strong a musical tissue.

I have been able to direct the prospective listener's attention to only a few of the features of Berlioz's greatest work. There are others worth noting, as the reader will realise when he hears the famous septet, the curious little nostalgic song of the young Phrygian sailor at the masthead, the big aria of Aeneas, and the moving scene of Dido's despair and death. *Les Troyens* is far beyond the present capacity of any of our opera organisations. All the more welcome, then, are the broadcasts of it which the BBC has had the imagination and the courage to give us.

1 June 1947
8 June 1947
15 June 1947
22 June 1947

4

Towards Covent Garden

THE GREAT EVENT of the year, we all believe, will be the production of *Les Troyens* at Covent Garden next June, an event towards which, maybe, the shade of Berlioz is already looking forward with hope and apprehension mingled. Even if I knew Hector's present address I would hardly trouble him with a questionnaire on the matter, for I can be fairly sure what his replies would be. He never had a high opinion of either musical performers or the musical public *en masse*: most of the singers he held in particularly low esteem, not because they could not *sing* but because few of them were capable of conceiving and reproducing what a composer had had in his mind when he was putting certain notes on paper.

Almost exactly 100 years ago, when the *Troyens* score was nearing completion, he was fretting his heart out over all this, despairing especially of finding the Dido or the Cassandra of his dreams. It was only a partial consolation that all his great predecessors had been in the same miserable plight: "We don't know what they may have suffered", he wrote, "from their 'interpreters'." By "interpretation", of course, he meant intellectual understanding; on the purely technical side the Paris of his day was rich enough in virtuosi of all species.

In this same letter he tells his correspondent how a day or so earlier he had been fortunate enough to hit upon a clarinet phrase adequately expressive of the tragic Andromache. A visitor called; it was the cornetist Arban, whom Berlioz describes as possessing an unusual gift for melodic expression: "He sang the melody finely and I was in the 17th heaven." A day or two later he had another caller, this time the leading clarinettist of the Opéra, on whom, by the way, would have devolved the execution of the melody had *Les Troyens* been accepted by the national opera house—"a virtuoso of the first order", says Berlioz, "but frigid".

This gentleman played the mournful melody on his own instrument, according to Berlioz quite inadequately; his phrasing of it, says the composer, was "only *à peu près*," though the man was condescending enough to describe it as *très joli*. He left poor Berlioz in the depths of despair, utterly out of tune with Andromache, Astyanax, and everyone else, and tempted to throw his score into the fire. "What a horror this *à peu près* is in the performance of music," he wailed; all he could hope for was that he might be able to knock some understanding of the clarinet solo into the frigid virtuoso by coaching him in it note by note.

*   *   *

The first point to be insisted on is that *Les Troyens*, like *The Ring*, must be apprehended in its entirety. To listen to it as just a conventional nineteenth-century collection of arias, ensemble pieces and so on is to approach it from quite a wrong angle. Berlioz planned his work on big lines, with one great "motive" determining the individual parts and the relation of these to each other and to the whole. The subject of the opera is not Cassandra or Aeneas or Dido or anyone else. The work does not aim at giving us a first picture, for its own sake, of the fall of Troy, then a second picture, also for its own sake, of the romantic and disastrous love of Dido and Aeneas. To perform either *La Prise de Troie* or *Les Troyens à Carthage* just by and for itself is to misconceive Berlioz sadly.

He intended us to take the title of his huge work seriously and in its fullest implication. His theme is from first to last not individual Trojans but "the Trojans": in one of his letters to Princess Wittgenstein we see him rejecting a variety of possible titles as being inexpressive of the totality of his scheme, which is purely and simply that of Vergil. The poet's over-riding purpose in his epic had been to voice the self-flattering Roman belief of the Augustan age that the Romans were the true heirs of the Trojans, their virtues having culminated in the founding of a city that should be eternal and an empire on which the sun would never set. That, in essence, was Berlioz's conception and plan also.

Each artist insists heavily on it, the poet at the beginning of his work, the musician at the end of his. Vergil announces his plan in his opening lines—"Arms and the man I sing who fled first from ruined Troy and after many buffetings by land and sea arrived in Italy, there to provide his native gods with a new and greater home. . . ."

Berlioz, of course, could not begin *his* work—a stage work—in that fashion. But he does in reverse precisely what Vergil had done; in the *concluding* stages of his opera he flaunts before our eyes and ears the key-words "Italia" and "Roma", insisting heavily on the point that the attainment of these objectives by the Trojans is the be-all and end-all of his dramatic scheme. So intent is Berlioz on conveying this message to us in the audience that towards the end of his work he introduces two Trojan soldiers discussing in their own naïve way their leader Aeneas's plans for leaving pleasant Carthage—a soldier's paradise—for a crazily fanciful "Italy".

Yes, the spectators must realise from the commencement that what the composer has designed to set before their eyes is not the tragic classic love of a Cassandra and a Corœbus, or the tragic romantic love of a Dido and an Aeneas, or this or that scene of antique horror or heroism or pathos or pageantry, but the vast epic of the Trojan race and the slow realisation of the Trojan destiny. The listener will judge for himself to what degree Berlioz has achieved this ambition as an artist; but, let me repeat, unless he apprehends, and constantly bears in mind, that this *is* the composer's ambition he has not even begun to see *Les Troyens* as its creator conceived it.

*   *   *

This is not to say, of course, that we are committed to taking his actual achievement at his own estimate; each of us will react to it in terms of his own artistic build-up. The fact that Berlioz has deliberately done so-and-so at this point or that of some big work of his need not deter us from deciding, to our own satisfaction, that thereby he has damaged or spoiled it. All we can contend, with reason, is that the closer we can get to following up on our own account the psychological lines on which we know Berlioz himself to have proceeded when creating his work, the better qualified we shall be for judging it objectively.

The composer's cultured father had made a fair Latin scholar of him, and from boyhood Hector had been hypnotised by the characters and the episodes of the *Aeneid*; apart from Shakespeare, indeed, Vergil was the most dominant figure in his whole literary life. In the middle-fifties of the nineteenth century Vergil obsessed and possessed him completely. The best preparation for listening to *Les Troyens* today is to re-read the first four Books of Vergil again a few times; to do this is to realise how completely the composer had made the poet the centre of his own artistic universe for the time being.

The explanation of one curious feature of the opera after another is to be found in Berlioz's desire to make his work wholly Vergilian—wholly and solely concerned with the story of the mission decreed by the gods for Aeneas and his compatriots of founding a new Troy (Rome) that should be an even greater glory than the old. So it comes about that the casual spectator who is primarily anxious to get to Dido and Aeneas is not allowed to do so until the third act.

Berlioz himself had quite early become aware that the first act of his opera alone would run to some 80 minutes in performance, with Aeneas hardly figuring in the matter at all so far, and Dido,

of course, not at all; 80 minutes entirely concerned with the mis-
fortunes of Troy! Berlioz did not turn a hair at the spectacle of the
pre-Carthage preliminaries of his drama running to such dangerous lengths. To him it was simply a matter of doing justice to
Troy; Dido and Aeneas and the rest of them could wait.

As I have mentioned in an earlier article, Berlioz, at a late
stage of his work, introduced a scene in which two Trojan soldiers
discuss serio-comically the queer kink in their leader's mentality
that makes him bent on leaving pleasant Carthage for adventures
and perils unknown upon the seas. Berlioz rather plumed himself
on the invention of this episode because it would bring once more
home to the spectator the compelling urgency of the gods' order
to the Trojan hero to depart from Africa and from Dido.

At a still later stage of his composition he seems to have felt that
the work had now become overlong, and in his score he inserted a
footnote authorising the omission of a late episode or two and a
leap to the finale. The strange thing is that while this cut means
the sacrifice of an impassioned scene in which the desperate
Dido bids farewell to life, Berlioz preferred even this sacrifice to
the loss of the episode of the two soldiers.

He was manifestly possessed by the Trojan subject more completely than he had been by any previous one or was to be
possessed by any future one; and I sometimes wonder whether,
unsuspected by them all, Wagner had not played some part in the
conception and the shaping of the opera. The two men had met in
London earlier in that decade, and Wagner could hardly have
failed to speak then to his French colleague of his own plans in
connection with the vast *Ring* saga. It is inconceivable also that a
few years later, when Berlioz and Liszt were seeing so much of
each other in Weimar, the latter should not have spoken of the
ambitious Wagnerian scheme.

So we cannot rule out the possibility, I think, that the mere
knowledge of such a plan incubating in his German rival's mind
may have done something to build up in Berlioz a similar
dramatic structure of cosmic scope. It would not be surprising if
that were so.

In the fifties he was at the very height not only of his musical but his intellectual powers, and it may conceivably have occurred to him that he would achieve realisation of all these powers in combination only in some dramatic theme of super-operatic reach, and, he being what he was, that the *Aeneid* was a theme heaven-sent to him for that purpose. It is not without a certain significance that even before *Les Troyens* was off his hands his imagination had begun to play on an opera on another subject of vast scope of time and place, that of Christopher Columbus.

★   ★   ★

The listener to whom the work is almost entirely new has no easy musical task before him. It is not so much that there are inequalities of inspiration in the score; one can hardly expect, with reason, anything else in a work of this length. The fundamental trouble is rather that the musical style is not homogeneous throughout, and moreover, that a good deal of the opera is couched in the Gluckian-Berliozian idiom with which our British public is relatively unfamiliar.

I myself am conscious of three musical styles in the work—the "classical," to which I have just referred (this is the style that prevails in the two acts located in Troy); the "romantic", which warms itself, especially in the Dido and Aeneas scenes, at Shakespearean fires; and a third style, new for Berlioz, which I cannot adequately characterise in the few lines open to me in the present article, a style that points towards a quite new development in him as a composer, a style of easy conversational flow, not relying on set forms but seeming to follow the natural contours of melodic dialogue, and so to anticipate later operatic achievements such as some of those of the mature Bizet.

The cardinal example of this style in *Les Troyens* is the exquisite quintet (Dido, Anna, Aeneas, Iopas, Narbal) in the fourth act, in which Anna sows in her sister's heart the seeds of forgetfulness of her dead husband (Sychaeus) and of a passion for the dazzling Trojan hero who has descended upon her Carthage.

Berlioz never wrote anything more remarkable than this quiet ensemble. Never yet, however, have I heard it anything like fully realised psychologically in performance.

It is, however, the Gluckian idiom of the first two acts (*La Prise de Troie*) that is likely to prove the main difficulty for the ordinary listener. To say that Berlioz deliberately adopted this idiom for his Troy scenes is rather to misrepresent the facts. It was a matter with him not of cool choice but of urgent inner necessity. Nor will it do to surmise that after having exploited this "classical" musical idiom for the Troy milieu he had abandoned it by the time he came to the "romantic" Carthage scenes. This facile assumption is negatived by the dates of composition of the various sections of the score. Berlioz did not work straight through Troy, finish with it, then put all that away and concentrate on Carthage; on the contrary, he kept going back to the composition of Troy episodes long after he had completed or almost completed some Carthage matter; and always, when he went back to Troy, the Gluckian idiom came uppermost in him once more as a simple matter of course. It was a fundamental part and parcel of him.

The spectator of today, then, must make a special effort not to be estranged by this "antique" style in the early stages of the opera, for if he is he will fail utterly to see Cassandra and Corœbus and the Trojans in general as Berlioz did and intended us to do. This, indeed, is the hardest task of all for us today, for Berlioz, being a cultured Frenchman, had roots in the classical French drama that are beyond the grasp of most theatregoers today. For Berlioz, as his letters and articles testify, the then contemporary stage was still to some extent the stage of Corneille and Racine, and—a point of which we must not lose sight—he often thought *musically* in terms of classical French declamation.

In 1859 he and Wagner met in Paris, and Berlioz read the poem of *Les Troyens* to his German colleague, who has left us his impressions of it all. He was not merely unimpressed by the subject but alienated by Berlioz's "dry and artificially theatrical delivery" of the poem. We have no difficulty in imagining what purely French forms that "delivery" took; in one of his Wittgenstein letters Berlioz, speaking with obvious satisfaction of some lines he had just drafted for his opera, declares his intention of getting the celebrated actress Rachel to declaim them for him in the true French classical style. Considerations of this kind were undoubtedly at the back of his mind when he was writing much of his Troy music, and it is consequently often difficult for us of today to *hear the music* of certain lines precisely as the composer must have heard them inwardly. Even with the French text before us this is difficult enough for us; and it goes without saying that no translation into any other language can reproduce the precise physical and mental inflections of the original.

14 April 1957
21 April 1957
5 May 1957
19 May 1957

5

"Les Troyens" and "The Ring"

THE READER WILL know that Berlioz received the greatest
encouragement in the composition of *Les Troyens* from the Princess
von Sayn-Wittgenstein; but there may possibly be more in that
simple historical fact than meets the casual eye. There can be little
doubt that the Princess, who hated Wagner, if only because he
was so dangerous a rival to Liszt as a composer, had hopes of
helping to bring into the world a massive French masterpiece that
could stand up to and perhaps outbalance the huge *Ring* on
which everyone knew Wagner to be engaged after the turn of the
mid-century. To this plan, even if it were not formulated in so
many words, Berlioz would not have been likely to have any
objection.

He did not immediately perceive that the Vergil subject had
two main aspects, the lyric and the philosophic—which it would
take considerable dexterity to reconcile on the stage. As to his
preoccupation with the epic and philosophic bearings of the
subject there can be no doubt. As I have said, at no time did he
think of his opera as the simple love story of Dido and Aeneas.
It was always, for him, *The Trojans* in the first place and the
lovers in the second. As Miss Helen Waddell has pointed out in
her delightful book *The Wandering Scholars*, Vergil's story presents
a modern poet, novelist or dramatist with a ready-made, complete self-existent work of narrative art and we are able to understand the fascination it had for many a good early Christian
Father whose interests were not wholly theological.

The philosophical element, however, is another and a very different matter. Vergil's subject had really been the foundation by the vanquished Trojans of a new and greater Troy in Italy. This was Berlioz's thesis also; and no one today can get an adequate idea of what he was driving at if he fails to recognise this simple fact. Berlioz, however, lacked the peculiar constructive musical faculty that would have been necessary for the perfect realisation of the Vergilian Troy-Rome theme to the full.

The point I am trying to make will, I think, be at once clear to the reader if he will take a fleeting glance at the *Ring*: there the cosmic ground-plan is visibly more important than any individual character. The whole thing evolves logically from a single psychological germ; we are conscious of the whole in each of the parts and vice versa. This faculty was never dominant in Berlioz; and the consequence is that he never quite succeeds in bringing the Dido and Aeneas element and the Troy-Rome element into a perfect balance: the closing moments of his opera, indeed, rather raise a smile by their naïveté.

But if he never quite realised in his musical and dramatic construction the cosmic theme as both he and Vergil had done imaginatively, he certainly never lost sight of it, and his poignant public lament for the failure of the gigantic work was concerned not with the romantic Dido and Aeneas, but with his "noble Cassandra"—the human symbol, for him, of all that Troy had stood for.

29 July 1958

6

The "Royal Hunt and Storm"

MOST PEOPLE KNOW by this time, as a concert piece, the "Royal Hunt and Storm" from *The Trojans at Carthage*. Listening to it again the other evening at Glasgow, this time in conjunction with the stage action, I was more than ever convinced that the latter, so far from helping us to appreciate the music, actually stands in the way of our appreciation. Berlioz gives us, in his score, the most detailed specification of the scene and the mimed action he had planned to accompany the music.

Dido and Aeneas having gone hunting in a forest near Carthage, Venus arranges for a storm to occur that will drive the doubting pair to some intimate shelter or other and so bring about a mutual recognition of their love. We see rocks and a grotto and a purling stream in the forest. Naiades appear and disappear. The fanfares of hunting horns are heard in the distance, and the Naiades disperse in terror. The hunting troupe traverses the stage: a solitary hunter, alarmed by the distant mutterings of the coming storm, first takes shelter under a tree and then plunges into the forest in the direction from which the horns are sounding. The storm breaks: the young Ascanius and a few hunters, on horseback and on foot, enter and scatter in various directions: then come Dido and Aeneas, who seek refuge in the grotto. Nymphs, fauns, satyrs and other sylvan creatures dance madly to the storm: the lightning strikes a tree, which crashes in flames. The woodland folk disappear in a thick mist that descends upon the stage:

229

the storm gradually dies down: the mist disappears, and the music ends in the tranquil mood of the opening.

Now the less we see or even think about all this the better. We realise the unique quality of this music best in the concert room, where we just say to ourselves at the commencement, "A Hunt, a Storm, the Storm subsides", and then think no more about the programme but let the music speak for itself. And when we do that, we see this music for what it is—not merely a marvellous piece of expression but one of the most perfect creations of form that the art can show.

"Form", in the text-books, means virtually only sonata form— a matter of exposition, working-out, and recapitulation, the whole being controlled by certain key-relationships and contrasts. I have more than once pointed out that this conception of form is so popular in conservatoires and among the writers of textbooks because form of this kind can be analysed and taught: no matter how the prescribed procedure may be varied or subtilised by individual genius, there remains a basic constant something that can be demonstrated, standardised, and made up from recipe. Form in the freer sense of the term is not taught in the conservatoires because it cannot be taught, for the very good reason that here form and content are one and indivisible, and occur in combination (or rather interfusion, interpenetration) only on that one occasion, without any possibility of the final result ever being made into a system and reproduced elsewhere.

An example of form in this superlative sense is the seventh symphony of Sibelius. Here a particular quality and sequence of ideas find their natural, inevitable expression in a form that never existed till that moment and can never exist again. "Form", in fact, here takes on a new meaning. It no longer implies pattern: it now means simply function: the idea could not possibly have taken any shape but this, and the resulting outer shape would have no meaning in connection with any other idea, so that no re-application of it in other circumstances is conceivable. It is form of this kind, the outward and visible sign of an inward organic life that begins and develops and passes away in obedience to no law but its own, that we see to perfection in the Chasse Royale when we listen to it simply as a piece of self-subsistent music.

Our present conception of form has been too much dominated by the very restricted specimens afforded us by what we call first-movement form in the classical sonata or symphony; and it is astonishing how blind the victims of scholastic tradition can be at once to the merits of freer forms and to the structural faults in some of the most admired examples of the pattern forms. Even the towering genius of a Beethoven or a Brahms sometimes fails to solve the problem of conciliating the claims of free invention, letting the wind of the spirit blow where it listeth, with those of the transmitted pattern. Nothing could well be more mechanical, for instance, than Beethoven's fumbling for a while at the critical point in the "Adieux" sonata. Brahms gets into the same difficulties at very much the same point in one first movement after another: a cardinal example is the commencement of the development section in his second symphony. Here, as in so many other instances, the lost aviator flies blind in the fog until he can see his way clear again: he manipulates his theme according to formula until his imagination can get to work again on something vital.

In the smaller men the mechanics of this kind of padding becomes positively painful—in the working-out section of the Tchaikovsky B flat minor piano concerto, for instance, or that of Borodin's *Prince Igor* overture. When imagination does get a free rein in Brahms, when, instead of laying standardised brick to standardised brick according to formula, his imagination goes on creating organically, the ideas unconsciously achieving their own inevitable form, he is unsurpassable, as the reader will see if he compares the feeble mechanics of such a passage as I have mentioned with the superb last few pages of the first movement of the second symphony or with the whole handling of the piano Rhapsody in G minor (op. 79).

It would be difficult to imagine a more perfect example of organic form of the freer kind than the "Chasse Royale". There is not a bar of padding, of mechanised structure, of surrender to convention: things happen as they do simply because they could not happen otherwise, and what is finally done is done once for all, without reliance on precedent and without the possibility of reproduction later either by anyone else or by Berlioz himself. Shakespeare, says Coleridge, "goes on creating, and evolving B out of A, and C out of B, and so on, just as a serpent moves, which makes a fulcrum of its own body, and seems forever twisting and untwisting its own strength". These words of one of the greatest of critics are applicable to the Berlioz of the "Chasse Royale" as they are to few composers and few works. If, for all that the text-books may say or omit to say, this piece is not form in the very highest sense of the term, the word has no meaning for me.

The trouble is that musical criticism has hardly realised as yet that there is more than one order of musical imagination and therefore more than one method of procedure in creation. The great German art critics have learned to distinguish between the different orders of imagination among painters, some of these being predominantly linear, for instance, some predominantly colouristic. It should be evident by this time that while some composers tend towards the architectural, others tend towards the poetic or the pictorial. By this latter term I do not mean that they indulge in the realistic painting of actualities, after the manner, for instance, of Bach's serpents or Schubert's spinning wheel. I mean that the poetic or pictorial composer's imagination works from starting-point to finishing-point along other lines than those of the more architectural composers, and that we must judge his achievement in terms of itself instead of in the totally inapplicable terms of a completely different order of music. To call the composer of the "Chasse Royale" an amateur merely because he does not rely for the organic connection of his music on the formalised technical devices natural to a Brahms or a Beethoven is an impertinence excusable only on the plea of ignorance—ignorance of the immense variety of forms and colours that the musical imagination can assume.

Our main difficulty in arriving at anything like a fully satisfactory aesthetic of music comes from the fact that the art is as yet only in its infancy. We can study the evolution of the other arts in Europe, Asia and elsewhere, over a period of twenty centuries, during which every variety of pictorial or sculptural or architectural imagination, every variety of design, has had time and opportunity to realise itself. But musical form, as at present understood, is an affair merely of some two hundred years, a mere segment of the vast arc that will ultimately be traversed; and we are too apt to assume that because sonata form was the ideal solution for certain eighteenth and nineteenth-century problems of musical structure it is the ideal solution for all other problems.

The day will come when sonata form will be regarded, as Greek architecture is now, as merely the result of the intensive concentration of a particular epoch upon a particular—and transient—body of material and the problems of design it presented. For other imaginative material other forms will have to be discovered in music; and along that path, as along so many others, Berlioz will some day be regarded as a pioneer.

31 March 1935

VII

Berlioz's Writings

1

Berlioz as Journalist

THE FIFTIETH ANNIVERSARY of the death of Berlioz has
passed almost unnoticed in the English musical press. He is not a
composer in whom the British public takes much interest, for the
British public knows little of him except *The Damnation of Faust*,
and has no idea of his whole range. But I should have thought that
my colleagues on the press, even if they do not care greatly for his
music, would have remembered him on this occasion affection-
ately as a musical critic and journalist. Berlioz as a composer was
too original for his own day, and more especially for his own
country. His music, even with the proceeds of his foreign tours
as a conductor, hardly sufficed to keep him; and for many years
he had to supplement his income from these sources by writing
musical criticisms for the *Figaro*★ and the *Journal des Débats*,
Apart from his famous *Memoirs*, his collected prose writings are
contained in three volumes—*A travers chants* (mostly pieces of
serious criticism), *Les Grotesques de la Musique*, and *Les Soirées de
l'Orchestre*. Of these the last is in many respects the most interesting today. The serious critical studies are well worth reading,
because it is always fascinating to see an artist who is himself a
skilled practician running an expert, sensitive anger over the
work of others. But some of Berlioz's subjects are a little *passés*
now; and his insight into Beethoven, for example, is not as
marvellous and as modern, so to speak, as Wagner's. The *Soirées*

★ Berlioz did not write for *Figaro* (P.H.).

237

de l'Orchestre, on the other hand, is a book that can never grow old; readers will still be chuckling over it a hundred years hence. Someone ought to translate it into English, if he can be trusted to do so in a style as finely-pointed as Berlioz's own.*

Berlioz ought to be specially dear to the hearts of musical critics everywhere, for in him they will recognise a great fellow-sufferer. It is bad enough to be a musical critic in, say, Birmingham, and to have to listen to for the thousandth time, and to write about for the thousandth time, always in fresh words, the same symphonies, the same suites, the same overtures, the same songs, the same singers, the same fiddlers and pianists. But most of the music the modern critic has to sit through, if stale in his ears, is at least fairly good of its kind; while poor Berlioz, in the unmusical Paris of his time, had to listen professionally to new operas and operettas and vaudevilles that were so beneath contempt that not even the names of them have survived for us to smile at. We can dimly guess at the feelings of the composer of *Faust* and *Les Troyens* and the *Te Deum* as he sat through this sort of thing week after week, and tried to concoct a *feuilleton* upon the monstrosities. He necessarily took refuge, as every critic has sooner or later to do in an unmusical town, in irony; the only way, as Figaro said, to keep oneself from crying is to keep laughing; the only way to prevent yourself going mad at certain concerts is to find amusement in the antics of the lunatics who have written the music or those who are performing it. Every musical critic has to work out for himself a sort of technique of endurance if he wants to survive to a reasonable old age. The value and the charm of *Les Soirées de l'Orchestre* are that here Berlioz lets us into the secret of his own concert and opera technique. Upon the feebleness and fatuities of the composers and performers whom he had to criticise he turned an abundant humour and the finest of irony. He could slay with an epigram; he could convey the most damaging censure by the simple process of conveying nothing. Hugo Wolf could be delightfully and dexterously contemptuous at

* *Evenings in the Orchestre.* Translated by C. R. Fortescue, 1963. Penguin (P.H.)

times—as when, by way of criticism of some inferior artist or other, he merely quoted the first line of one of the famous Mignon songs of Goethe—"Heiss' mich nicht reden, heiss' mich schweigen". But Wolf's touch at its best had not the delicacy of Berlioz's. Asked, after a performance of *Don Giovanni*, what he thought of the baritone who had been playing the part of the wicked hero, he replied, "I think he deserves the prix Monthyon." (The prix Monthyon, let me explain for the benefit of the English reader, is a prize given annually in Paris for virtue.)

Berlioz could not have survived his awful experiences as a musical critic but for this gift of his for seeing absurd things humorously instead of angrily; and in the pages of the *Soirées de l'Orchestre* the critic of today may learn how to face his own troubles as a man and a humorist. For in these matters it is only the names and the forms that change: the diseases are perenially the same—the singers, the pianists, the violinists, the audiences, the agents, the bad composers, and all the rest of them. Berlioz had his Aerbut Paerks, though he would know them under another name; and then, as now, the real musicians in any concert or operatic performance were the orchestra, the singers, for the most part, being just—singers. The scene of the *Soirées* is set in an opera house that is mostly given up to inferior works. When one of these is being performed, the orchestra keep just the big drum and a brass instrument or two going, while the bulk of the band read books or talk. It is during performances of this sort that the stories of the *Soirées* are told by Berlioz himself (sitting in the front row of the stalls)* to the orchestra, or by the orchestra to him. There is the story of the grocer's assistant who hissed *Der Freischütz*, who died in the hospital, and whose skeleton was sold to the Opera, where it paid for its one-time owner's *lèse majesté* by appearing night after night in the *scène infernale* of *Der Frei-schütz*; "at the moment when Samiel cries 'Here I am,' there is a thunderclap, a tree falls into the abyss, and our grocer, the enemy of Weber's music, appears in a red light, brandishing, full of enthusiasm, his flaming torch. Who could ever have divined the

* In the orchestral pit (P.H.).

dramatic vocation of the joker?" There is the story of the prima
donna with the acid voice who was practising at her open window
one morning when a milkwoman passed. "Ah," sighed the
milkwoman, "Marriage isn't a bed of roses." Returning in the
afternoon, she hears the same agonising sounds. "Mon Dieu,"
she says, crossing herself: "Poor lady! It's now three o'clock, and
she has been in childbirth since this morning!" There is the
delicious skit, in the story of Barnum and Jenny Lind's American
tour, of the never-changing advertising methods of the prima
donna's agent. The American newspapers are full of accounts of
the agitation of the ocean when the Swedish nightingale crossed
it, and of the deaths by suffocation in the huge crowd that awaited
her landing at New York. The crowd turns its eyes towards the
sea, and beholds a marvellous and affecting sight. "The dolphins
and the whales, who for eight hundred (some say nine hundred)
leagues had taken part in the triumph of the new Galatea and had
followed the ship, spouting fountains of perfumed water, fell
into convulsions in the harbour, ravaged by despair at not being
able to come on land with her; old sailors, shedding great tears,
abandoned themselves to the most lamentable wailing; while
seagulls, frigate-birds, and other savage birds that inhabit the vast
solitudes of the ocean, more fortunate than the whales and
dolphins, hovered fearlessly around the adorable singer, lighted
on her pure shoulders, circled about her Olympian head, holding,
in their beaks, enormous pearls, which they offered to her in the
most graceful fashion, cooing sweetly the while." Even this is not
enough. Barnum has invented for Jenny Lind the "claque à mort".
Before her arrival he has sought out a number of poor devils who
were tired of life, and pointed out to them that they would be of
more value to their families dead than alive. He guarantees the
heirs of each of them two thousand dollars the day they carry
out their agreement with him, which is to fling themselves out of
high windows when the prima donna passes, crying with their
last breath, "*vive* Lind", or under her horses' feet, or under her
carriage wheels, or to stab or shoot themselves after she has
sung her second aria, declaring loudly that they can no longer

endure prosaic existence after such paradisiacal delights; and so on.

There is a delicious calculation, again, of the value of each note emitted by an operatic tenor who, with a salary of 100,000 francs, appears on an average seven times a month, or eighty-four times per annum. "Supposing a role to consist of 1,100 notes or syllables, this figures at one franc per syllable. Thus in *William Tell*—"Ma (1 franc) présence (3 fr) pour vous est peut-être un outrage (9 fr). Mathilde (3 fr) mes pas indiscrets (100 sous) ont osé jusqu'à vous se frayer un passage (13 fr)"; while the prima donna who plays Mathilde, having only a beggarly 40,000 francs, replies at the rate of merely eight sous a syllable: "On pardonne aisément (2 fr 40 c) des torts (16 sous) que l'on partage (2 fr). Arnold (16 sous), je (8 sous) vous attendais (32 sous)." Yes, Berlioz as a journalist was great. The *Soirées de l'Orchestre* ought to be the *vade mecum* of the young musical critic. One particularly valuable wrinkle he will find there—how to convey his opinion of a wretched new work without discussing it.

* * *

A young musical critic in another town asks me for further particulars as to that feature of Berlioz's journalistic technique to which I referred at the close of last week's article—how he conveyed his opinion of a wretched new work without discussing it. My friend thinks the tip might be of service to himself and others who are engaged in the nefarious business of musical criticism. As hardly any one in this country seems to know anything of the delightful *Soirées de l'Orchestre* I have pleasure in exhibiting in closer detail one of the most fascinating chapters of that book.

There is the usual platitudinous opera being performed, and the musicians of the orchestra have time to talk among themselves and with the gentleman in the stalls (Berlioz himself). Corsino, the leader, thinks this opera just the sort of work on which Berlioz could exercise his "talent of saying nothing" in his criticism. Berlioz protests with mock seriousness. "What do you mean?

I always try to say something in my miserable *feuilletons*. I merely vary the form; what you call saying nothing is often a way of speaking very clearly". Corsino goes out and returns with a collection of the critic's articles, extracts from which he reads to the orchestra, as specimens of the art of criticising by saying nothing. For instance, "if he wants to scoff at the author of a libretto without making the least observation on his poetry, he employs the atrocious means of telling the plot of the work in rhymes that run along as prose". Examples are quoted. Berlioz gravely repudiates the charge that these are "atrocious". "I had no malicious *arrière-pensée*. It was the run of the rhythm that made me write like that. The opposite of Molière's M. Jourdain, I made poetry without knowing it. After having listened to a barrel-organ playing the same air for an hour, don't you find yourself singing the tune in spite of yourself, no matter how ugly it may be? So it's quite simple that after listening to an opera containing such verses as those my prose should drop into verse and that I should be able to dis-rhyme myself only by an effort." He speaks of all the disagreeablenesses of the critic's life—the necessity of hearing poor works, the necessity of writing about them, of giving the public some idea of a thing that itself was destitute of ideas, of never repeating oneself in precisely similar circumstances, of telling the truth without wounding suscepti-bilities, and so on.

After ten minutes or so of this, Corsino pulls him up. "You resort to irony", he says, "to prove that you never resort to irony. But here are the proofs, and I call the orchestra to witness." He proceeds to read one of Berlioz's articles. It is about an opera called *Le Phare* (*The Lighthouse*), produced on December 27, 1849. "The scene represents a square in the village of Pornié. Breton fishermen are about to set sail with Valentin, the pilot. They sing a chorus . . ." The critic begins to give the story of the drama as it gradually enfolds itself. But after six lines he stops. "I fear I should weary the reader if I were to go into further details as to the music and the verses of this work. I will just add a word on the *mise en scène*." It seems that at the back of the stage another drama was

being enacted, unknown to the audience. The scene represented
a sea in a furious storm. It is explained, with great elaboration,
that this realistic effect is produced by a crowd of poor devils
crouching under a painted canvas, and making the waves by
contortions of their backs and legs. Comparison are made
between this instrument of torture and the famous cage invented
by Louis XI, in which prisoners had no room to stretch their
limbs. The waves have, however, one advantage over the
prisoners of Louis XI. They can talk to each other. They quarrel;
each thinks the others are shirking their work and putting too
much upon him. The repartees are fast and furious; the alterca-
tion drifts off into an argument on social inequality and the
rights of man. Tempers rise, until there is a free-fight among the
waves. The effect, from the scenic point of view, is magnificently
realistic. "It was a water-spout, a typhoon. And the public
admires this fine confusion—the effect of politics—and becomes
enthusiastic over the rare talent of the machinists of the Opera."
It is all done with delicious wit and gravity. The reader is so
drawn into the story that he quite forgets that Berlioz began by
ostensibly discussing the production of a new opera; and by the
time the story is over, whatever interest the reader may originally
have felt in the opera has evaporated.

Even better is the account of "*Diletta*, opéra-comique in three
Acts", produced on Monday, July 22, 1850. Berlioz begins his
article thus: "It is very sad to have to think about opéras-comiques
on a Monday, because Monday is the day after Sunday. Now on
Sunday you go to the Nord Railway Station. You get into a train
and you say to it, 'Take me to Enghien.' When you descend from
the obedient vehicle you find some good friends, true friends,
of the sort whose name you don't know very well, but who don't
couple yours with an opprobrious epithet when your back is
turned, and someone asks who you are". At Enghien they talk
of what they are going to do this delightful Sunday; some are
going in a boat on the lake to fish. The friends come to cross-
roads and part. Then Berlioz is inspired to a rhapsody on friendship. "O true friendship, sister of republican fraternity!" And so

on. He strolls over the plain of Enghien. He becomes appro-
priately conscious of all the sights and sounds and silences of the
place. In the distance church bells are heard: they cease, and the
silence is profounder than before. "You stop; you listen; you
look into the distance—towards the West. You think of America,
of the new worlds springing up there, of virgin solitudes, of
vanished civilisations, of the grandeur and the decadence of
savage life. Then the East—memories of Asia crowd upon you;
you think of Homer and his heroes, of Troy, of Greece, of Egypt,
of Memphis, of the Pyramids, of the court of the Pharaohs, of
the vast temples of Isis, of mysterious India and its sad inhabitants,
of China in decay, of all these ancient mad, or at any rate, mono-
maniac, races." A bird flies from a bush and soars into the sky,
singing joyously. "It seizes a gnat and goes off with it, thanking
God, whose beneficence, it says, is spread over all nature, for it
does not disdain the providing of nourishment for the young of
birds—a naïve sort of gratitude which perhaps the gnat does not
share." Piquant Parisiennes pass. The bells again call the faithful
discordantly to church. You decide to go to vespers, and the
inevitable description of the pretty little church follows. In a
corner of the wall you find three words discreetly carved:
"Lucien: Louise: toujours."

The inscription sets you thinking. What tender romance do
they half conceal, half disclose? You become very romantic
yourself; you think of when you were eighteen, and you look
into space, trying to see again a vanished form. "The organ plays;
a simple melody reaches you through the walls of the church.
You wipe your right eye and say again, 'Bah! I'll go to vespers'.
And you enter." There follows a description of the church, the
congregation (thirty women and children), the curé, the choir
("all singing out of tune in a way that would rot the teeth of a
hippopotamus"), the organist, who has no knowledge of harmony, the barbarous music. You are set dreaming now of art;
how nice it would be to own a charming little church of this
kind, to give sweet music in it, to retire into it to pray, to evoke
the past, to smile, to weep. Your meditation is interrupted by the

organist playing a dance tune from an old ballet. It drives you out. You go into the cemetery, find a tombstone with the right slope, recline against it, and read Vergil. You hear sobs. A little girl on crutches comes into sight, weeping bitterly. She tells you, at great length, the sad tale of herself and the swallow with the broken leg. You put your book away, light a cigar, and make your way to the train for Paris, some saucy final impudence of the child who has not had the tip she expected, rankling in your mind. "And that is why I am so little disposed to give you an account today, Monday, of the new opéra-comique. Today's idyll has stupefied me. Tomorrow, then!" But the next day's *feuilleton* gets us no nearer the subject. "It is always sad", it begins, "to have to think about opéras-comiques on a Tuesday, because Tuesday is the day after Monday." The reader is again led gently off the track of the opera by means of a long story. At the end of this, "Now let us come to the principal object of this article. We must never put serious matters off till the morrow: it is always so sad to have to think of opéras-comiques on a Wednesday. *Diletta* . . . but . . . very . . . the music . . . always . . . paleness . . . platitude." And an editorial footnote is appended: "The author's manuscript here becomes indecipherable by any of our readers. We are thus forced to print his criticism of the charming opera *Diletta* in a slightly incomplete form." That is all; but Berlioz has managed to convey what he really thought of *Diletta*.

THE BIRMINGHAM POST. 17 March 1919
24 March 1919

2

On the Riviera

No GOOD BERLIOZIAN can be on the Riviera without thinking of Berlioz, for this coast was one of the few places on earth where that unhappy soul could forget its troubles and feel that life was worth living. It was at Nice, it will be remembered, that an unusually intelligent Providence, if we may believe Berlioz's rather tall story, saved him from being lost to history as merely one of the crowd of commonplace perpetrators of the *crime passionel*. He had set out from Rome in 1831, at the age of 28, to wreak vengeance on the faithless Camille Moke and his friend Pleyel. His preparations had been made in the very best romantic tradition: having left a note on the manuscript of the *Symphonie fantastique* that the flute was to be doubled at the last entry of the main theme, he loaded his pistols, put in his pockets two bottles, one containing laudanum, the other strychnine, bought a complete lady's-maid outfit, including a green veil, and set off to Paris on his errand of vengeance; having penetrated into the Pleyel household by means of this impenetrable disguise he would shoot Camille and her husband, despatch the lady's mother with a third bullet, and then, if his pistol missed fire at the fourth attempt, saturate himself with strychnine and laudanum.

But by the time he reached Nice his fury had evaporated. He had no objection to ridding the earth of the Pleyel-Moke vermin, but to have to die himself was a trifle unpleasant: would it not be better to remain alive and write some more music? At Nice (I am telling the story from memory, and the reader will forgive me if I am not quite accurate in all my details) he became wholly rational again, wrote to the Director of the Academy at Rome admitting how foolish he had been, and then settled down to what he calls the twenty happiest days of his life in the neighbourhood of Nice (which at that time must have been a delightful little town, not at all like the present awful combination of Brighton and Birmingham), bathing in the sea, sleeping on the as yet unspoiled hills overlooking Villefranche, and writing his *King Lear* overture.

He came to Nice again for a respite from his worries at a later date—it must have been some time after 1840 in which year Paganini, who is the hero of the story he tells in the *Soirées de l'Orchestre*, had died at Nice preparatory to setting out on the most remarkable tour ever undertaken even by a fiddle virtuoso. According to the story told by Sir Frederick Treves in his book *The Riviera of the Corniche Road*, the Church refused to allow the body of the great violinist, who had neither lived nor died in the odour of sanctity, to be buried in consecrated ground. The body remained for some days in the cellar of a house of "a friendly" (but presumably mad) "hatter", and was then removed to a hospital. Paganini's son having lost his action against the bishop, the body was taken to Villefranche and deposited in a lazaretto.

"In about a month the smell emitted by the corpse was complained of, and accordingly the coffin was taken out of the building and placed on the open beach near the water's edge. This gave great distress to the friends of the dead artist, and so one night a party of five of them took up the coffin and carried it by torchlight round the bay to the point of Cap de St. Hospice." Anyone who will take that walk, as I did the other day, from Villefranche along the narrow strip of footing between the rocks and the sea and then on to St. Jean, will realise that the endurance of the coffin-bearers must have been equal to their piety. "Here they buried it close to the sea and just below the old round tower which still stands on this spit of land." This was not by any means the end of Paganini's posthumous pilgrimage, but we need not, for our present purpose, follow the further peregrinations of the body before it finally found rest in the church of the Madonna della Stacata in Parma in 1876.

In the *Soirées*, Berlioz tells us that one day when he was returning by boat from Villefranche to Nice, the young fisherman who was rowing him showed him on the bank "an isolated villa of somewhat strange aspect" (apparently the "lazaretto"), in which as the boy naïvely expressed it, "Paganini lived for three years after his death." (The "month" of Sir Frederick Treves, it will be observed, has become three years in the expansive imagination of Berlioz.) That night, he goes on to say, he slept in the tower of the Ponchettes—the ancient Bellanda tower that is still one of the sights of Nice—"that is stuck like a swallow's nest against a rock two hundred feet above the sea". Here a strange and romantic thing happened. He heard Paganini's Variations on the Carnival at Venice being played on a violin. "Just imagine E. T. A. Hoffmann in my place; what a touching and fantastic elegy he would have written on this strange incident!" After this, it is a sad descent to earth to learn that there was nothing supernatural about the nocturnal performance; the violinist was Paganini's friend, the Comte di Cesole who had been his companion in the last months of his life in Nice.

I am prepared to accept most of this, including, at a pinch, the sleeping in the Bellanda tower, uncomfortable as it must have been; for Berlioz, as a romantic, felt it obligatory upon him to do the romantic thing and what are old towers for except for romantics to sleep in, even at the cost of a little comfort? But with the best will in the world I find it difficult to swallow the story about the Comte di Cesole coming there at night to give a violin recital. The reference to Hoffmann seems to me to give the story away. Berlioz did not tell lies to serve purely personal ends, as Wagner did in his autobiography; but the border-line between fact and fancy in his reminiscences is occasionally a thin one. I have sometimes wondered whether the explanation may not be, at times, a physical one; in the latter half of his life Berlioz had to be continually dosing himself with laudanum to still the pains of what he calls his intestinal neuralgia, and it would not be surprising if, in his opium state, he occasionally dreamt something that afterwards emerged into his waking consciousness and imposed itself on him as a memory. But in the Comte di Cesole case I fancy that he had persuaded himself in advance that the occasion and the scene was admirably Hoffmannesque, and his lively imagination did the rest.

We are inclined to forget, when we read some of the early Berlioz's wild romantic outpourings, that certain portions of the earth were still, at that time, romantic for even the most moderately romantic minded. The Italy in which his years as *Prix de Rome* were spent was still a land of brigands and passions of the true romantic type. Berlioz was naturally predisposed to people his world with men and women and scenes and adventures of this type, and, as his *Memoirs* show, his Italian sojourn must have given him ample material for his luxuriant fancy to play upon. It is likely, also, that his youthful experiences in the hospitals in Paris, and particularly in the dissecting room, had intensified his sense of the macabre.

The youthful Flaubert passed through a very similar stage. But the average reader of *Madame Bovary* or *L'Education Sentimentale* knows nothing of the earlier and more romantic Flaubert; whereas the musical public still constructs its Berlioz on the basis of the juvenile *Symphonie fantastique*, though the mature Berlioz mastered in time the romantic and the macabre in him as completely as the mature Flaubert outgrew the Flaubert of the first callow years.

19 January 1930

3

New Letters

PROFESSOR JACQUES BARZUN of Columbia University, now the world's highest authority on Berlioz biography, has just laid us under a fresh obligation by the issue of a volume of Berlioz letters hitherto unknown or imperfectly known. (*New Letters of Berlioz, 1830–1868*, with Introduction, Notes and English Translations by Jacques Barzun: Columbia University Press, New York, and Oxford University Press, London.) The letters are copiously annotated, and the editor's linking remarks make the book a partial biography of the composer from 1830, when he was twenty-seven, to his death in 1869.

The correspondence is in the main more interesting to the Berlioz student than to the general reader, being largely concerned with the composer's preparations for, or the results of, concerts of his works in Paris and abroad; indeed, apart from the illuminating correspondence about *The Trojans* with the Princess von Sayn-Wittgenstein, which has not yet appeared in English, he does not talk very much in his letters about his own creative processes.

The reader who follows at all the contemporary course of Berlioz criticism can hardly have failed to note that in what may be called official Berlioz circles the composer is now in danger of being as uncritically over-valued as he was critically under-valued at one time. We are given to understand by his present loyal bodyguard that he was the fountain-head of all that is really vital in the music of the nineteenth and even the twentieth centuries. Professor Barzun quotes approvingly a remark of Mr. W. H. Auden that "whoever wants to know the nineteenth century must know Berlioz". Pontifical utterances of that sort from quarters more literary than musical do not help us very much; whoever "wants to know the nineteenth century"—a rather tall order, surely—must know a hundred or two musicians, artists, men of letters, philosophers, politicians, etc., etc., in addition to Berlioz.

We stand, in fact, sorely in need of a new study of Berlioz the composer. He has survived without much damage the stink-bombs of the thugs; we can only hope that he will survive the incense burned all around him just now by the less critical of his thurifers.

The reader of the book under review must be put on his guard against accepting at its face value the interpretation put there on the Wagner-Berlioz controversy of 1860, à propos of the former's three concerts in Paris. The too-partisan Berlioz propagandists of today may just as well resign themselves to accepting the simple facts, out of which Berlioz does not emerge with credit. The root of the trouble was the congenital inability of a genius of his type to follow the workings of a musical mind of the type exhibited in the *Tristan* prelude. In his article in the *Journal des Débats* he set up a scarecrow of his own construction which he tried to persuade the Parisian public was an authentic statue of Wagner: he put into the mouth of this figment of his own imagination a number of ridiculous doctrines which he falsely implied were Wagnerian, then rose to his feet and declaimed grandiloquently, "If this is the new religion I am far from practising it. . . . I raise my hand and swear *Non credo*."

Wagner had no difficulty in disposing of all this nonsense in his reply in the *Débats*. His open letter was quietly reasoned and temperately phrased. Berlioz prudently refrained from comment-ing on it publicly; but in a letter to Charles Hallé (included in the present volume) he brazenly described it as "tangled and turgid", "a letter presumably of explanations in which nobody understood anything", that had "done Wagner more harm than good". All this was simply the old scarecrow dodge over again; he must have known that he had publicly placed himself in the wrong *vis-à-vis* Wagner, but could not bring himself to admit it.

Plenty of excuses can be made for his conduct in this sad affair. He was a very sick and unhappy man, disappointed and frustrated. After having the doors of the Paris Opéra closed in his face year after year, and with his own great *Trojans* ready for performance, he had to undergo the humiliation of seeing an interloper from Germany welcomed with open arms by the powers that were, and that not for artistic but for merely political reasons—the desire of Napoleon and his ministers to get on the right side of Austria and Germany. For Wagner and his *Tannhäuser*, as he and all Paris were soon to discover, no expenditure could be too prodigal. Berlioz would have had to be more than human not to allow all this to influence him in his attitude towards Wagner in 1860.

Though he never really understood his German colleague's art, it is pleasant to find him making some sort of approach to it after hearing a good performance of *Tannhäuser* at Weimar in 1863. "There are truly beautiful things in it," he wrote to a friend, "especially in the last act; it is profoundly sad but in the grand style." That is to say, it was not until 1863, six years before his death, that he had got so far as beginning to understand the Wagner of 1845; and that, I imagine, was about as far as he ever got where Wagner was concerned.

9 January 1955

VIII

Barzun's "Berlioz and the Romantic Century"

Barzun's "Berlioz and the Romantic Century"

A NEW BIOGRAPHY of Berlioz has long been needed. Adolphe Boschot's three-volume work, which appeared during the early years of the present century, still commands respect for its painstaking documentation; but most people have risen from a reading of it with a puzzled feeling that the biographer was not in entire sympathy with his subject and did not wholly understand him.

The field was consequently open to some biographer who would approach Berlioz and his epoch from another angle, which an American writer, Mr. Jacques Barzun, has now done with conspicuous ability. His *Berlioz and the Romantic Century* has just been published in two large volumes by Little, Brown and Co., of Boston, in a format calculated to make authors on this side of the Atlantic turn green with envy. The price, twelve dollars fifty cents, may stand in the way of a re-issue in England, but I hope that little difficulty can somehow be overcome; for this is by far the most important contribution to Berlioz biography that has ever appeared.

Mr. Barzun, who knows his subject inside out—and that subject, as the title of his book indicates, is not only the man and musician Berlioz but the Romantic milieu in which he lived and thought—has done his work with a thoroughness that is beyond praise. He has corrected several errors in current Berlioz biography and shed a new light on the long familiar documents. He gives us a copious—perhaps over-copious—bibliography of books and articles on the composer, or bearing in any way on him and his epoch, in various languages during the last hundred years or so; it is not quite up to date in some small respects, but there is nothing like it in existence anywhere else, running as it does to nearly fifteen hundred entries.

He gives us a racy "Index to Misconceptions about Berlioz and their Corrections". Following in the footsteps of that consummate Berliozian, the late Tom S. Wotton, he devotes about twenty-five pages to a critical examination of the twenty volumes of the Breitkopf and Härtel Collected Edition of Berlioz's works, dealing drastically with the many errors of judgment and misrepresentations of fact in it, and the lack of qualifications of its editors, Weingartner and Malherbe, for their difficult task; his summing up is that "this German edition is a true counterpart of Boschot's French biography—indispensable but untrustworthy".

There is no subject, indeed, connected with Berlioz as man and artist about which Mr. Barzun has not something new and pertinent to say. He deals with particular effectiveness with some of the gross misconceptions of his idol that, by dint of sheer thoughtless repetition, have come to be accepted as gospel truth about the matter both by writers on Berlioz and by the musical public. He grinds to powder the nonsensical legend that Berlioz was simply a composer of original and vivid imagination but imperfect technique and inadequate self-direction; the real Berlioz no more conforms, in fact, to the current adjective "Berliozian" than Sappho or Epicurus does to the slick adjective "sapphic" or "epicurean".

Mr. Barzun sees the composer clearly against the "Romantic" background of the 1830s, which explains many of the things he said and did and the way he deliberately chose to say and do them. *Lélio*, for instance, seems to the superficial observer of today a mere hodge-podge of absurdity both of matter and of form. But, as Mr. Barzun rightly insists, it was the only way in which, in 1831, Berlioz could deliver himself of a number of things which it was a burning necessity to him to say and advisable for the Parisian public to hear.

On the biographical and historical sides, then, Mr. Barzun's book is wholly admirable; but on the musical side I must permit myself some criticisms.

His central thesis is that Berlioz was "the fountainhead of modern music as Delacroix is of modern painting." "Broadly speaking, after the death of Beethoven, Weber and Schubert (all before 1830), the one seminal mind in music was Berlioz"; though, as Mr. Barzun generously admits, "he was ultimately seconded by a small army of coadjutors, from Liszt and Wagner in the thirties to Saint-Saëns and the Russians in the sixties, all of whom had their awakening or drew their inspiration from Berlioz."

And so *ad infinitum*. Wagner in particular, it appears, simply could not have paid his musical way if he had not been able to draw so liberally on Berlioz's current account. The last movement of the *Death of Cleopatra* of 1839 is "a subtly scored death scene, here and there suggestive of the love-philtre music in *Tristan*, thirty years ahead." The "delicate orchestration" of the *Lohengrin* prelude was "borrowed" by Wagner from Berlioz's *Tempest* overture. The March in *Harold in Italy* "is built on a pattern which has since become familiar through its use by Wagner in his preludes, and which consists of a phrase brought by development to a high point of intensity and then gradually diminished to its first elements—in a word, crescendo-diminuendo"; apparently so titanic a feat of musical construction would have been beyond the dwarf capacity of Wagner and all the rest of the humble "coadjutors" if Berlioz had not shown them how to perform it.

So it goes on. The *Requiem* "opens with a brief orchestral introduction, a repeated rising scale in the strings, which admirers of the prelude to *Parsifal* will recognise at once as having engendered the 'Eucharist' theme with which that work begins." Benvenuto Cellini's "account of his adventures" when he returns "puts one in mind of Tannhäuser's Rome Narration." "Opera-goers will scarcely have failed to notice that between Cellini and his *maîtres-ciseleurs* and Walther and the *Meistersinger* there is that same 'strange coincidence' which critics have noted between part of the music and Tannhäuser's Rome Narration . . . beyond a doubt the dramatic substance of *Die Meistersinger* is a *bürgerlich* transposition of Berlioz's original." The design of the vocal finale of the French composer's *Romeo and Juliet* "is that of a gradual crescendo, which incidentally served as the model for Wagner's practice in *Tannhäuser* and elsewhere." "As in *Benvenuto Cellini*, also in *Romeo and Juliet*, the leitmotif plays its role—Wagner heard it there. . . ." The allegro melody of the Apotheosis of the *Funeral and Triumphal Symphony* "makes one think at once of Mendelssohn's War March of the Priests and Wagner's *Kaiser-marsch*, both subsequent."

Nor, according to Mr. Barzun, was Wagner the only com-poser who managed to turn out some of his best things only by "remembering" something or other of Berlioz's. The "new atmosphere" of the opening of the Waltz movement in the *Fantastique* was "remembered by Johann Strauss when he wrote *The Blue Danube*," while that of the pastoral adagio of the symphony was "remembered by Wagner in *Tristan*, Act 3 . . . Indeed, from Wagner ('Thought' motif) to Paul Dukas (*Sorcerer's Apprentice*) composers seem to have found these five movements [of the *Fantastique*] a storehouse of musical material, while as some-one has said, the Witches' Sabbath, with its Stravinskyesque sonorities and the orchestra playing in two keys, is the first piece of Russian music." You may think that both the expression and the form of Richard Strauss's *Don Quixote* were generated quite naturally by the nature of the Cervantes subject. But according to Mr. Barzun you are wrong; the *Don Quixote* is "patterned after Berlioz's *Harold*." Moreover, the "anxious allegro [in the tomb scene of Berlioz's *Romeo and Juliet*], reminiscent of the 'quarrel' theme of the Introduction", was "later remembered by Tchaik-ovsky in his *Romeo and Juliet* overture." We are left with the impression that a great deal of what is best in the music of the last century or so would never have come into being if Berlioz had not written this, that or the other half-dozen bars, Stravinsky, Sibelius, Walton and Holst being among those who are, or were, "still drawing on the original inspiration" of Berlioz; and we begin to wonder how composers from Wagner and Liszt onwards managed to write all the original music they did, seeing how much of their mental energy must have been spent in "remembering" the great Frenchman.

The claim for Berlioz that he is the fountainhead of modern music will strike most people, I fancy, as rather high-pitched. Always Mr. Barzun marks the Berliozian hits, but rarely records the misses. It is perhaps one more proof that musical criticism, relatively to literary or artistic criticism, is as yet only in its infancy that enthusiasts for this or that composer mostly overwrite their subject; they are astronomers royal who cannot or will not see the spots on their own sun.

Where does Berlioz criticism stand today? It is now generally recognised that his was one of the most truly original minds in the history of music; the very qualities that at one time made it difficult for listeners who suffered from a congenital or acquired German or Italian mind-set—the individuality of his thinking, his purely personal harmonic syntax, his free asymmetries of rhythm, and so on—are now the very qualities that delight us. But there is a debit side to the account. Those of us who have always been drawn to him, and whose admiration increases as we sink ourselves more deeply in him, cannot deny that he sometimes misses his mark badly.

Like all the great poets, the great musicians have their occasional weaknesses: Bach is sometimes dull, Mozart sometimes does no more than give impeccable expression to a truism, Brahms sometimes calls on school-mechanics to keep the thing going until inspiration returns, Mahler sometimes pushes naïveté over the borderline that separates it from triviality, Schubert's fluency sometimes lands him in spun-out commonplace, Wolf sometimes fails to untie a harmonic or melodic knot into which the strands of a complex of ideas have somehow gathered themselves, and so *ad infinitum*. It would be unreasonable, therefore, to expect Berlioz to be invariably at his best.

When his music is relatively or absolutely bad it is in a way entirely its own, and I seem to remember having tried, in this column, to explain in just what that badness consists and how it comes about. Someone—I think it was Heine—hit the nail on the head when he said that the trouble with Berlioz was that he had not enough talent for his genius.

All the great masters have been lucky in the possession of a strategic reserve of talent that obligingly moves up when required to keep things going until their genius has got its second wind. They have a sort of hereditary or communal instinct to draw upon to keep the machine working until thinking, in the full sense of the term, can regain control. Bach or Mozart, for instance, can blandly keep on with the standardised routine until the divine spark is generated again, as it is sure to be sooner or later. But the very individuality of Berlioz's genius made this sort of utility near impossible for him. He could not pad; he could write either only at his purely Berliozian best or his purely Berliozian worst.

Not only was his artistic mind insulated for the most part from the music all around him but it was in some ways curiously inconsistent with itself. For example, at the very time when he was endowing music with a new rhythmic life, breaking up its conventional four-square symmetries, bringing in the accentual footfalls in all kinds of unexpected places and so giving the melodic line a new yet wholly organic articulation, Victor Hugo was fighting the same battle on behalf of French poetry, claiming for it the right to ignore the conventional scissors-snap at the end of each line or two and to carry on the sense without a break into the middle of a following line, thus opening the door to a new world of subtleties of verbal rhythm. One would have thought that Berlioz would have welcomed with open arms a development in a sister art so completely at one in essence with what he himself was consciously achieving in music. But no; he disagreed with Hugo for what he took to be a sin against "form," for doing in his own sphere precisely what Berlioz was doing in his.

"I find in it [Hernani]", he wrote to his sister, "certain things that are sublime, and other things and ideas that are ridiculous. . . . As for the verse, which I dislike any way in the theatre, these run-over lines and broken half-lines which enrage the classicists leave me quite indifferent. When spoken it all sounds like prose, and for that reason alone I could prefer it." Had Berlioz understood English he would have seen that Shakespeare's infinite rhythmic variety invited the same condemnation.

Berlioz's occasional failure to think consistently over the whole field of his art does not mean that he was merely the brilliant improviser that some of his opponents have tried to make him out to be. That legend has been blown sky high by Mr. Barzun. Berlioz put a good deal of hard cerebration into the designing and elaboration of his larger works.

All the same, there are times when he puzzles his warmest admirers by a failure to come to real grips with a problem, and his complacent acceptance of a formula that is really no solution at all. What is the explanation of these lapses of his? Was he so completely absorbed in his inner vision of a situation that he could not see it objectively, as it would look from the listener's point of view?

The problem may be illustrated from the opening scene of the Second Part of his Romeo and Juliet. The structure is entirely instrumental. We do not see Romeo in the flesh but have to visual-ise him in imagination; nor are we given any continuous verbal clues to his state of mind, as would be the case in opera. Berlioz merely writes at the head of his score, "Romeo alone: Sadness: Distant Sounds of Music and Dancing: Grand Fête in the Capulet Palace."

Romeo is in the garden, dreaming of his Juliet. The opening "andante malinconico e sostenuto" depicts his solitariness and dejection. From the palace come the first sounds of the revelries within; and as they die away Romeo pours out his ardent, suffer-ing young soul in an inexpressibly moving oboe solo (larghetto) that is one of the rarest of Berlioz's creations. Then the music of the fête returns, in greater force than before, and for the time being Romeo passes beyond our field of vision.

But it is essential to Berlioz's dramatic design that in due course we shall be made conscious again of his presence. In case we might not notice his little technical device—this is hardly likely, though he may have been right in thinking that the Parisian audiences of his day would need some guidance in such a matter—he writes at the head of the next section "Combination of the two themes, that of the larghetto and that of the allegro." The tempestuous theme of the fête is given its head in the strings and flute, while underneath it the larghetto melody thrusts itself on our notice in wide augmentation (notes of much greater length).

No doubt it was necessary for Berlioz to remind us at this point that his hero is still there, looking up at the palace windows and brooding upon Juliet; but could anything be more naïvely tasteless than the way he goes about it? Mr. Barzun does not dwell on this aspect of the matter. He justly points out in a footnote that "certain analysts" have been wrong in describing the love theme as being entrusted to "the trombones bellowing fortissimo"; the larghetto melody, he says, which "joins and tops" the "glitter and agitation" of the fête music, is scored simply for "*one* trombone and wood winds, all marked forte". (Actually the trombone melody is given out also by cornets and horns.)

What amazes and distresses the true Berliozian is not merely the tastelessness of the musical effect here but the helplessness of the technical handling of the problem: how a man so sensitive to the finest shades of colour values could persuade himself that an exquisite cantilena, born of the very soul of the oboe, remains the same melody when translated into the more robust tones of trombone, cornets and horns, and further—in order to make it contrapuntally workable—stretched out on a Procrustean bed of augmentation, is simply beyond our comprehension. Romeo is no longer the poetic dreamer of the oboe solo, but an angry young fellow doing his best to shout the festive music down.

The final Berlioz criticism, I think, will have to do something else with such lapses of taste on the composer's part as these than maintain a benevolent silence with regard to them.

24 December 1950
31 December 1951
4 February 1951
11 February 1951

EPILOGUE

Ernest Newman, 1868–1959

A Memoir by Peter Heyworth

Ernest Newman, 1868–1959

WHAT, I ASK myself, made E. N. such a giant among pigmies? There have been brilliant and witty critics, there have been profound and penetrating musical scholars; there have been musicologists noted for their breadth of grasp of a whole period, and others no less remarkable for the meticulous detail of their learning; there have been writers on music who have won respect from experts in some chosen field and there have been journalists with an ability to fire the interest of the ordinary reader. Ernest Newman had all these gifts. He was beyond question the greatest music critic who has practised his craft in the English language. A composer once pointed out that no city has yet raised a statue to a critic. That may be. But long after the works of many of the minor composers of today have become no more than material for musicological doctorates, men will still turn to the writings of Ernest Newman.

Greatness of this sort is not just a matter of being right—and Newman was often wrong and biased in his assessment of composers and performers; nor is it a matter of intellectual brilliance, which not even his worst enemy denied him, nor even of great learning. All these attributes play their part, of course. Yet the heart of the matter lies elsewhere: Newman was a great critic because he was a big man. It was this that gave him a unique authority over a huge readership, the majority of which had only a very marginal interest in music. They read Newman, not only because he was lively, entertaining and informed, but because that vigorous prose carried with it a vast sense of character.

When he was finally obliged by ill health to retire on the eve of his ninetieth birthday, no less a man than Sir Thomas Beecham wrote the birthday tribute that appeared in the *Sunday Times* and from all over the world famous musicians paid homage to his achievements. When he died, it was as though some landmark had passed away. Men felt lost as they did after the death of Queen Victoria, simply because hardly anyone could remember the time when she was not there.

Ernest Newman was born in Lancaster in 1868, an auspicious year that saw the first performance of *Die Meistersinger* at Munich. *The Ring* was still uncompleted, Wagner's son was conceived but not yet born, the Festspielhaus at Bayreuth still lay in the womb of the future and so did all the symphonies of Brahms and the operettas of Gilbert and Sullivan. England was rich and powerful, but musically the country was a German colony, dominated by the memory of Mendelssohn and dedicated to polite drawing room songs and sacred oratorios. The musical climate was provincial, genteel and pious.

Newman's true name was William Roberts, and it is told that he acquired the *nom de plume* by which he was to become famous when an editor, casting about for someone to cover a concert said, "What about that earnest new man?" William Roberts was not educated for a musical or literary career. His original intention was to enter the Indian Civil Service and when ill-health prevented this he joined a bank. It was not an auspicious background to scholarship or criticism, yet in 1895, when Newman was still only in his middle twenties, he published a full-scale study, called *Gluck and the Opera*. This book surveys the composer, then very largely neglected, with careful scholarship against the background of his time and the evolution of opera. Yet it was written by a man with no formal musical education. Newman had never been abroad; he lived in a provincial city to which the alien art of opera rarely penetrated and the works of Gluck never. It was an astonishing triumph over circumstances.

Gluck and the Opera was followed in 1899 by the first of New-man's many books on Wagner. It is one that in later years he came to disown, for in it he presented a thesis that Wagner's mind was entirely musical, and that his creative processes were the exact reverse of his theory that drama was the master and music the servant. But if Newman argued his case in an extreme form, he was none the less a great deal nearer the mark than those pious Wagnerians who took Wagner's writings on the subject at their face value. (In later years he was to produce in *Wagner as Man and Artist* (1914) a far more penetrating examination of this subject, and one that has stood the test of over half a century virtually unscathed.) Granville Bantock, who was head of the Midland Institute of Music at Birmingham, saw the promise of these books and in 1903 invited Newman to join the staff. Two years later another book appeared, a collection of long essays called *Musical Studies*.

It is worth seeking, for it gives a first-hand impression of the impact that Newman had on the English musical scene in the early years of the century. The style is extraordinarily trenchant and vigorous, and the subjects proclaim the author's sympathies. Essays on Berlioz, Strauss, Faust in Music, reveal an absorption in high romanticism. There is no trace here of the circumscribed horizons of English musical life at the turn of the century. At this time of his career Newman was a fierce and effective ad-vocate of what was then considered "modernism". He fought for the symphonic poem, and in particular for a wild young revolu-tionary called Richard Strauss, he had already proclaimed his admiration for the music of Berlioz, and he was a staunch advocate of Elgar. Finally in 1907, a bare four years after the composer's death, he produced the first full study of Hugo Wolf in English. In it he not only claimed that Wolf was a song writer second only to Schubert, but that in some settings he had achieved a greater profundity. Today, Wolf's music is oddly neglected, partly because there are so few singers able to do justice to his subtlety, and partly because there are fewer people with enough of the German necessary to proper understanding of songs in which test and music are woven into an organic unity. But time will, I believe, bear out many of the claims Newman made for him.

In 1905 Newman was invited to become music critic of the *Manchester Guardian*. It was a time when the great figure of Hans Richter, who was conductor of the Hallé Orchestra, dominated the musical life of Manchester. As a friend and intimate of Wagner and a participant in the first performances of *Die Meistersinger* and *The Ring* he was already an historic personage. For a young critic to challenge so august a figure needed exceptional courage.

Richter had in fact raised music-making in Manchester to a high level and he was an advocate of the music of two younger composers, Strauss and Elgar, in whom Newman was especially interested. But Newman was in no way prepared to endorse every performance conducted by the great conductor, and, when he found fault, he was not a man to mince his words. Tension soon rose between the Hallé and the earnest new man, and it reached bursting point when, after a performance of Berlioz's *Romeo and Juliet*, Newman wrote that it was "obvious" that Richter did not know the score. The performance, he said, was "completely bad, in almost every respect . . . merely to say that it was bad, indeed, is to express oneself quite mildly about some parts of it . . . a great part of it could scarcely have been played in a more apathetic or slovenly way." The next year Newman moved to the *Birmingham Post*.

There he remained until 1919. In his autobiography Neville Cardus, who first met Newman in 1917, describes him at that time as an immaculate dresser. "In those days Newman had not renounced the world, but was much a man of it; his very walk, debonair and leisurely, told of the connoisseur in delectable experiences—told as much as his heavy lips, lidded eyes, and the way he flavoured every word he uttered. . . . When he removed his Homburg hat, revealing raven-black hair, a vision of Disraeli invaded the imagination." It is a picture that stands in striking contrast to the withdrawn, detached scholar I knew in his later years, although even in extreme old age, when he could only move with difficulty, Newman's elegance of manner never left him.

Finally in 1919, at the age of fifty-one, Newman arrived in London to become music critic of *The Observer*. He only remained with it for a year and was then successfully wooed by *The Sunday Times*. Here, together with James Agate, the dramatic critic, and Desmond MacCarthy, the chief literary reviewer, he became part of a trio as formidable as any newspaper has assembled in living memory, and one that persisted unchanged for a generation until the deaths of Agate and MacCarthy after the Second World War. It was at *The Sunday Times* that the final pattern of Newman's life took shape. On a Sunday paper he was able to stand a little aside from the rough and tumble of daily journalism, to pick and choose the concerts and operas he attended. It was the period when Newman finally matured into the position of *doyen* of English music critics. His influence was immense, his position unchallenged.

Yet I doubt if this was in fact Newman's greatest time as a critic. The First World War had brought to a head a great crisis in the development of music. When the fighting finished it was discovered that, not only had empires fallen, but a new and revolutionary generation, headed by Schoenberg, Berg, Stravinsky and Bartók was making the pace, and that men of Newman's generation, such as Mahler, Strauss and Elgar were either dead or had slackened as creative forces. Newman's fundamentally romantic taste never really understood this new generation. He was too inquiring intellectually to dismiss it out of hand, but it was too late for him to bring to it the aesthetic sympathy that he had for composers of his own time. All this is natural enough. It is given to few of us to understand and enjoy the music of generations later than our own. That at the age of fifty-seven Newman was still able to welcome a work as revolutionary in its day as *Wozzeck* is evidence that he preserved an exceptional elasticity of mind. On the other hand, he played a large part in the astonishing over-valuation of Sibelius, who, between the two wars in England and America, came to be widely considered the outstanding composer of the age.

But his position on *The Sunday Times* brought Newman something that he valued much more than journalistic influence: it brought him the means and leisure for scholarship. In the late twenties he started work on his monumental biography of Richard Wagner. It was to occupy him for almost twenty years, for it was not until 1947 that the last volume appeared. This book is beyond dispute the greatest musical biography in the English language. Its learning is prodigious in its breadth as in its depth. Meticulous and detailed though Newman was as a scholar, he was always complete master of his material. Indeed *The Life of Richard Wagner* has about it something that recalls *The Ring* itself. Not only is it in four volumes, but, like *The Ring*, it grows in richness and range from the relatively simple beginnings of Wagner's life and early career at Dresden, until it embraces an entire epoch of European music. Newman seizes the countless themes, threads and motives and weaves them into a great narrative tapestry with a mastery worthy of his subject.

This great biography is the high point of Newman's achievement. By the time he had completed it he was almost eighty and it might have been supposed that his work was done. But to it he added *Wagner Nights* (1950), by far the most searching commentary and analysis that exists in English of the Wagnerian music dramas, and as late as 1954, when he was eighty-six, there came a successor to his earlier *Opera Nights* (1943). Even then he was not finished, for he was a man incapable of inactivity. He spoke to me of his desire to write two books, one on Berlioz's music and another on Beethoven's late quartets, and probably only the failing eyesight that plagued his last years prevented him from doing so.

By the end of the last war Newman had become something of a recluse. He was delighted to receive visitors, but, although he visited Covent Garden until the last year of his life, few concerts attracted him to London. He turned out for two evenings in 1952 at which his beloved Toscanini gave unforgettably radiant performances of the Brahms symphonies, and the following year a complete performance of Wolf's *Italienisches Liederbuch* lured him again to the Festival Hall. At the age of eighty-five he was still extraordinarily dapper and spry. As soon as the curtain was down at Covent Garden he was out of his seat like a scalded cat. Over coffee in the interval or in the foyer afterwards the old wit would still crackle. "I sometimes wonder", he murmured to me sadly after a particularly awful performance of the one-act *Salome*, "which would be nicer—an opera without an interval, or an interval without an opera." Gradually, as his legs grew unsteady, his appearances grew fewer, though until he was in his ninetieth year he rarely missed a Wagner revival. But when in January 1958 he failed to appear at Sadler's Wells for *The Merry Widow* (a particular favourite), it was clear that old age had caught up even with Ernest Newman.

Apart from these increasingly rare excursions, he spent almost all his waking hours in an extraordinary retreat that he had built in the garden of his house at Tadworth. This was nothing less than a small village hall, and in it Newman worked and read from dawn to dusk, surrounded by his great library, two pianos, a harpsichord (if I remember rightly) and a battery of gramophones of varying vintages, and far removed from all mundane disturbances such as vacuum cleaners, door bells and telephones.

To sit with him when he was relaxing there in the evening was a memorable experience. His mind was so prodigiously learned, his experience of life and people so wide and his judgement so shrewd and witty, that it was as though one were sitting at the feet of some great sage, heavy with years and wisdom. In print, Newman conjured up an image of a fierce and even ferocious figure. To meet he was surprisingly gentle, urbane and immaculately courteous. He was not a cynical man, but he was sardonic and sceptical, notably where the motives of conductors and singers were concerned (the *mot*, "the higher the voice, the smaller the intellect" was his). While he lovingly savoured his Havana cigar and sipped at a whisky and soda, his old, blue eyes staring into the middle distance, jokes, wisdom and learning mingled in an easy flow. As for the mad world outside, it was "Wahn, Wahn, überall Wahn".

There was nothing of the blinkered, *weltfreund* scholar about Newman. He was devoted to boxing, and on rare occasions wrote about "the other Ring"; he was vice-president of the local football and cricket clubs (it was characteristic of him that he would accept those offices but refused to sit on musical committees); he was a strong rationalist of Victorian mould and in his younger days contributed to J. M. Robertson's *The Free Review*; he had written papers on Ibsen and on "inherited characteristics"; the chapters on Nietzsche in his life of Wagner are evidence of his far from dilettantish interest in philosophy (indeed at one time he planned a separate book on the subject), and I remember that when I visited him shortly before I first went up to Oxford after the war, he particularly asked me to let him know what new books on philosophy were attracting attention in that stronghold of logical positivism. It was, I think, the breadth of the man that enabled him to establish such a hold on his readers in *The Sunday Times*. And he for his part never lost his sympathy with what he liked to call the Plain Musical Man. It was in such a capacity that I first visited him, and I shall not forget the simplicity and lack of condescension with which he discussed matters on which he was an authority and I either an ignoramus or the merest amateur, nor the prompt and enchanting replies to letters, written in an elegant hand which strikingly recalls that of Wagner himself.

Yet the affection and respect with which he was regarded by the general public did not always extend to the inner sanctums of the musical profession. He had trodden on too many toes, he had mocked too many sacred cows; he was too detached from, and too obviously contemptuous of, the day-to-day mechanics of influence and musical politics. He served on no committees, he ground no axes and contributed to no lexicons, not even to Grove. He was too big a man to chain himself to causes. When in the first quarter of this century the folk song revival and a new and necessary desire to fight free of German hegemony brought on occasions a rather strident chauvinist note into English musical life, Newman remained aloof from the tendency to overpraise native composers because they were native, or young composers because they were young. "My dear boy," he said to me once when I had rashly taxed him with not doing enough to encourage young composers, "You may help a lame dog over a style, but he is still lame on the other side."

I think that in the thirties there was probably a time when, for all the public admiration he commanded, Newman was regarded as a vaguely archaic figure, out of touch (as indeed he was) with the new worlds of Stravinsky and Schoenberg and obsessed with a composer whom many people had come to regard with repugnance. It was his good fortune to live long enough to laugh at Wagner's denigrators. For the end of the last war brought another change in musical climate. A new generation arrived, who looked at the great romantic composers, and above all at the giant figure of Wagner, with fresh interest and fascination. And when we turned to inform ourselves on Wagner (and on Berlioz, Liszt, Mahler, Strauss and Elgar) we discovered that one man above all others had written truly. It was, of course, Ernest Newman. The fact that today Wagner has been purged of the excesses of the old guard Wagnerians is, first and foremost, the fruit of *Wagner as Man and Artist*. And this reform has nowhere been more evident than at Bayreuth itself. Paying a public tribute to Newman on his ninetieth birthday, Wieland Wagner wrote, "I owe to Ernest Newman what one may perhaps describe as the scientific basis of the New Bayreuth."

Through all the years when few minor composers and critics could let a month pass without some jibe at the unfashionable figure of Wagner, when he was held responsible for anything from the evils of Nazism to the collapse of diatonic music, Newman held faith unflinchingly. He never for a moment faltered in his belief that Wagner was the creator of some of the greatest dramas conceived by the human mind. He lived to see him purged of ideological and political excrescences, to witness Bayreuth reopened (he travelled to the first post-war festival); and to find himself a legendary and revered figure, who, more than any other man had raised the study of Wagner above a level of adoration and abuse, and had thus finally enabled his hero to take an unchallenged place among the greatest of the great. It was a heroic task, heroically accomplished.

Index

Index

Works not by Berlioz are indexed under their authors or composers